BARE
ESSENTIALS

BRAS

CONSTRUCTION AND PATTERN DRAFTING FOR LINGERIE DESIGN

Publication by
Fairbanks Publishing LLC
dba Porcelynne

THIRD EDITION

Jennifer Lynne Matthews - Fairbanks

Book Design by Designarchy
Cover Photography by Ashley Burke
Interior Photography by David Fairbanks
Written by Jennifer Lynne Matthews-Fairbanks

Universities and wholesale purchasing:
Fairbanks Publishing offers special rates for universities and for wholesale purchasing.

Wholesale purchasing is available through Ingram Distributing or directly through Porcelynne.com.

Updates:
Information contained in this book was current at the time of publishing. For updates, check our blog. https://blog.porcelynne.com

Contact Us:
Fairbanks Publishing LLC, DBA Porcelynne
info@porcelynne.com

Your feedback is always welcome. Let us know if we can do anything to improve this title.

Copyright First Edition © 2012 Fairbanks Publishing LLC dba Los Angeles Fashion Resource
Copyright Second Edition © 2016 Fairbanks Publishing LLC
Copyright Third Edition © 2019 Fairbanks Publishing LLC dba Porcelynne

Publication by Fairbanks Publishing, LLC dba Porcelynne.

All rights reserved. No part of this book may be reproduced electronically or by other means without permission in writing from the author, except by a reviewer who wishes to quote passages in connection with a review written for inclusion in a magazine, newspaper or digital press medium.

First Edition: ISBN: 978-0983132844
Second Edition: ISBN: 978-1533623539
Third Edition: ISBN: 978-1074526238 - Black & White Paperback
        ISBN: 978-1733274005 - Color Spiral Bound Paperback
        ISBN: 978-1733274012 - Color Paperback

CONTENTS

PREFACE 11

BEGINNER

CHAPTER 1

INTRODUCTION TO BRA CONSTRUCTION 15

Anatomy of a Bra 15
Tools & Supplies 16
Notions for Basic Bra Patterns 18
Fabrics Types 20
Fabrics Characteristics 20
Fabrics for Bra Making 21
Machines & Stitches 22
    Woven Fabric Stitches 22
    Knit Fabric Stitches 23
    Specialty Machine Stitches 23
    Specialty Feet Attachments 23
    Needles 23
Stretch and Patterns 24
Elastic for Patterns 24
Bra Patterns 26
    Why is it so hard to find a bra that fits? 26
    Traditional Measuring for US Ready-to-Wear Bras 28
    Determining the Cup Size 29
Understanding Fit 30
    Choosing a Pattern 32
    Choosing Wires 32
    Understanding Wire Shapes 32

CHAPTER 2

BASIC BRA CONSTRUCTION.. 33

- Cup Construction 33
- Band Construction 37

CHAPTER 3

BAND ALTERATIONS FOR ELASTIC 47

- Part 1: Pattern Manipulation 47
- Part 2: Construction Method 49

CHAPTER 4

FRAMELESS BRA 55

- Part 1: Pattern Manipulation 55
- Part 2: Construction Method 58
  - Cup Construction 58
  - Band Construction 59

INTERMEDIATE

CHAPTER 5

INTRODUCTION TO PATTERN MANIPULATION 65

- Tools. 65
- Supplies 65
- Pattern Styles 66
  - Padded Bra 66
  - Demi Cup Bra 66
  - Strapless Bra 66
  - Stylized Bra Cup 67
  - Nursing Bra 67
  - Mastectomy Bra 67

CHAPTER 6

PATTERN ADJUSTMENTS FOR FIT ... 69

- Adjusting Patterns for Torso Shape ... 69
- Adjusting Patterns for Wire Size ... 74
- Adjusting Patterns for Bust Point Position ... 75
  - Change the Vertical Bust Point ... 76
  - Change the Horizontal Bust Point ... 77
- Adjusting Patterns for Wire Spring ... 78

CHAPTER 7

PADDED BRA ... 81

- Padded Seamed Cup ... 81
  - Part 1: Pattern Manipulation ... 81
  - Part 2: Construction Method ... 82
- Padded Inserts ... 84
  - Part 1: Pattern Manipulation ... 84
  - Part 2: Construction Method ... 85

CHAPTER 8

FRONT CLOSURE DEMI BRA ... 87

- Method 1: Demi Underwire ... 87
- Method 2: Custom Cut Wire ... 91

CHAPTER 9

STRAPLESS BRA ... 93

- Part 1: Pattern Manipulation ... 93
  - Variation 1: Basic Strapless Bra ... 93
  - Variation 2: Backless Strapless Bra ... 95
- Part 2: Construction Method ... 101

CHAPTER 10

STYLIZING A BRA: SEAM LINES 103

- Changing Style Lines 103

CHAPTER 11

STYLIZING A BRA: SLASH AND SPREAD 107

- Gathers 107
  - Part 1: Pattern Manipulation 107
  - Part 2: Construction Method 109
- Pintucks 110
  - Part 1: Pattern Manipulation 110
  - Part 2: Construction Method 111

CHAPTER 12

NURSING BRA 113

- Part 1: Pattern Manipulation 113
- Part 2: Construction Method 115
  - Variation A: Nursing Clip 117
  - Variation B: Adjustable Hook & Eye 118

CHAPTER 13

MASTECTOMY BRA 119

- Part 1: Pattern Manipulation 119
  - Fitting into a Cup 119
  - Designing the Pocket 120
- Part 2: Construction Method 122

ADVANCED

CHAPTER 14

INTRODUCTION TO PATTERN DRAFTING AND GRADING 127

- Tools 127
- Terminology 128
- Fabrics, Elastics and Stretch 128
- Wire Selection 130
- Measurements for the Porcelynne Pattern Drafting Method 134
  - Drafting Measurements 134
  - All The Math I Did 135
  - The Calculation 136
  - Adjustment for Breast Asymmetry 137
- Slopers & Pattern Manipulation 137
  - Bralette 138
  - Non-Wired Soft Bra 138
- Patterns and Labeling 138
- Grading & Grade Rules 138
  - Grading for Nonstretch 138
  - Band Grading 139

CHAPTER 15

BRA BAND PATTERN DRAFTING 141

- Drafting by Hand 141
  - Wire Draft 141
  - Breast Spacing 143
  - Wire Styles 143
  - Front Band 150
  - Back Band 151
- Drafting on Illustration Software 157

CHAPTER 16

BRA CUP DRAFTING: PORCELYNNE PATTERN DRAFTING METHOD ... 165

- Drafting By Hand ... 165
  - Wire Circumference ... 165
  - Lower Cup Bust Depth ... 167
  - Torso Shape Adjustment ... 170
  - Cup Curves ... 172
  - Wire Line ... 177
  - Strap Placement ... 180
- Drafting by Illustration Software ... 181

CHAPTER 17

PATTERN DIRECTIONS ... 189

- Seam Allowance by Hand ... 189
  - Bra Band ... 189
  - Bra Cup ... 191
- Seam Allowance by Illustration Software ... 192
- Grainlines ... 193
  - Grainlines vs. Direction of Greatest Stretch ... 193

CHAPTER 18

CREATE A SLOPER: PORCELYNNE PATTERN MANIPULATION METHOD ... 195

- Cup Sloper ... 195
  - Guidelines ... 196
  - Cup Curves ... 197
- Front Band Sloper ... 199
- Back Band Sloper ... 200

CHAPTER 19
PORCELYNNE PATTERN MANIPULATION METHOD..................203

CHAPTER 20
PATTERN MANIPULATION: BRALETTE..................209

CHAPTER 21
PATTERN MANIPULATION: NON-WIRED SOFT BRA..................215

CHAPTER 22
BRA BAND GRADING..................219

- Grade Rules..................219
- Grading By Hand for Wire Sizes..................222
  - Band Front..................222
  - Back Band..................227
- Grading by Hand for Band Sizes..................229
  - Front Band..................229
  - Back Band..................230
- Wire Line Adjustments..................231
- Grading in Illustration Software..................232
- Grading By Software for Wire Sizes..................233
  - Front Band..................233
  - Back Band..................236

CHAPTER 23

BRA CUP GRADING 237

- Sister Sizing a Cup Grade 237
- Grading By Hand 238
  - Radial Grading Method 238
  - Grid Grading method 241
- Adjustments for Cup Patterns 244
- Grading on the Computer 246
- Grading in Illustration Software 247

PATTERNS

CHAPTER 24

PATTERN INSTRUCTIONS 251

APPENDIX A

POLYPATTERN® BY POLYTROPON 279

- About the Program 279
  - Pattern Features 280
  - Special Features 280
  - Grading Features 281

PREFACE

As a lingerie designer and educator, I felt there was a gap in educational texts for lingerie design. I compiled this information for educational purposes, from personal experience and experimentation. This book series is designed to take an individual through the process of sewing lingerie, developing pattern modifications and drafting from measurements.

This book covers many different aspects of the design process and is divided into three basic sections. As one progresses through the book, the directions become more complex, allowing each individual to master the art of lingerie design through construction, pattern manipulation and pattern drafting.

I wrote the third edition to cover additional topics that were previously uncovered by the first and second editions. While the drafting and grading instructions were thorough in both earlier editions, I received feedback from my readers that determining the measurements for the draft proved difficult.

With this feedback, I have re-approached the drafting process in a more mathematical manner. The math in this book is a little complex, but since math doesn't lie, I felt this was the best approach to make the most accurate drafts possible. This new method of drafting is referred to as the Porcelynne Pattern Drafting and Manipulation Method, named after my business acumen.

Within this edition, I introduce information for varying body shapes and create a pattern manipulation concept that I believe anyone can follow and achieve a great first test fit.

Enjoy your venture into designing and creating your own lingerie.

-Jennifer Matthews-Fairbanks

Jennifer Lynne Matthews-Fairbanks was an instructor at the Fashion Institute of Design and Merchandising in Los Angeles and San Francisco for nine years. She owned and operated her own lingerie design business, Porcelynne Lingerie, for 10+ years and has been working freelance as a pattern maker for nearly 20 years.

A special thanks to my husband, David Fairbanks, for being there for me every step of the way, and to my beautiful daughter Emily, for being the unstoppable force of a stubborn duplicate of myself.

Additonal thanks to my valued team of testers: Jane Ramsey, Crystal Gilbertson, Meg Delafave, Klaudia Prusinska, Ivy Pugh, Paula Jean, Becky Allhands and Karey Harrison. I could not have done this without each and every one of you.

BEGINNER

Chapter 1: Introduction to Bra Construction............................15

Chapter 2: Basic Bra Construction 33

Chapter 3: Band Alterations for Elastic 47

Chapter 4: Frameless Bra 55

CHAPTER 1
INTRODUCTION TO BRA CONSTRUCTION

A bra is a complicated feat of breast support engineering. The best course of action when beginning this journey is understanding bra construction and the components inherent in their structure.

The introduction chapter of each section details the tools, supplies, notions and materials used for the projects in that section. The recommendation is to work through this book, from the beginning, to get a better understanding of construction and manipulation.

ANATOMY OF A BRA

There are three general parts to a bra: the cup, the band and the bridge. The band is generally in two parts for the front and back. The front band and bridge are often combined as one pattern and is referred to as the frame.

Cup - A cup of a bra can be seamed or molded, with a variety of coverages: full coverage, demi cup, half cup or quarter cup. The high point of the cup is referred to as the apex or bust point.

A seamed cup contains one or more seams to shape the bust and is generally in a stable fabric without stretch. This seam can be horizontal, vertical, diagonal or any design in between. The key is proper seaming with one seam intersecting the apex of the breast.

All seams on a bra should be shielded from the body. Irritation can occur if there is no lining or seam covering.

A side panel in a cup is referred to as a power bar. The power bar can be part of the seamed cup or a completely separate fabric sling on the inside of the cup to help support larger breasts.

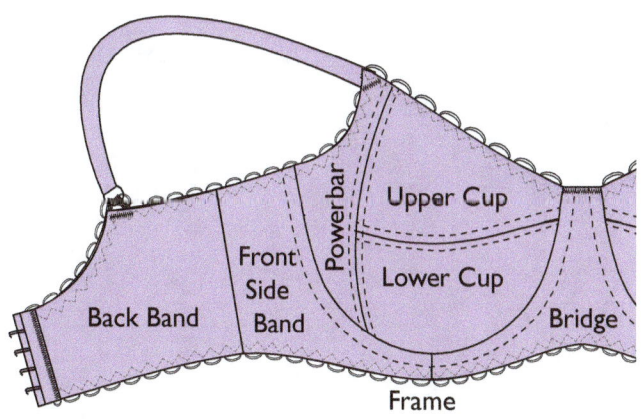

A molded cup is another type of cup, but as a designer or maker, design of the cup is limited due. Specifications of a cup design is made by the manufacturer of the cups. Molded cups can be with or without padding.

Band - The band can be in multiple pieces, joining under the cup and/or at the side seam. A band that contains a side seam generally has two distinct differences: the front band contains no stretch (and is stabilized) and the back band is constructed of a stretch fabric such as power net. Larger cup sizes may contain a piece of boning at the side seam for additional support of the bust.

A band can also be constructed without a side seam. The entire band in this scenario would be constructed of a stretch material. The center bridge would be stabilized, even if the entire band and frame is constructed out of a stretch fabric.

Bridge - This is the center of the bra that connects the two cups together. The bridge can be incorporated into the band to form the frame. It can also be freestanding on its own for a "frameless" design. The bridge is stabilized to keep the fabric from stretching.

TOOLS & SUPPLIES

For seasoned sewers, many of these tools may already be present in sewing kits. For those just starting out in the field of sewing, this is a suggested shopping list.

Dressmaker Pins - There are a variety of different pins one can use in sewing. Some are very pliable and made from less than quality materials, while others are sturdy and strong. In the varieties available, be sure to get pins that are appropriate for the project. Silk pins are recommended for delicate fabrics.

Fabric Shears and Scissors - The words shears and scissors can be interchanged, although shears is the industry standard term. Be sure to purchase a pair of quality shears and designate them for fabric use only.

French Curve - A French curve is used for making small and tight curved shapes. French curves are available as stand alone rulers or as part of a variety pack, containing multiple curved shapes.

Paper Scissors - As one should have a pair of scissors specific to fabric, a pair specifically for cutting paper products is also necessary.

Pattern Paper - Pattern or dot paper is what we use in the industry for drafting. The markings may not be dots, but may contain numbers and letters on a grid. This type of

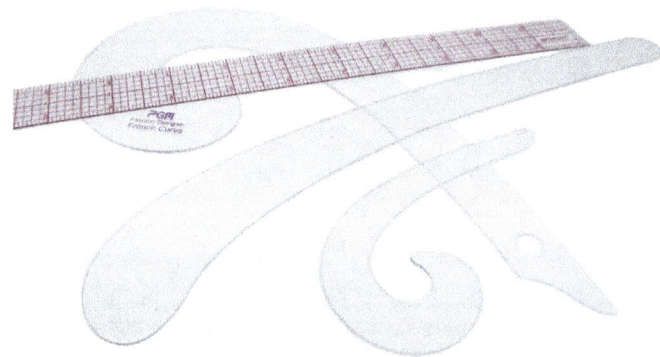

paper is referred to as alpha-numeric paper. Pattern paper may not be available in all areas. Poster paper, craft paper or tracing paper can be used as acceptable alternatives.

Pattern Weights - Pattern weights can be in the form of small bean bags or as bars of steel. They are versatile and can be used to stabilize a pattern, whether tracing a pattern piece or using it to hold down fabric.

Pencils - In order to get accurate shapes and edges, a mechanical pencil or a pencil with a very sharp point is necessary. A few colored pencils are handy to help differentiate pattern line changes.

Rotary Cutter and Cutting Mat - When working with small and detailed designs, using a large pair of shears is not always practical. Use of a rotary cutter or an X-Acto® knife ensures a precise cut every time.

Be sure to use a cutting mat under all work. Cutting mats come in a variety of sizes from letter size to table size. The use of rotary cutters and cutting mats is commonly used when cutting bras and delicate laces.

Straight See-Through Grid Ruler - This is important for drafting. These are generally available for both the imperial and metric systems.

For the imperial system (inches), measurements are taken in 8ths. The complexities of a bra reference 16th and 32nds of an inch. The table on the next page converts fractions to decimals. This chart will prove handy when using this book in conjunction with computer aided design programs such as Adobe® Illustrator®.

The metric system (centimeters) references 10th of a centimeter, making conversions easier than the imperial system.

Tape Measure - A soft tape measure is needed for taking measurements. Many tape measures have the imperial system on one side and the metric system on the other. Double check all tape measures against a straight ruler. Cheap tape measures may not be as accurate as one would think.

IMPERIAL MEASUREMENT CONVERSION CHART
Measurements in Inches

1/32	0.03
1/16	0.06
3/32	0.09
1/8	0.13
5/32	0.16
3/16	0.19
7/32	0.22
1/4	0.25
9/32	0.28
5/16	0.31
11/32	0.34
3/8	0.38
13/32	0.41
7/16	0.44
15/32	0.47
1/2	0.50
17/32	0.53
9/16	0.56
19/32	0.59
5/8	0.63
21/32	0.66
11/16	0.69
23/32	0.72
3/4	0.75
25/32	0.78
13/16	0.81
27/32	0.84
7/8	0.88
29/32	0.91
15/16	0.94
31/32	0.97

NOTIONS FOR BASIC BRA PATTERNS

Bra making supplies are not regularly found at local fabric shops. Some items may be stocked, but for a more extensive inventory of choices, online bra making resources are available. Our supply business, Porcelynne, carries a wide selection of these supplies. For more information on our supplies, go to Porcelynne.com.

Boning - Boning can be acquired in plastic or metal. For bra construction, 1/4" or 6mm width is recommended. Ridglene boning can also be used, which is a type of boning tape that can be sewn through. Boning is not always used, but can help reinforce the side seam of the bra. Adding boning to a bra is optional.

Boning Casing - Casing can be sold with boning as a set. To create custom casing, use a 1" or 25mm wide strip of soft woven fabric (flannel or similar) either straight grain or bias cut. Fold both edges in by 1/4" or 6mm and press to reveal a 1/2" or 12.5mm piece of casing.

Hook & Eye Tape - Hook & eyes generally have three columns of eyes for adjusting the fit. Hook & eye tape can contain one or more rows. One row is typically used for small cup sizes. For larger cup sizes, hook & eyes contain two or more rows. Strapless bras generally contain four or more rows to provide additional support.

Seam Tape - Seam tape is a thin piece of nylon tricot that is soft and is stitched over a seam to avoid irritation of the seam against the skin. A commercial version can be found under the name Seams Great™ by the brand Dritz®.

Slides and Rings - Slides are used for making a strap adjustable and resemble an "8" shape. Rings are used to attach straps to the body of the bra. Both are available in a variety of sizes and materials. Slides and rings are sized by the width of the strap elastic, not by the outer dimensions.

Straps - Straps vary in width from 1/4" to 1" (6mm to 25mm). Some straps are constructed using fabric and some include padding, but most are comprised of elastic. Straps contain a slide and ring for adjusting the strap length.

Underwire - Underwires come in a variety of shapes and sizes. If a design requires an underwire between sizes, one can cut down a full coverage or long wire. Underwires may be coated in nylon or are comprised of plain carbon steel, but they always have capped ends to ensure that the wires do not poke through the bra.

Underwire Channeling - Channeling is used to encase the underwire around the cup. Channeling has a brushed texture.

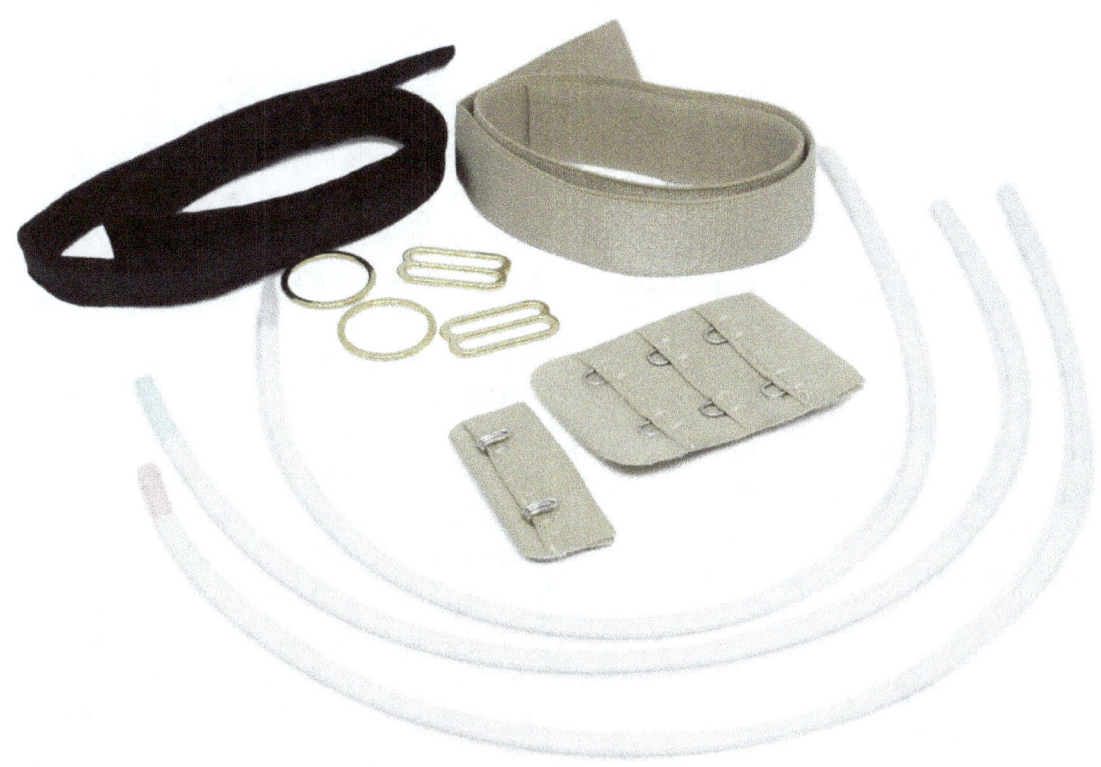

FABRICS TYPES

Fabrics generally fall into two main categories: woven and knit.

Woven Fabric - Woven fabrics are comprised of threads intertwining from perpendicular directions.

Knit Fabric - These fabrics are created by a single yarn that is looped on a course. The yarn is pulled through loops to create a knit stitch on one side and a purl stitch on the other side. The knit side appears as lines of "V's" and the purl side is compiled of loops.

FABRICS CHARACTERISTICS

Every fabric has different characteristics. Many of these characteristics can be attributed to the grainlines of the fabric.

Selvage - The selvage of a fabric is the finished edge of the fabric that runs the length of the fabric. This is found in both woven and knit fabrics.

Length Grain - This refers to the length of the fabric. This grain is parallel to the selvage and is called the warp grain in the fashion industry. It is also referred to as the straight grain.

Knit fabrics technically do not have grainlines, but many knit fabrics have the same characteristics of a woven fabric. The length in a fabric generally contains no stretch. On occasion, the fibers knitted into a fabric may contain more stretch in the length than in the span of the fabric from selvage to selvage.

Cross Grain - When a fabric is woven, the threads on the length grain are generally stationary and weft threads are woven back and forth, from edge to edge, creating the finished selvage. This weaving action causes the cross grain, or weft grain, of the fabric to have more pliability than the straight grain.

The cross "grain" of a knit usually is the stretchiest part of a knit fabric, but this is not always the case. On occasion the length stretches more than the cross section. This is important to note when cutting pattern pieces out.

Bias - The bias of a fabric is the stretchiest option when using a woven fabric. Bias aligns at a 45 degree angle from the selvage. Using the bias on a knit fabric is not recommended as it does not generally provide additional stretch and produces unnecessary fabric waste.

Direction of Greatest Stretch (DOGS) - The term "direction of greatest stretch" or "DOGS" is used in home sewing patterns and by independent pattern designers. DOGS is not common terminology in the apparel manufacturing industry. Many home sewing patterns are labeled with what appears to be a grainline (or the direction of least stretch), but is actually the DOGS. This can cause complications if the guide line on the pattern is not clearly marked as the grainline or the DOGS.

Check with the pattern directions to determine if the markings on the pattern are for grainlines or DOGS. The patterns in this book use a traditional grainline that follow the selvage on the parallel (they follow the direction of the least stretch). DOGS are generally in a direction that is horizontal on the body which allows for stretch across the body.

FABRICS FOR BRA MAKING

When creating custom patterns, many different fabrics can be incorporated into a design, but how the patterns fit will vary based on their stretch.

In custom bra making, cup fabric is stable and does not stretch. Smaller cups can get away with having some stretch in the cups, but larger cups need the support that stable fabrics provide.

Tricot - Tricot is a type of knit that is commonly used in lingerie design. It can have stretch in one direction, two directions or in no directions. The most common tricot used in bra making is a thicker, more stable, tricot with a weight of 7-ounces or more. It is generally stable with only a mechanical stretch in one direction. This type of tricot is also called duoplex, sport tricot or dazzle tricot.

Lighter weight tricot with a stretch in one direction can be cross cut with two pieces of opposing "grains" to stabilize the fabric. A thinner tricot is what many shops call "bra lining" because of its soft handle.

Power Net - This is generally a nylon/spandex net mesh. Power net is used on the back band and has a firm stretch with great recovery. Stretch fabrics other than power net can be used for the back band, but tend to stretch out more than a band constructed with power net.

Power net is often referred to as power mesh. Many retailers label a very stretchy net mesh as power mesh. Double check with the retailer on the weight of the mesh. Medium to heavy weight are most appropriate for bra making. Light weight mesh is not appropriate for any form of bra making.

Spandex Knits - Spandex knit is a jersey knit with Lycra® or spandex fibers that allows for stretch in athletic and swim wear. Spandex can be used in place of power net.

Stabilizer - This fabric is sheer, rigid and should not stretch in any direction. It is generally a nylon net and is used on the front band and center bridge of a bra. If this fabric contains stretch in one direction, cut the required pattern pieces to restrict stretch across the body.

Lace Fabric - Laces can be created by either woven or knit construction. Depending on the stretch of the lace, lace can be treated as either. Woven lace is recommended for cup construction. Knit laces are recommended for the back or areas of stretch, but can be used on nonstretch areas when stabilized.

Bra Tulle - Bra tulle is a nonstretch mesh that is stable in all directions. If it is rough against the skin, line with a soft tricot. Mesh fabrics may vary with one side softer than the other. Cut the pattern pieces for the soft side to lay against the skin.

MACHINES & STITCHES

A bra can be constructed with a combination of knit and woven fabrics. Various stitches are required for proper construction.

WOVEN FABRIC STITCHES

Straight Stitch - A straight stitch is needed when constructing the cup and attaching encasements for underwire and boning.

Bar Tack Stitch - A bar tack stitch is a very tiny zigzag stitch and can be sewn with most sewing machines. This stitch is used when attaching the straps, hook & eye closures and at the ends of the underwire channeling.

Most home machines have zigzag functionality to them. The setting for this stitch is similar to the stitch size used to sew a buttonhole. The spacing between is very small and narrow.

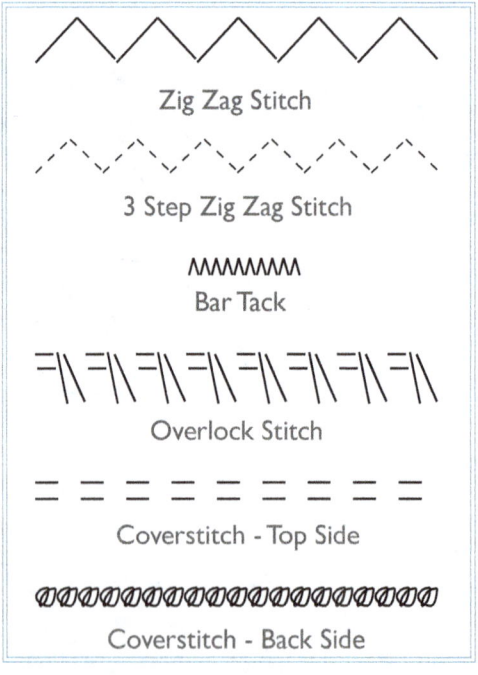

KNIT FABRIC STITCHES

When sewing stretch fabrics and elastics, avoid using a straight stitch. If a stretch material is sewn with a straight stitch and the fabric stretches beyond the length of the stitch, the thread breaks.

Zigzag Stitch - A zigzag stitch is the recommended stitch for sewing stretch fabrics. The zigzag allows the fabric and elastic to stretch without threads breaking.

Three Step Zigzag Stitch - The three step zigzag stitch allows for stretch, but also secures the thread in the stitch.

SPECIALTY MACHINE STITCHES

Overlock Stitch - An overlock or serger machine cuts and finishes the edge of fabric. A similar stitch, called an overcast stitch, can be sewn on a home machine. The overlock machine generally utilizes four threads, two threads reinforce the seam and two threads form an overcast on the edge of the fabric, leaving a clean finished edge.

Coverstitch - Coverstitch machines utilize three to four threads. A coverstitch is used in hemming garments, as well as attaching elastic around the neck and hemline of a bra.

This stitch is not as secure as a three step zigzag. If a coverstitch thread breaks on a garment, the entire stitch can unravel.

SPECIALTY FEET ATTACHMENTS

Edge Stitching Foot - An edge stitching foot is used to join laces and trims together. It generally has a series of guides for joining different fabric layers.

Roller Foot - A roller foot is used in sewing knit fabrics. It helps roll the fabrics through the machine without stretching the fabric. It is not necessary to use such a foot, but it does make sewing knits much easier to handle.

Walking Foot - A walking foot helps evenly feed fabric through a machine. This foot is especially helpful when sewing thick layers together.

NEEDLES

The size and type of needle is dependent on the fabrics being used. Each size has a different purpose.

Smaller numbers indicate a finer needle and should be used for more delicate fabrics. Larger numbers are thicker in size and are used for heavier fabrics.

Needles are labeled with two numbers. This indicates both the American and European size. For bra sewing, a 10/70 or 12/80 are ideal sizes.

NEEDLE SIZES

American	European
8	60
9	65
10	70
11	75
12	80
14	90
16	100
18	110
19	120

Sharp Needles - Sharp needles are used for woven fabrics. It creates straight accurate lines of stitches.

Ballpoint Needles - Ballpoint needles are used for knits. The rounder point allows the needle to safely glide between the loops of the knit without disturbing the fibers. The stitch is not as straight as sharp needles which allows for some give on the stitch.

Universal Needles - Universal needles have many of the characteristics of both a sharp needle and a ballpoint needle. It falls in the category between sharp and ballpoint. These can be used on either woven or knits, but if skipped stitches occur on a knit, switch the needle type to ballpoint.

Stretch Needles - This needle is similar to a ballpoint needle, but is specifically recommended when sewing Lycra®, spandex or swimwear. This needle helps in avoiding skipped stitches. Some elastics require the stretch needle due to their fiber content.

STRETCH AND PATTERNS

Not all patterns are created equally, nor are they created for all fabrics and notions. The patterns included in this book were designed to use two different kinds of fabrics. The front of the bra, including the cups and band, were drafted for a fabric without stretch. The back band was created for a power net and elastic with a stretch of 50%.

To test the stretch of a fabric, fold the fabric approximately 4" or 8cm* away from the cut edge of the cross grain. Place two pins 5" or 10cm* apart from each other. Use the ruler on the next page, placing one pin at the 0 mark and pull the fabric to a stretched point that meets resistance. This is not the full stretch of the fabric, but the normal stretch of the material. Make a note of this amount. The ideal fabric to use with these patterns stretch 7.5" or 15cm*.

Elastic stretch can be measured in a similar manner, place two pins in a length of elastic 5" or 10cm* apart. Stretch to determine the stretch amount. The ideal elastic to use with these patterns stretch 7.5" or 15cm*.

These measurements are only suggestions based on how these patterns were developed. Use own discretion in deciding appropriate fabrics for these projects.

ELASTIC FOR PATTERNS

The elastics in a bra are used for support around the cup and band.

The elastic on a bra is treated differently than elastic on panties and other lingerie. Bra elastic is sewn at the exact length of the finished garment, no stretching or the bra could be too tight.

Band Elastic - This elastic contains one side that is decorative and one side that is brushed for a soft touch to the skin. There is often a picot or decorative edge to one edge of the

*These numbers are intentionally not an equal measurement translation.

Beginner / Introduction to Bra Construction | 25

elastic.

Clear Elastic - Clear elastic or Lastin can be used for reinforcement on a garment to keep the integrity of a stretch lace edge. This is generally made of Polyurethane. For the examples in the book, we use this elastic behind the edges of lace to keep the stretch stable.

Picot Edge Elastic - Picot edge elastics are available in many varieties. The picot description is of a decorative loop-type edge on an elastic. These come in every color under the sun. This elastic is typically available in widths of 3/8" to 5/8" (10mm to 15mm), although wider and narrower picot trim can be found. The elastic itself without the decorative edge is usually 1/4" or 6mm wide.

Strap Elastic - One side of the elastic is brushed for comfort and the other side has a decorative finish. Strap elastic can be in widths of 1/4" to 1" (6mm to 25mm).

BRA PATTERNS

In the back of this book, a basic pattern is included for the projects in this book. These patterns are used as a teaching aid, in learning basic sewing of bras. These patterns were created from the drafting and grading instructions in the advanced section of this book.

The patterns may not fit properly without alterations. The intermediate section covers basic fitting changes for bra patterns.

The first bra made by anyone is never a wearable bra. The recommendation is to use inexpensive fabrics and trims for the first sewn bra.

It is commonplace to recycle parts from existing bras, whether they are from older, worn out bras or bras purchased at second hand stores. If repurposing an existing bra, the straps, hook & eye, underwire casing and occasionally the underwire are all salvageable.

WHY IS IT SO HARD TO FIND A BRA THAT FITS?

Nearly every woman has been measured for a bra at least once in her life. It is a frustrating process in which 80% of the time, the bra fitter places an individual in a bra that just does not fit right. Incorrect bra fitting happens for these three main reasons:

Reason 1. *Bra fitters do not know how the measurements being taken, relate to the bra. This can vary for the brand being fit into.*

Reason 2. *Manufacturers have different criteria for fit models in which they design their bras around.*

Reason 3. *Accurate measurements are difficult to take while wearing ill-fitting bras. This is the Catch 22 scenario.*

Reason 1

To address the first reason, answer this question: What does the number of a bra size mean? The numbers on a bra have different meanings in different countries. This also varies by the manufacturer.

In France, the number on the bra usually indicates the measurement of the chest, which is the area above the breast tissue.

In Europe and other international countries (not including the UK), the number on the bra indicates the measurement taken directly below the bust on the rib cage.

Italian and Australian bra sizes do not have any relationship to either of these measurements, just international sizes in general.

That just leaves US and UK sizing. US/UK sizing is not as simple as French or international sizing, but it does relate to both of those measurements. US/UK sizing is based on the average between the two measurements.

The next column has a basic conversion chart to show band size and common cup size conversions for different countries.

BAND SIZE CONVERSION

US/UK	Europe/Japan	France	Italy	Australia
28	60	75		6
30	65	80	0	8
32	70	85	1	10
34	75	90	2	12
36	80	95	3	14
38	85	100	4	16
40	90	105	5	18
42	95	110	6	20
44	100	115		
46	105	120		
48	110	125		
50	105	130		

CUP SIZE CONVERSION

US	UK/Italy/Australia	Europe/France	Japan
AA	AA	AA	A
A	A	A	B
B	B	B	C
C	C	C	D
D	D	D	E
DD/E	DD	E	F
DDD/F	E	F	G
G	F	G	H
H	FF	H	I
I	G	J	J
J	GG	K	K
K	H	L	L
L	HH	M	M
M	J	N	N
N	JJ	O	O
O	K	P	P

Some manufacturers create their own standards and do not follow any standard chart.

Reason 2

The second issue is likely the biggest issue. Not all women are shaped the same, but someone at the manufacturer level has to choose their "perfect" fit model. Many times, manufacturers choose what they consider to be average.

Women's torso shapes vary, but bras generally do not accommodate these differences. A wide v-shaped torso may have a 6" or 15cm difference between the chest measurement and the under bust measurements. A straighter torso, may have the same measurement for both the chest and under bust.

If a bra is drafted for an individual that has a 6" or 15cm increase for the chest, but an individual with no difference is trying on the bra, the neckline will likely gape at the neckline and slide down on the back due to the downward hike created by the torso shape.

The torso height can also be an issue for individuals. Since the bra takes up the space between the under bust and the chest, the measurement down the center front of the body between these two areas can also vary drastically. This measurement is considered the chest height.

Individuals with the chest height measurement of 3" to 4" (7.5cm to 10cm) generally need a shorter wire and cup, but not a smaller cup. Individuals with a taller chest height of 7" to 8"

(17.5cm to 20cm) might need a much longer wire and taller cup, but not a larger cup.

The question remains, what measurements did the fit model have? See my blog at Blog.Porcelynne.com for details on an experiment I did to determine what sizes a handful of bras were drafted for.

Reason 3

To address the third issue, bra fitters take measurements to determine the cup size by measuring the bust circumference. This may not be very accurate as women may not be wearing the correct size bra in the first place. I call this the "Catch 22" scenario. Without a great fitting bra, the right measurements are impossible to take, but they are needed to achieve correct measurements to get into the right bra.

The full bust measurement remains unreliable until the perfect fit has been met, as it depends on where the breast is sitting. If the bust sags due to age or incorrect bra size, the full bust circumference will vary, as will the recommended cup size.

TRADITIONAL MEASURING FOR US READY-TO-WEAR BRAS

Taking ones own measurements can be difficult and inaccurate. It is ideal to take measurements without outer clothing on. If taking the measurements over clothing, consider the bulk in the measurement and subtract about 1/2" for clothing.

1. Take a snug measurement under the bust. (This is more accurate without wearing a bra.)

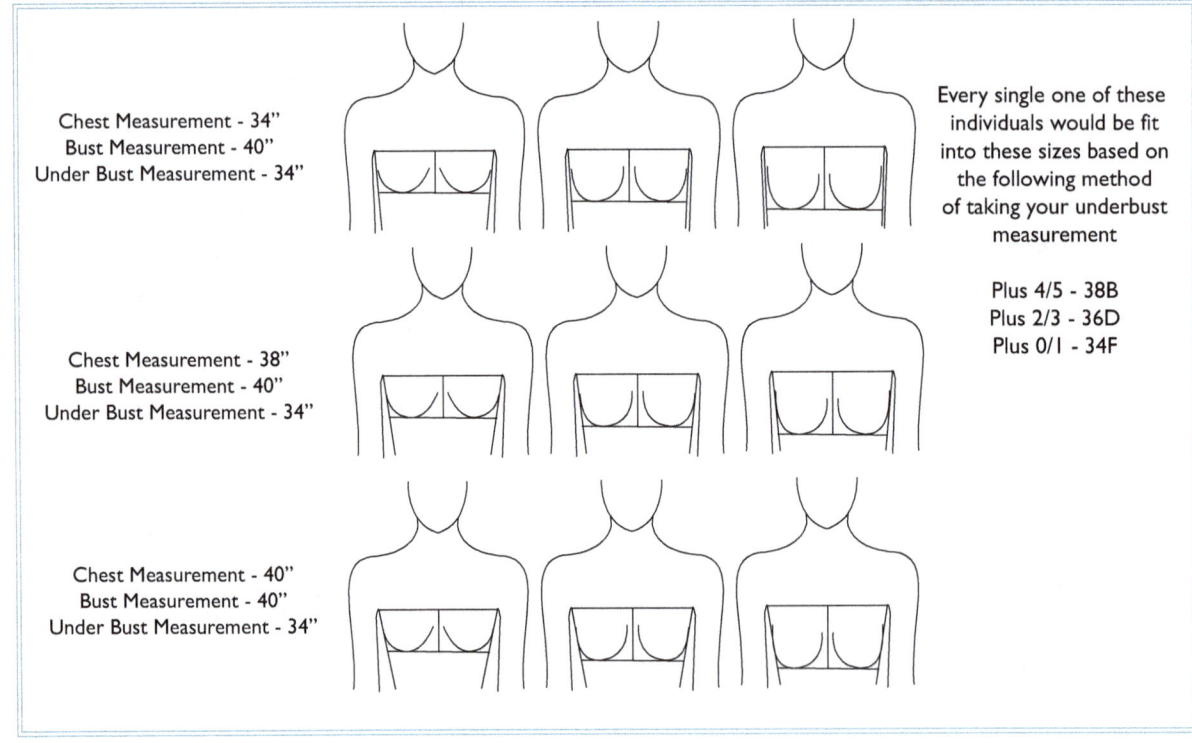

2. The chest measurement is taken above the breast tissue. This measurement should also be snug. (This is more accurate without wearing a bra.)
3. Take the full bust measurement across the widest point on the bust. (This measurement is most accurate wearing a well fitting bra).

> Under Bust Measurement
> Chest Measurement
> Bust Measurement

This next part is tricky. Some manufacturers have individuals take the under bust measurement and add 4" or 5" to that number for an even number band size. (This method does not generally apply for international brands.)

For many higher end ready-to-wear in the US, the best measuring guide is to take the under bust and add 2" or 3" for an even number band size. (This method does not generally apply for international brands.)

It is best to consult the manufacturers recommendations for fitting their own brand of bras.

For the patterns included in this book, follow the sizing instructions in the back of this book. These sizing instructions coincide with my own patterns (Porcelynne branded patterns) and do not follow either of the aforementioned methods.

Always confirm the sizing instructions by the pattern designer. To determine what torso shape a manufacturer drafted a bra for, see my blog, at Blog.Porcelynne.com, for my bra sizing experiment.

I have provided two example charts on the following page to show how sizes can vary based on how a bra size is calculated. Not all sizes are included in these charts.

DETERMINING THE CUP SIZE

For US/UK bras, the general rule for determining cup size is to subtract the band size from the full bust measurement. For each 1" difference, add a cup size, starting with a 1" difference as an A cup.

If the band measures as a 36 band and the full bust measurement is 40", the cup size would count up four sizes.

If trying bras on in a store, take both the bra that measures with the +2/3 method and the bra that measures with the +4/5 method. See which measurement guide fits closer for each brand selected.

International sizes are similar in determining cup sizes based on the difference between the band size and the full bust measurements. Approximately, every 25mm (20mm for Australian sizies) is a cup size.

UNDERSTANDING FIT

First test that the band fits correctly. If the cups are too small, it may pull the band away from the body not allowing for a true fit of the band. A good fitting band will fit snug around the body and will not move when reaching arms up or when bending down to touch the ground.

Once the band fits, focus on the fit of the cups. Unfortunately, every manufacturer has a different take on fitting. The same process will need to take place for each brand that is explored in fit. Start with a larger cup size to ensure that the band fits the body snug and in the correct place.

US/UK BRA SIZE - IMPERIAL - PLUS 4 OR 5
Measurements in Inches

Under Bust Measurement	\multicolumn{11}{c}{Full Bust Measurement}
	31	32	33	34	35	36	37	38	39	40	41
27-28	32AAA	32AA	32A	32B	32C	32D	32E	32F			
29-30			34AAA	34AA	34A	34B	34C	34D	34E	34F	
31-32					36AAA	36AA	36A	36B	36C	36D	36E
33-34							38AAA	38AA	38A	38B	38C
35-36									40AAA	40AA	40A
37-38										42AAA	42AA

US/UK BRA SIZE - IMPERIAL - PLUS 2 OR 3
Measurements in Inches

Under Bust Measurement	\multicolumn{11}{c}{Full Bust Measurement}
	31	32	33	34	35	36	37	38	39	40	41
27-28	30A	30B	30C	30D	30E	30F					
29-30			32A	32B	32C	32D	32E	32F			
31-32					34A	34B	34C	34D	34E	34F	
33-34							36A	36B	36C	36D	36E
35-36									38A	38B	38C
37-38											40A

The fit of a bra can be very challenging. These are examples of a bad fit.

1. **The back of the band is yanked up high.** If the band is not level around the body and is lifted higher in the back, the band is either too big and/or the straps are too tight.

2. **The straps are digging into the shoulder leaving an indentation in the shoulder.** This is usually due to the band and cup fitting incorrectly. 90% of a bra should be supported by the band. If the straps dig in, loosen the straps to their fullest and see how the bra performs.

3. **The band is not sitting flush to the skin.** The band holds up the cups and is supposed to be snug on the body. If the wearer lifts their arms and the band moves the band is too big or the cups are too small. Just the same, if a finger can be placed under the band at the center front, the bra has similar issues. Go down a band size and step up a cup size or two.

4. **The breast tissue is dented and overflows where the cup lays across the body.** This is especially visible in a snug tee shirt. This indicates that the cup is too small.

5. **Back fat bulging from under the band in the back or side seam.** This could either be a band that is too small or a band that is too big. A properly fitting bra should comfortably contain all "extra" skin.

US WIRE CHART - INTERIOR NUMBERS ARE THE WIRE SIZE

Band Size	A	B	C	D	E (DD)	F (DDD)	G	H	I	J	K	L
28	26	28	30	32	34	36	38	40	42	44	46	48
30	28	30	32	34	36	38	40	42	44	46	48	50
32	30	32	34	36	38	40	42	44	46	48	50	52
34	32	34	36	38	40	42	44	46	48	50	52	54
36	34	36	38	40	42	44	46	48	50	52	54	56
38	36	38	40	42	44	46	48	50	52	54	56	58
40	38	40	42	44	46	48	50	52	54	56	58	60
42	40	42	44	46	48	50	52	54	56	58	60	
44	42	44	46	48	50	52	54	56	58	60		
46	44	46	48	50	52	54	56	58	60			
48	46	48	50	52	54	56	58	60				
50	48	50	52	54	56	58	60					
52	50	52	54	56	58	60						

CHOOSING A PATTERN

There is no standard size chart that all manufacturers use. A bra size will vary based on individual pattern designers. Be sure to check the designer's recommendations for sizing before purchasing any patterns.

This book contains sizes 30A to 40F. The size chart for these patterns are located in the back of this book. These patterns are also available for a free download online at Porcelynne.com. For larger sizes, select a styled bra by any pattern maker or create a custom bra with the drafting directions in the advanced section of this book.

CHOOSING WIRES

Wires vary in size and shape. Wires generally come in two major classifications: regular and vertical. Additional wire styles such as demi, semi, half and monowires will not be discussed in this chapter.

Each pattern designer selects their base size and base wire for their draft. Utilize the designer's instructions when selecting underwires.

When altering the basic pattern for fit, having additional wire sizes and styles on hand, will be beneficial to experiment with. The patterns provided in the back of this book use the wire size chart on the previous page for wire recommendations.

UNDERSTANDING WIRE SHAPES

The shape of a wire can range drastically, but for general reference, a regular wire points out to the sides, as opposed to vertical wires, which point straight up at each end.

Regular wires are generally used for wider or smaller breast roots. The breast root is the shape of the breast against the body.

Vertical wires are generally for much narrower or larger breast roots.

CHAPTER 2
BASIC BRA CONSTRUCTION

There are many methods for constructing a bra. This chapter introduces the basics. Each subsequent chapter of this section, introduces alternative construction methods for further knowledge. The bra that is provided in the back of this book, is utilized for these exercises. This design has a simple 3/8" to 1/2" (10mm to 12.5mm) picot elastic trim applied to the neckline and waistline.

In preparation, cut two sets of cups (mirrored), one center front band on the fold and two side front bands out of a nonstretch fabric. Cut two mirrored back bands from power net. In a stabilizer, cut two side front bands and one center front band on the fold to reinforce the front of the bra

CUP CONSTRUCTION

1. With the right sides of the fabric together, place the two lower cup pieces together at the center cup seam.

Right Sides Together

Wrong Side of Fabric

2. Pin the edges together. Stitch together, without a back stitch, at 1/4" or 6mm with a straight stitch.

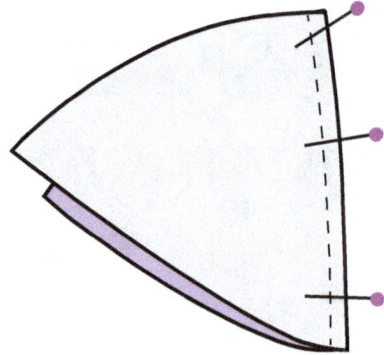

3. Open the lower cup seam and press the seam open.

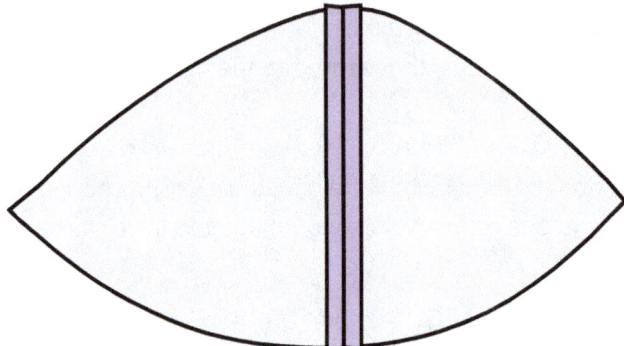

4. Trim down the seam allowance to 1/8" or 3mm. Place a shear strip of seam tape over the seam allowance and pin in place. For first time construction, loosely hand baste in place prior to stitching.

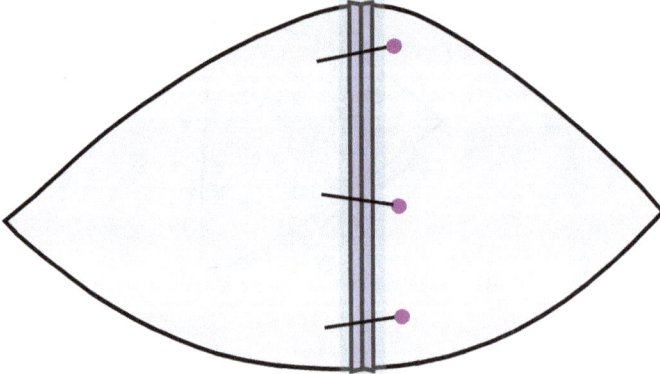

5. Sew two rows of stitches, one on each side of the seam, securing the seam tape over the seam allowance. If the seam tape is wide, the stitch can be placed anywhere on the seam tape, providing it holds the seam open.

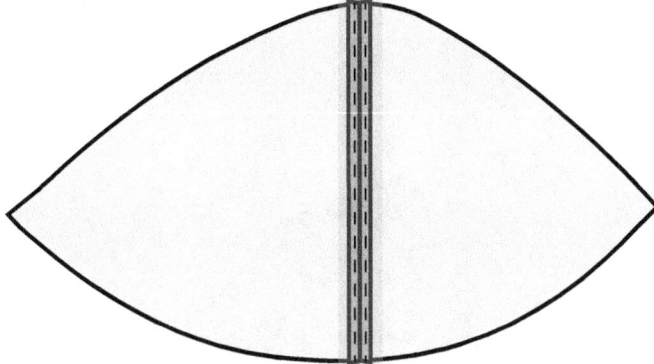

6. Attach the top cup to the bottom cup at the center horizontal seam with the same method as the bottom cup.

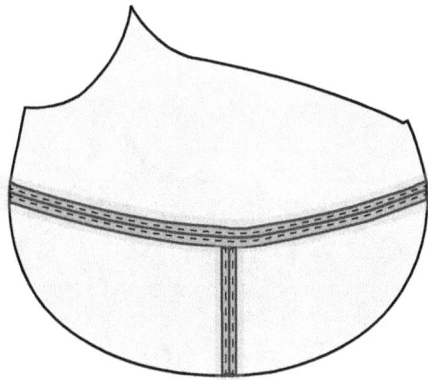

7. Before continuing to the remainder of the bra, picot elastic needs to be attached to the center neckline of the cup.

   a. Sew a sample of the elastic on a scrap prior to sewing on the bra. Place the decorative side of the elastic toward the right side of the fabric and stitch in place closely and evenly to the picot edge. This can be done with an overlock, zigzag or straight stitch. Do not stretch the fabric or elastic when sewing. Do not cut the elastic on the overlock machine. Cutting the elastic causes the elastic to lose its stability. This can result in the elastic stretching out rapidly.

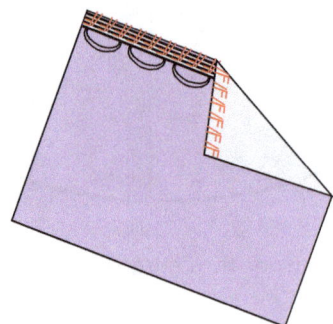

   b. Attach the elastic to the neckline of both cups with the right side of the elastic facing the right side of the cup.

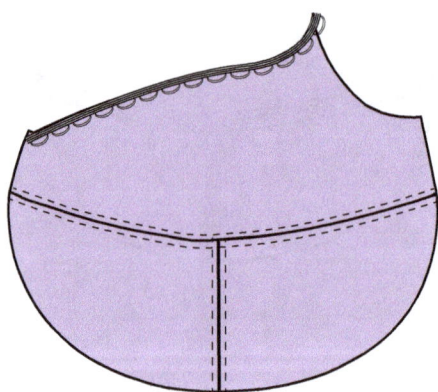

Beginner / Basic Bra Construction | 37

8. Flip the elastic so the stitched side appears on the back side of the garment. The decorative edge is the only part visible on the right side of the garment. With the elastic flipped, stitch in place with either a zigzag or three step zigzag stitch.

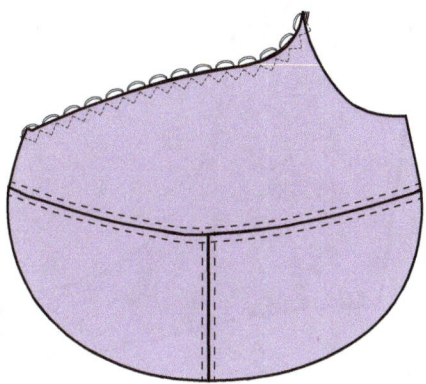

BAND CONSTRUCTION

9. For the bridge, place the stabilizer and fabric together with right sides facing each other and stitch the top seam at 1/4" or 6mm with a straight stitch.

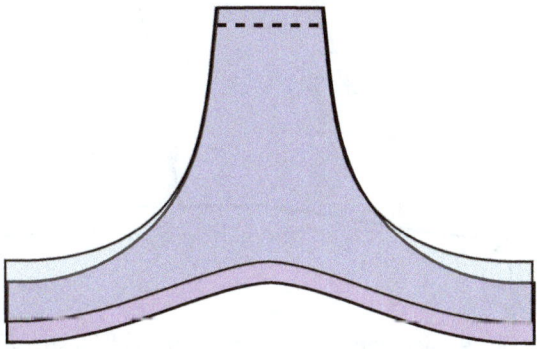

10. Flip the stabilizer to the back side of the band and secure in place by stitching around all the edges at 1/8" or 3mm. This helps in the construction steps when attaching the cups.

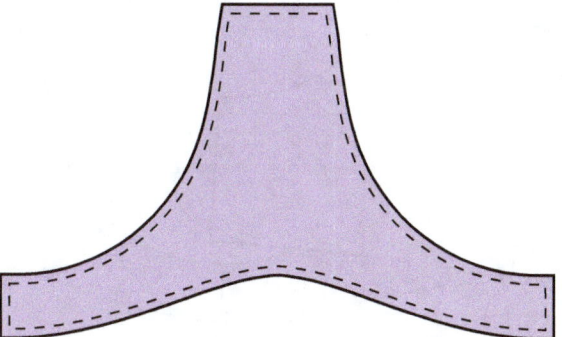

11. On the side front band, place the stabilizer behind the band with wrong side of the stabilizer facing the wrong side of the band. Stitch in place at 1/8" or 3mm to create a double layered pattern piece.

12. Connect the bridge to the side front band with right sides together at 1/4" or 6mm. Press the seams open.

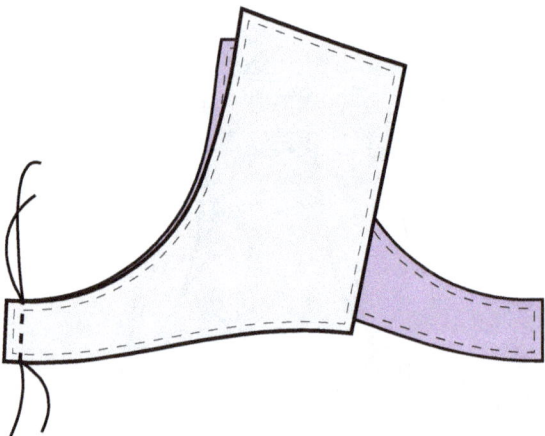

13. Attach the front band to the back band at the side seam with a straight stitch at 1/4" or 6mm and press towards the front.

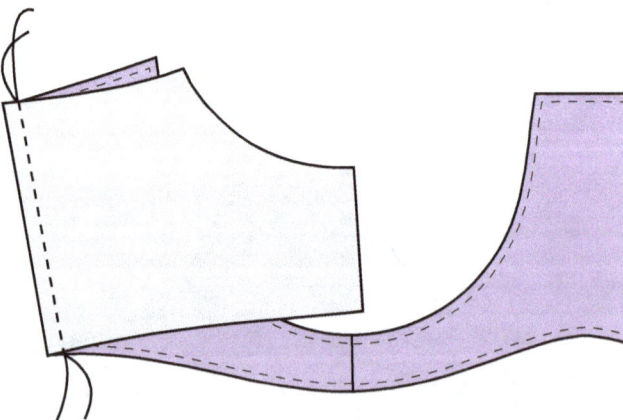

14. For added support on larger cups and bands, boning can be added to the side seam.

   a. Measure the side seam from top to bottom. Remove 1/2" or 12.5mm from the distance and cut this amount of casing. The boning should be approximately 1/4" or 6mm smaller than the length of casing.

Side Seam	
	- 1/2" or 12.5mm
Casing Length	
	- 1/4" or 6mm
Boning Length	

   b. Attach the casing edge to the seam allowance on the back side of the band, leaving 1/4" or 6mm at both the top and bottom.

   c. Fold the casing flat towards the front side of the band and top stitch the remaining side in place, stitching from the top edge of the band to the bottom.

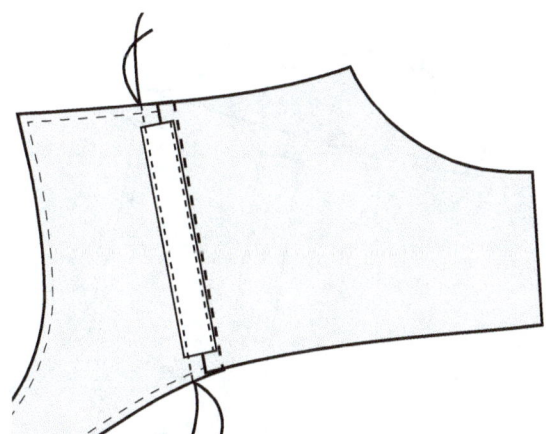

15. Attach elastic around the waistline with the decorative side facing the right side of the fabric.

16. Fold the elastic to the backside and secure with a zigzag or three-step zigzag stitch.

17. Attach the cup into the curve of the band with right sides facing each other. If this is the first time sewing a bra, the recommendation is to hand baste these pieces in place prior to sewing by machine. Stitch in place with a straight stitch at 1/4" or 6mm.

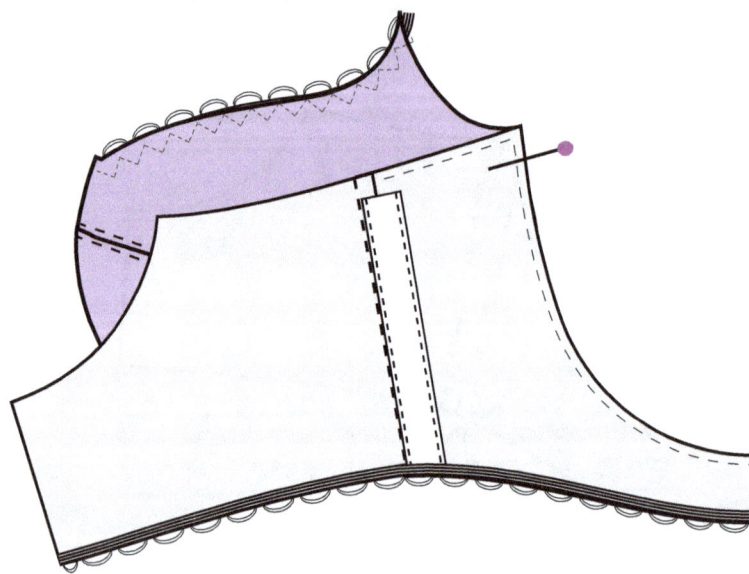

Beginner / Basic Bra Construction | 41

18. Measure the stitch line from the previous step. Subtract 1/4" or 6mm from the length. Cut this length in underwire channeling. We reduce it by 1/4" or 6mm for applying the neckline elastic under the arm.

Cup Seam Length	
	- 1/4" or 6mm
Channeling Length	

19. Take the underwire channeling and attach it to the seam allowance on the cup side as we did for the boning casing. Begin from the underarm 1/4" or 6mm away from the end and stitch it all the way to the center front neckline. This should end at the top of the bridge. Trim the casing to fit.

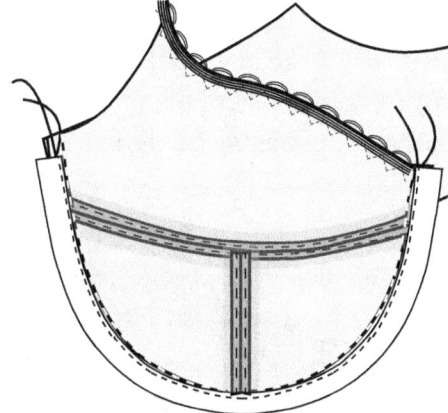

20. Fold the channeling towards the band and top stitch the remaining side in place.

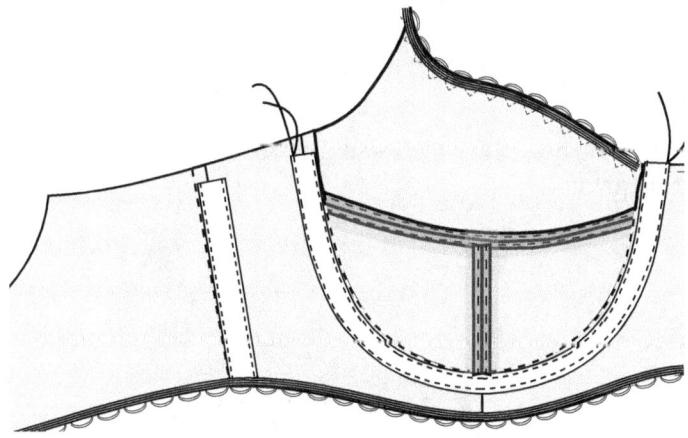

21. Attach the neckline elastic from the strap point in the back to the strap point of the cup.

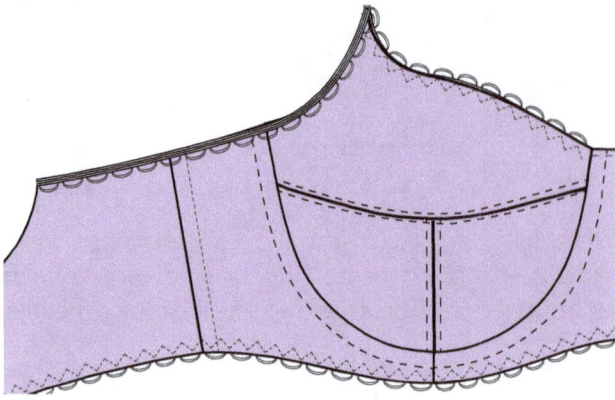

22. a. Insert the boning into the casing at the side seam.

    b. Flip the elastic to the backside of the bra and top stitch with a zigzag. Be careful, stitching through the boning is possible. As long as the boning is plastic, stitch slowly and it should not break the needle.

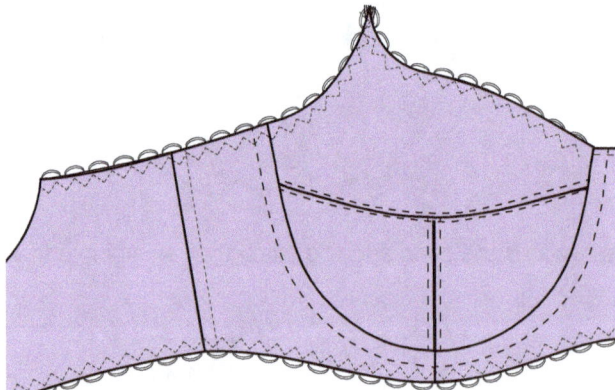

23. On the back band of the bra, attach the center back elastic. Leave an additional 1/2" or 12.5mm of elastic at the strap point.

24. To construct a strap, collect strap elastic, a ring and slide.

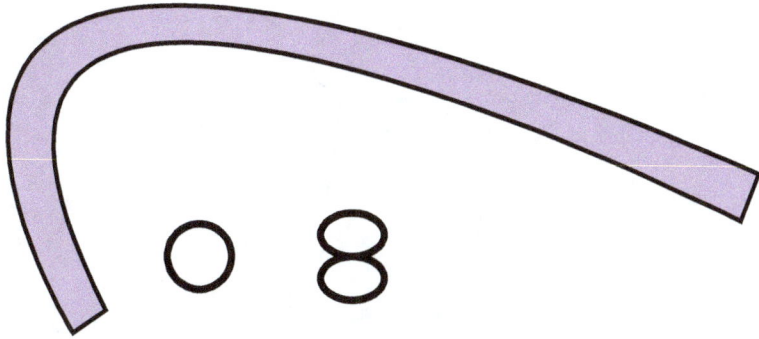

25. Loop the elastic through the center of the slide and secure in place with a bar tack or a shallow and small zigzag stitch.

26. Place the elastic through the ring and pass the elastic through the slide a second time.

27. Attach the strap end to the front neckline with the right sides facing each other. Line the strap up and stitch the strap to the strap point.

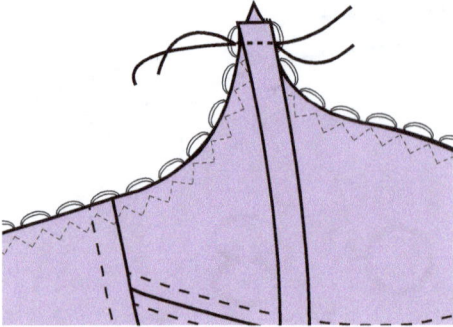

28. Flip the strap to show the right side and bar tack in place, securing the strap and cup seam allowance down.

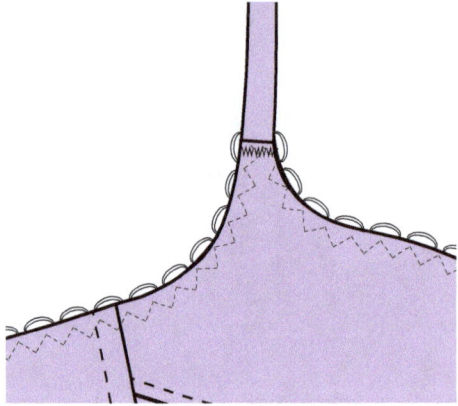

29. Attach the ring of the strap to the elastic at the back strap point by passing the picot end through the ring and securing it to the back side of the band. Bar tack in place.

30. Insert the underwire into the channeling at the center front of the bra. Bar tack the end of the casing at the top of the bridge.

31. Hook & eye tape usually has an open flap for placing over the end of the bra backs.

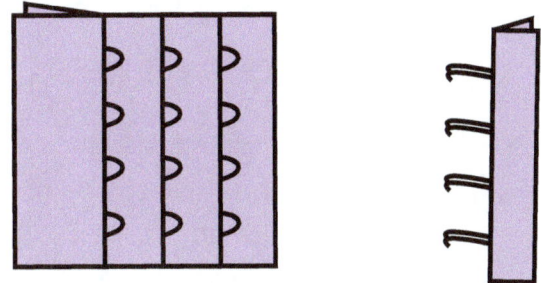

32. Use a zipper foot to baste the hook & eye tape in place. Use a regular foot or an adjustable zipper foot to zigzag over the edge to clean finish the flap. Attach the hooks on the left side of the bra and the eyes on the right side of the bra back.

CHAPTER 3
BAND ALTERATIONS FOR ELASTIC

All patterns are designed for specific notions. In order to alter something as simple as the elastic width, a pattern needs to be changed to accommodate it. For this exercise, change the elastic to a 3/4" or 20mm elastic for the waistline and center back neckline. Both elastics will be attached by an overlapping method, rather than the stitch and flip method demonstrated in the previous chapter.

PART 1: PATTERN MANIPULATION

1. Draw in the seam allowances on the front band and bridge at the joining seams, as pictured, at 1/4" or 6mm.

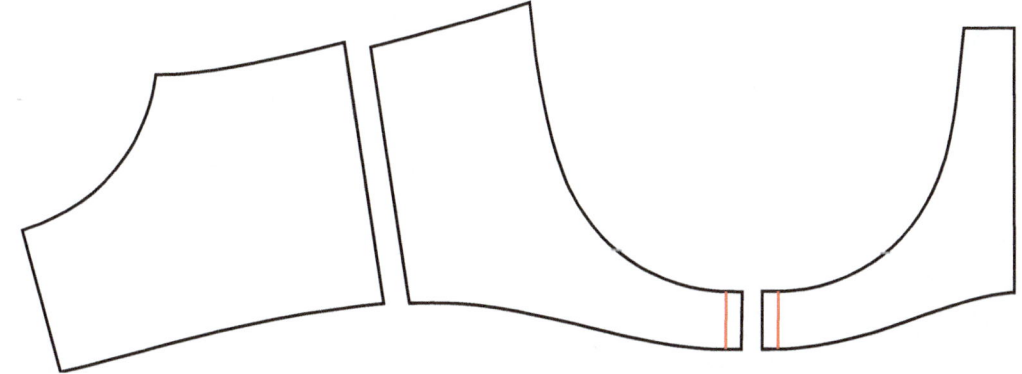

2. Overlap the front band pieces at the seam lines.

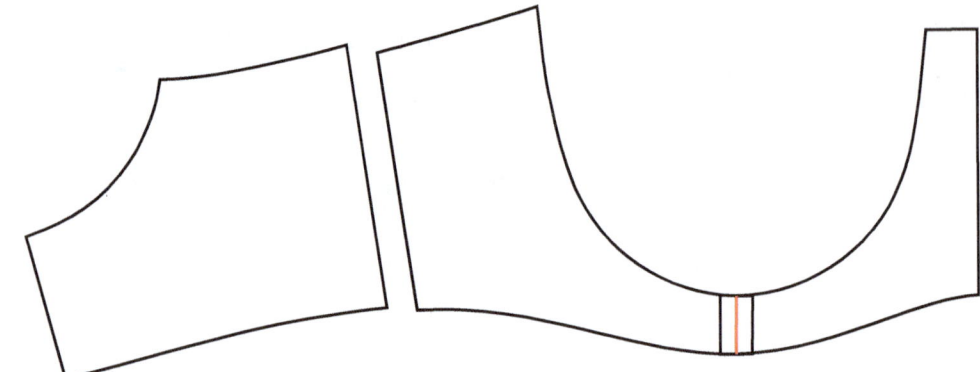

3. Remove 1/4" or 6mm off the waistline of the band. The 1/4" or 6mm is the maximum amount that can be removed from the waistline, of this pattern, and still allow the channeling to be attached properly.

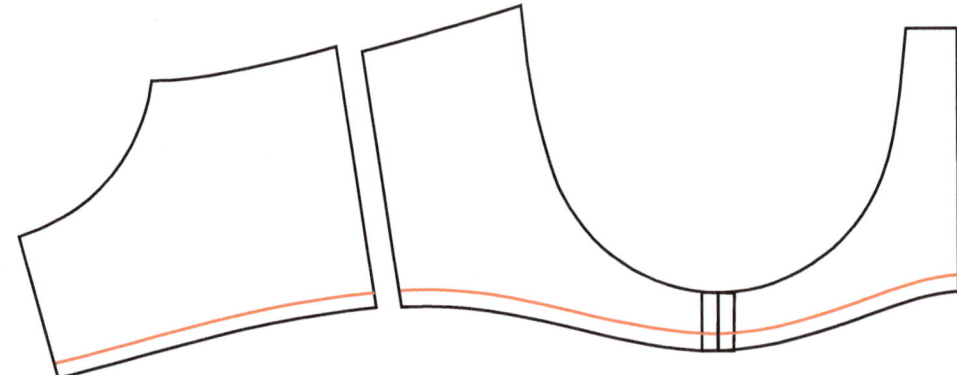

4. Remove 3/4" or 20mm off the back neckline from the center back to the back strap. The elastic will be overlapped by 1/4" or 6mm at both the back and waistline. The finished width of the elastics and back band must equal the original amount required to properly accommodate the hook & eyes. The back strap adjustment resolves the width needed for proper attachment.

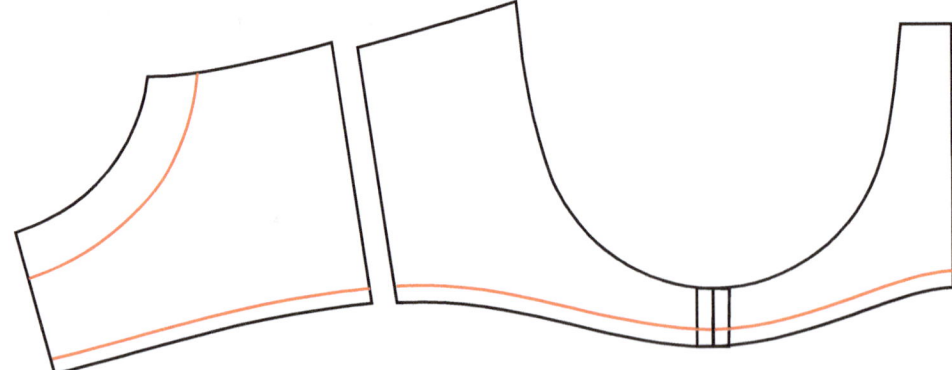

PART 2: CONSTRUCTION METHOD

This exercise introduces a different method in which to attach elastic to the waistline and adds an attached back strap to the back neckline. These directions also introduce a fully lined cup. A lined cup is used when the design fabric has too much stretch or if it might cause irritation to the skin.

1. Cut out two sets of patterns for the cup. One of the design fabric and one of the lining. Prepare the other pattern pieces as previously demonstrated.

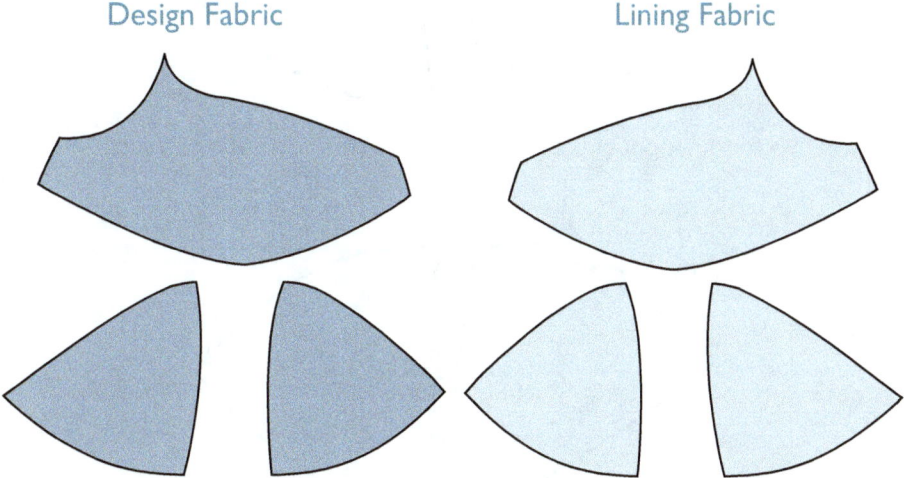

Design Fabric   Lining Fabric

2. Attach the two lower cups together at 1/4" or 6mm for both the lining and the design fabric.

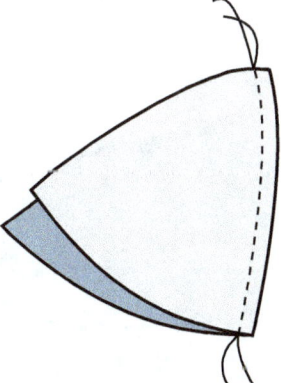

3. Press the seams open and top stitch the seams down close to the seam. The seam allowance can be trimmed down to 1/8" or 3mm to reduce bulk. Since the cup is fully lined, seam tape covering the seam is not necessary.

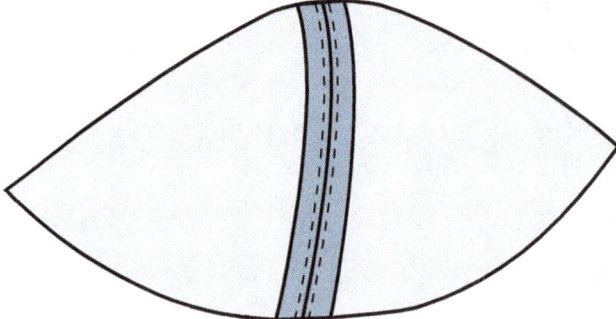

4. Sew the lower cup to the upper cup at 1/4" or 6mm. Press open and top stitch.

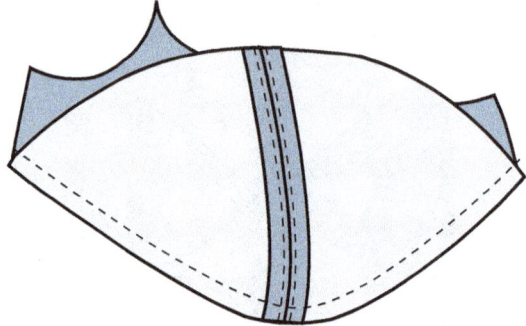

5. Take the right side of the design fabric cup and place the decorative elastic at the center neckline of the cup. Stitch in place.

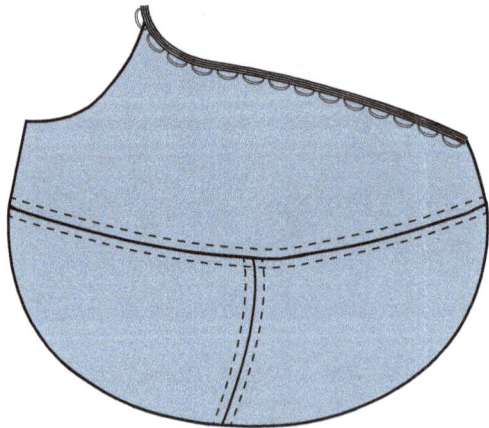

6. Place the right side of the lining towards the right side of the design fabric. Sew the necklines together at 1/4" or 6mm, sandwiching the elastic between the two layers. At the center front of the neckline, stop sewing 1/4" or 6mm away from the end (this will aid in attaching the cup to the band).

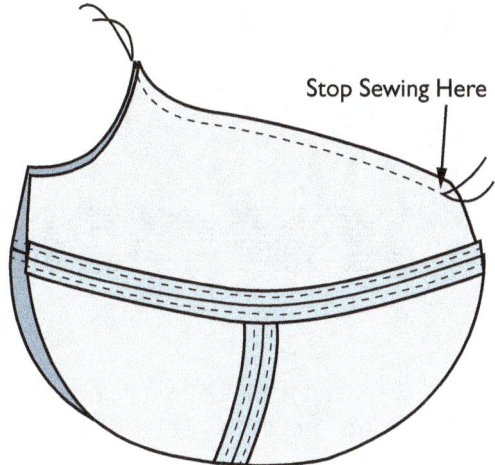

7. Flip the cup right sides out and stitch the edges together to hold the two layers in place.

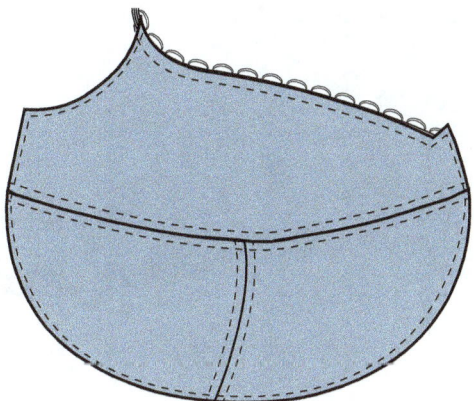

8. Attach the band pieces together as previously demonstrated.

    a. Instead of attaching the elastic at the waistline, as demonstrated in Chapter 2, overlap the elastic on top of the raw edge by 1/4" or 6mm. Use a 3/4" or 20mm elastic.

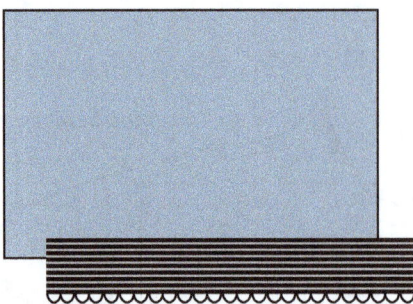

    b. Stitch in place with a zigzag or coverstitch. If a coverstitch machine is available, a coverstitch is ideal for this finishing because it covers the raw edge underneath the elastic.

9. Attach the cups, channeling and armhole elastics as previously demonstrated. To create an attached strap for the center of the back neckline curve, cut a length of elastic that will expand the back neckline and become the strap. A standard strap measures between 15" and 18" (38cm to 45cm).

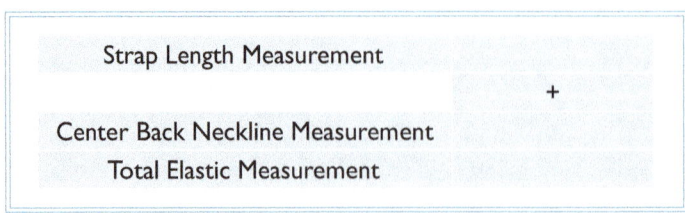

Strap Length Measurement

+

Center Back Neckline Measurement

Total Elastic Measurement

10. Prior to attaching the elastic to the back neckline, attached the strap hardware to the end of the straps, as previously demonstrated. Overlap the back neckline with the elastic by 1/4" or 6mm as instructed for the waistline. Attach the elastic and secure at the top of the back band with a bar tack.

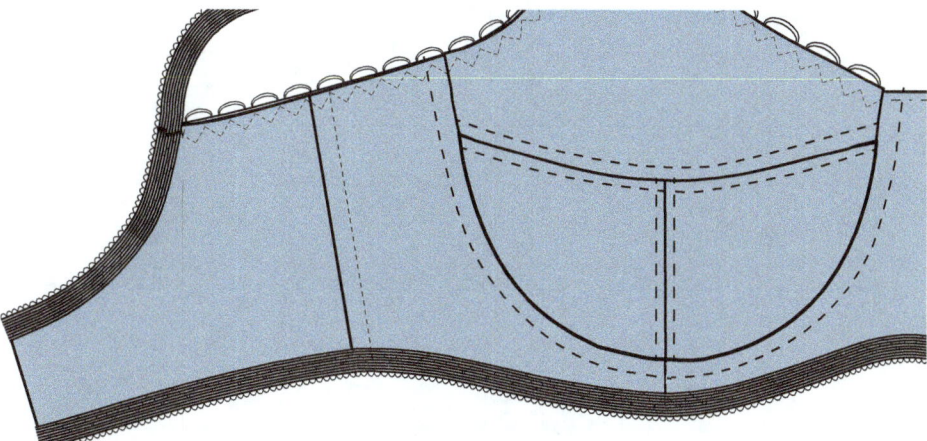

11. Attach the ring to the front of the bra by looping the strap point through the ring. Bar tack in place. Complete the hook and eye closure as previously demonstrated.

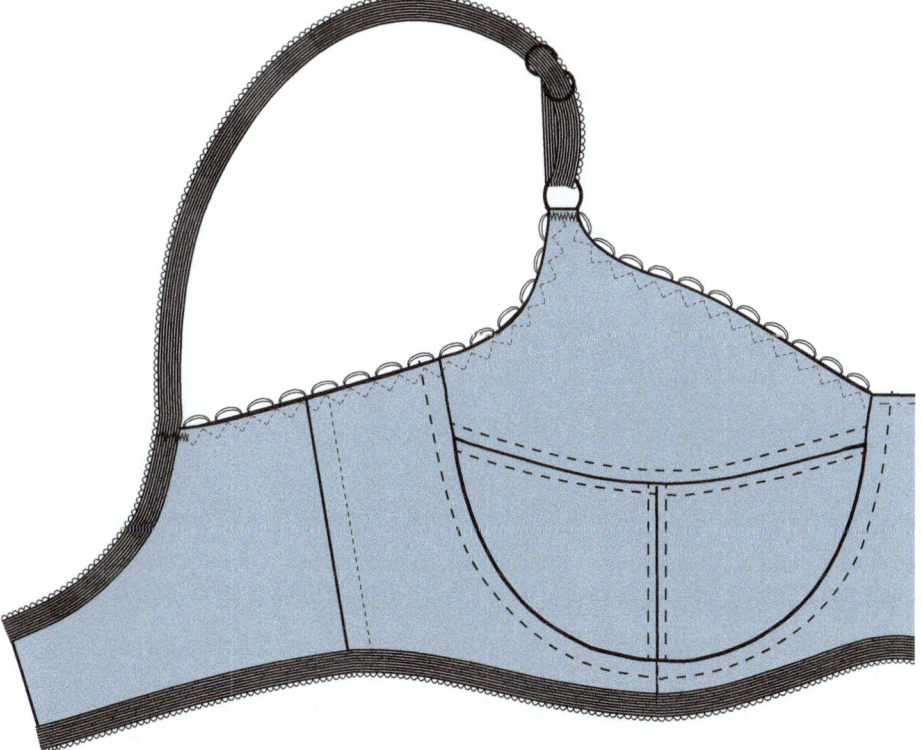

CHAPTER 4
FRAMELESS BRA

Some bra designs have only a partial band, meaning that the band itself is segmented on the sides of the cup. This chapter alters the basic bra pattern to create a bra with floating cups, where the band is not attached to the entire cup. For a construction variation, the cup neckline will use a decorative edge lace fabric and a variation for attaching straps to the back of the band. This type of bra is referred to as a "frameless" bra.

PART 1: PATTERN MANIPULATION

1. Normally the underwire channeling is folded outwards and stitched down to the band. Because this bra does not have a full band, the channeling must be sewn to the cup instead. As to not lose any volume in the cup, add the amount that is lost due to the underwire attachment. At the curve, where it is sewn to the band, add 3/8" to 1/2" (10mm to 12.5mm) for the width of the underwire channeling.

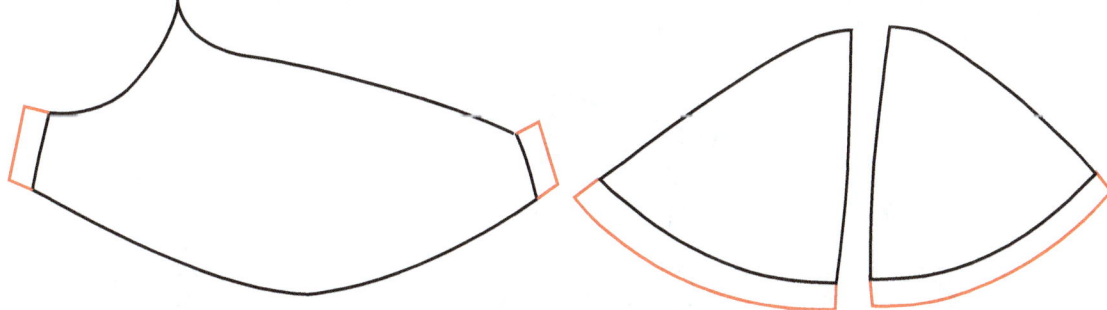

2. The next change is to alter the neckline for a straight edge lace. Draw a straight line from the right side of the strap to the center front neckline.

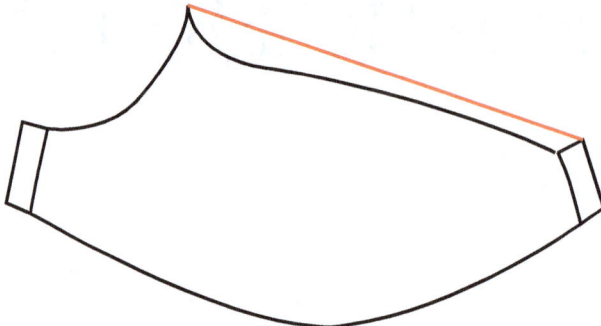

3. Trace all the band pieces and draw in the seam allowances at the side seam and joining band/bridge seam at 1/4" or 6mm.

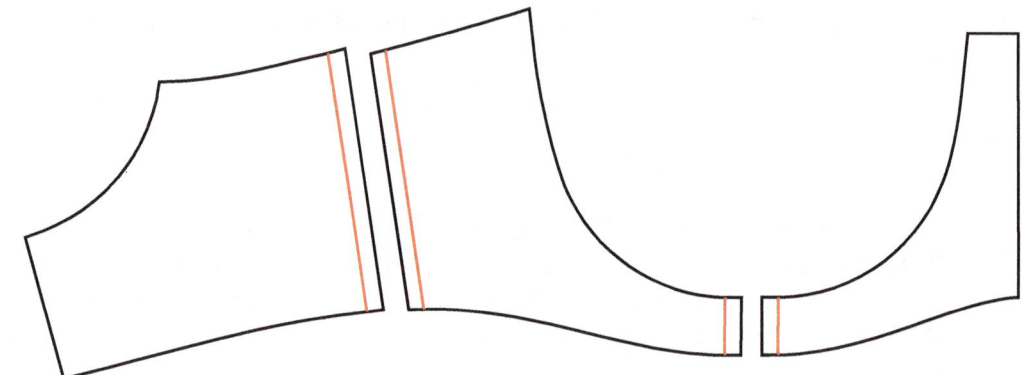

4. Connect the back band to the side front band by overlapping them on the seam lines. Connect the bridge to the side band in the same manner.

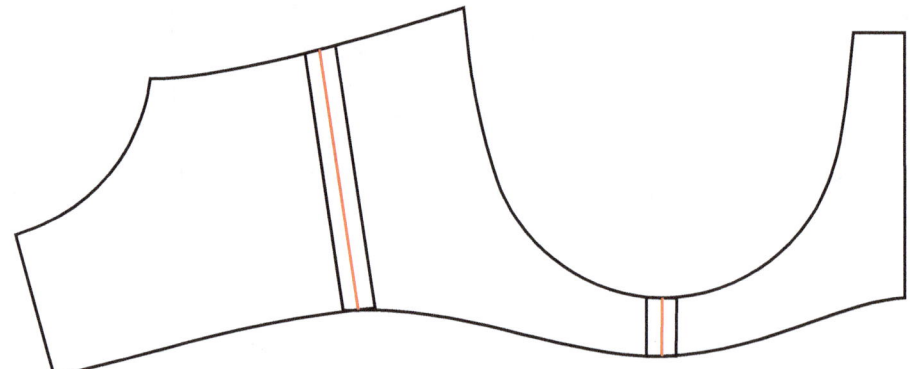

5. Keeping the top of the bridge and the hook & eye width intact, adjust the band shape removing the lower portion of the lower band.

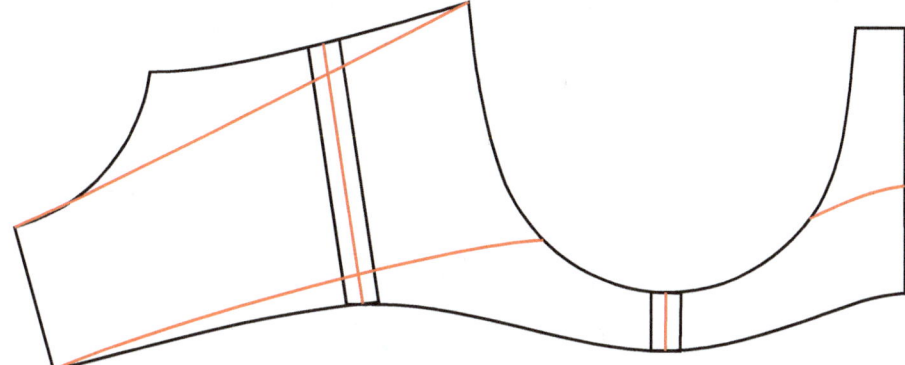

6. Separate the three pattern pieces.

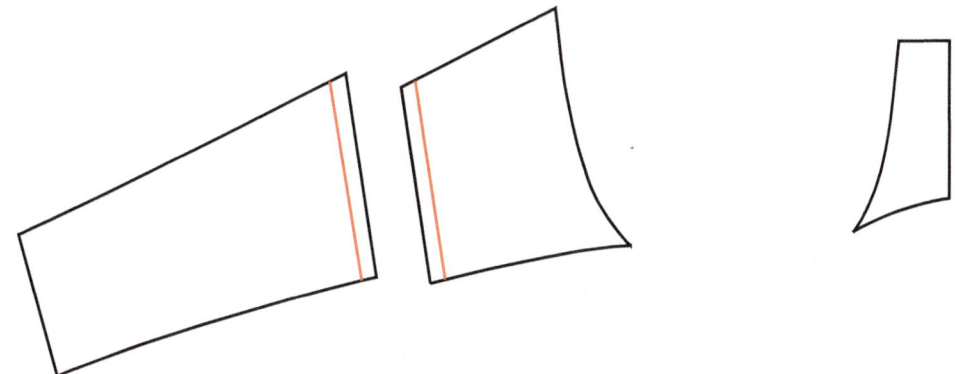

7. Volume was added to the cup, therefore the band needs to be altered to balance the amount that was added to the cup. Remove 3/8" to 1/2" (10mm to 12.5mm) from the band where the cup is inserted.

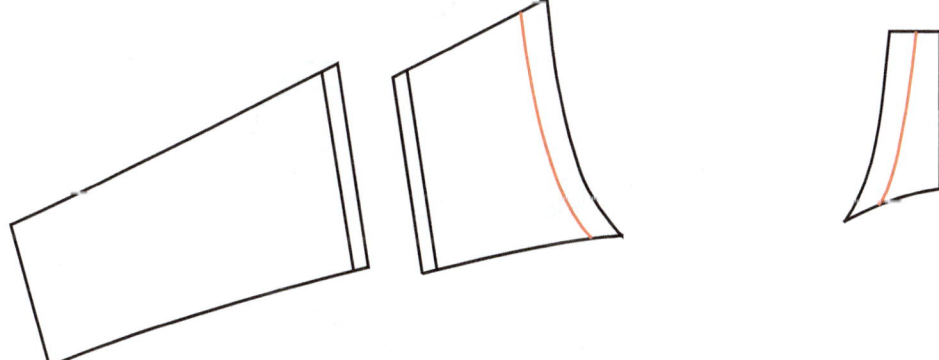

PART 2: CONSTRUCTION METHOD

Using a lace with a finished edge, line up the top front neckline to the edge of the fabric and cut out the top cup. If cutting the entire cup out of a stretch lace, it is recommended to fully line the cup in tricot or a bra lining.

CUP CONSTRUCTION

1. Attach the cup seams together as previously demonstrated. If fully lining the cup, seam tape is not necessary.

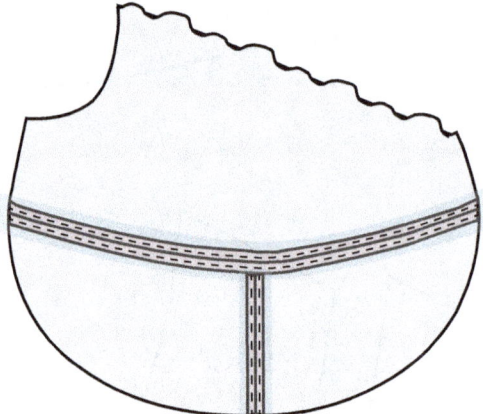

2. Due to the nature of lace, the edge needs to be reinforced by either clear elastic or seam tape. Both serve the purpose of securing the neckline. Elastic can be stitched with a zigzag, slightly stretched, to hug the neckline. Seam tape is stitched with a straight stitch, to secure the fabric from stretching. If fully lining the cup, fold the top down of the lining 1/4" to 1/2" (6mm to 12.5mm) away from the edge and stitch down. The neckline for a lined cup should also be reinforced.

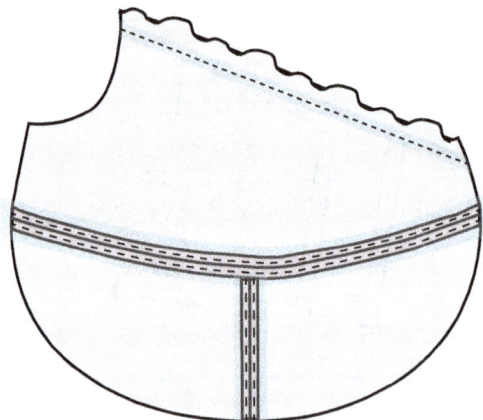

BAND CONSTRUCTION

3. Place the right side of the bridge to the right side of the stabilizer. Stitch the tops and bottoms together at the 1/4" or 6mm seam allowance.

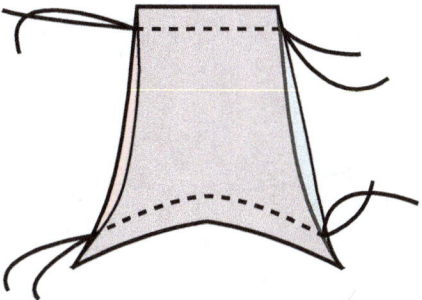

4. Flip the bridge with right sides out and stitch around the edges at 1/8" or 3mm.

5. For the side front band, stitch the stabilizer to the front band. Attaching the side seams, boning casing and the waistband elastic as previously demonstrated.

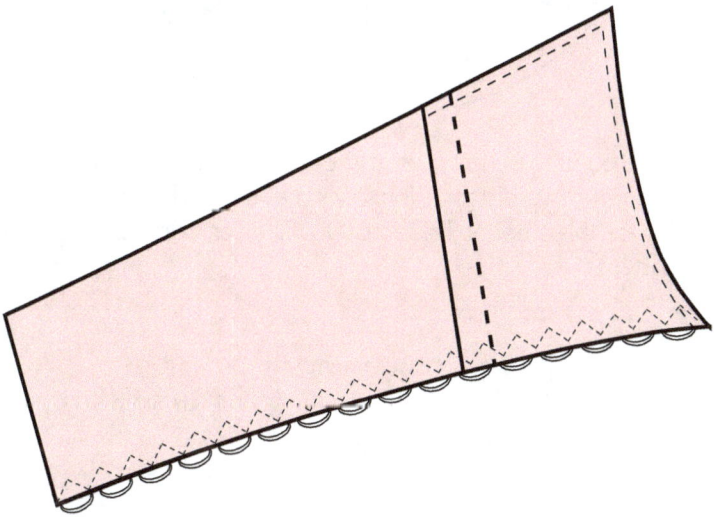

6. Beginning at the top of the cup in the center front of the bra, attach the bridge to the cup at the 1/4" or 6mm seam allowance.

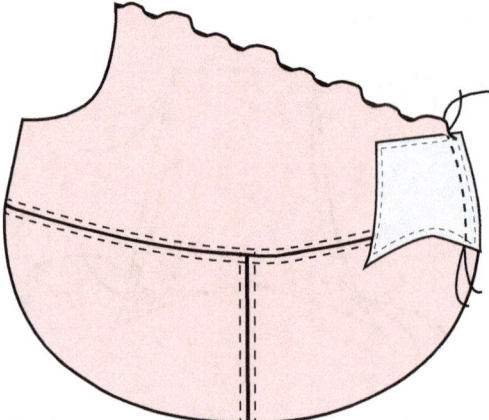

7. Attach the top of the side cup to the band at the 1/4" or 6mm seam allowance.

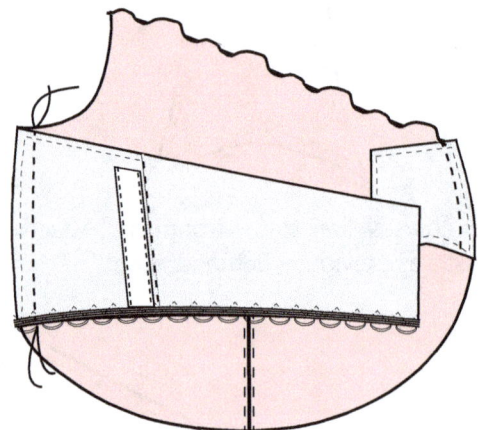

8. Measure the distance around the cup curve at the seam line (1/4" or 6mm from the cup edge). Remove 1/4" or 6mm from that distance, for spacing at the underarm elastic. Cut a piece of underwire channeling for this amount. This amount will differ from Chapter 2 due to changes in the cup and band patterns.

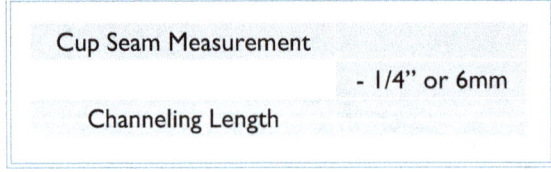

9. Take the underwire channeling and attach it to the seam allowance of the cup curve just short of 1/4" or 6mm. Instead of attaching it to the wrong side of the cup as we did in Chapter 2, attach it to the right side of the cup on the seam line. Start 1/4" or 6mm down from the side cup. The channeling should end at the center front neckline. If it extends past, trim down the channeling.

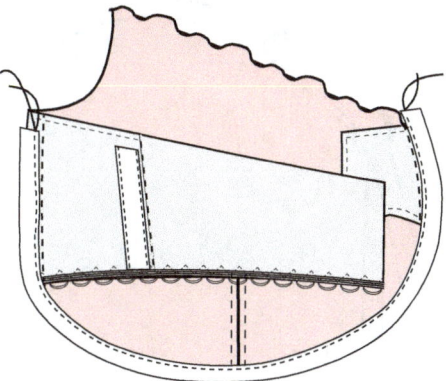

10. Fold the channeling inwards to the cup and top stitch the edge in place.

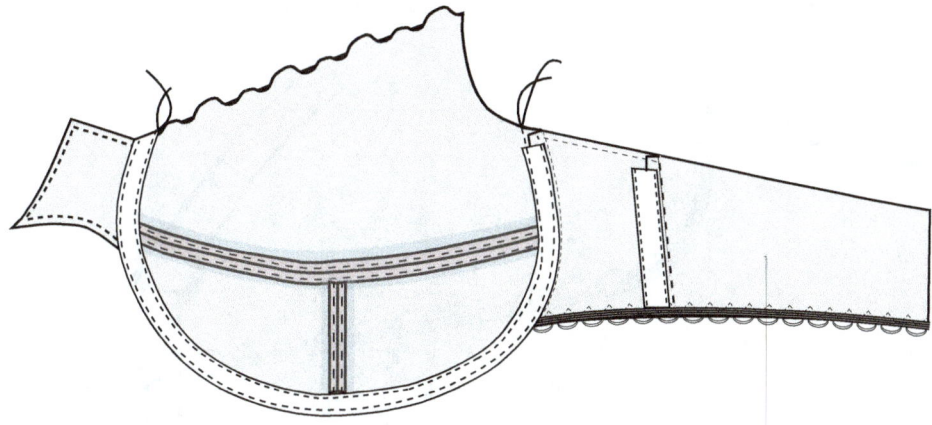

11. Attach picot elastic to the neckline of the back and side cup.

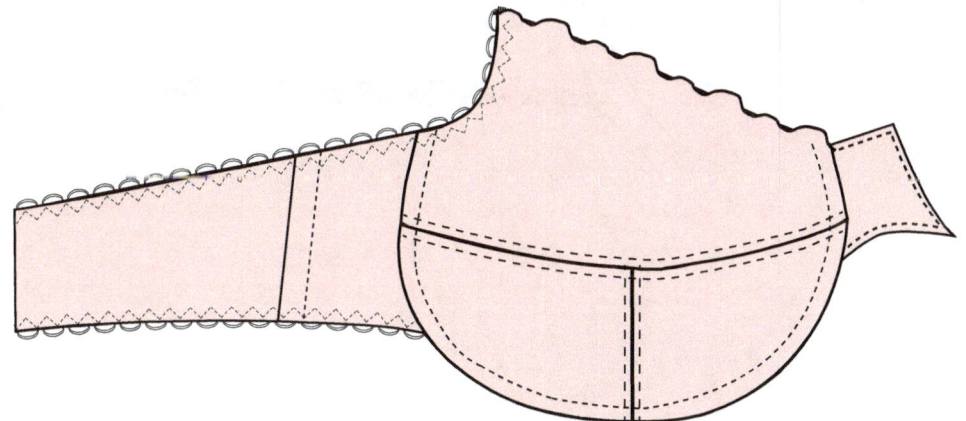

12. For the styling of the back band, it is recommended to use a reinforced strap. Create the strap as previously demonstrated. At the bottom of the ring, loop a length of elastic equal to twice the back band height plus 1" or 25mm. This strap is attached at the top and bottom of the band.

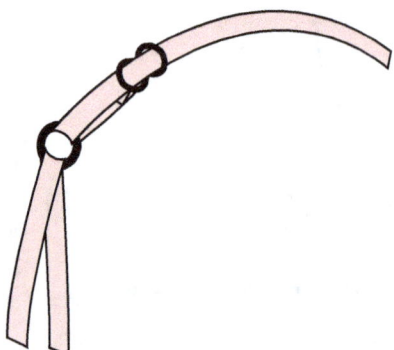

13. At the strap position of the back band, attach the bottom of the elastic to the bottom of the band with a bar tack. Reinforce the top of the elastic at the top of the band with another bar tack. Complete the remainder of the bra as previously demonstrated.

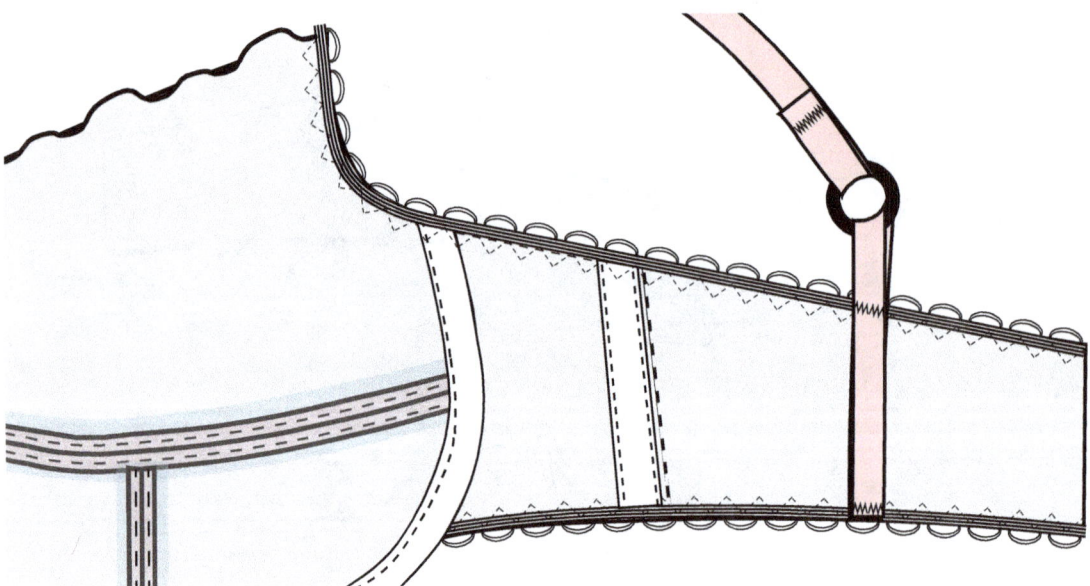

INTERMEDIATE

Chapter 5: Introduction to Pattern Manipulation. 65

Chapter 6: Pattern Adjustments for Fit. 69

Chapter 7: Padded Bra 81

Chapter 8: Front Closure Demi Bra 87

Chapter 9: Strapless Bra 93

Chapter 10: Stylizing a Bra: Seam Lines 103

Chapter 11: Stylizing a Bra: Slash and Spread 107

Chapter 12: Nursing Bra 113

Chapter 13: Mastectomy Bra 119

CHAPTER 5
INTRODUCTION TO PATTERN MANIPULATION

The intermediate section highlights how to perform more complex pattern alterations. These alterations include changing patterns for fit, creating simple style lines changes and adding design details. Specialty bras are also covered in this section, including padded bras, strapless bras, nursing bras and mastectomy bras.

TOOLS

Notcher - A notcher is a small handheld tool that places small cutouts on the edge of a pattern. It looks like a hole punch, but only snips the edge of a pattern. Select notching should be done on patterns to indicate stitch lines.

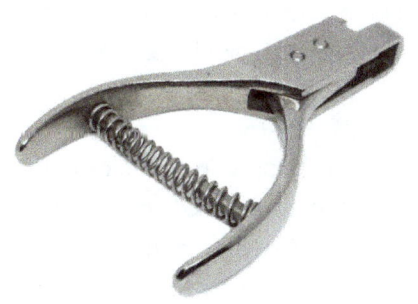

Wire Cutters - A small pair of wire bolt cutters or pliers with wire cutting capabilities are recommended to alter wire lengths to create custom cut wires.

Tipping Agents - When cutting down wires, a variety of tipping agents can be used. The first step to prep a wire for a tipping agent is to file down the edges to ensure a proper surface for adherence. Suggested mediums are Household Goop®, nail polish, latex paint or tool dip.

To tip with nail polish or latex paint, several layers may be required to properly coat the tip.

Some individuals have also found success in tipping wires with heat shrink tubing.

SUPPLIES

Foam & Batting - Batting or foam is used to pad a cup. Different weights and concentrations are available in widths of 1/8" to 1/2". Batting can be cotton, poly-cotton or 100% poly-fill. Spacer fabric can also be used as padding.

Front Clip - Front clips allow for an easy open and close functionality to a bra. A front closure does not allow a bra to adjust in size.

Gripper Elastic - Gripper elastics contain a narrow strip of rubber on the back side. Gripper elastics can be used on strapless bras.

Jersey Fabric - The most common knit is known as a jersey knit. Jersey knits are found in everyday clothing such as tee shirts and underwear. Jersey knits can be used on smaller cup bras, but offer little support for larger bust sizes. In this section, jersey fabric is used for a prosthetic pocket on a mastectomy bra.

Nursing Clip - A nursing clip is a specialty clip which allows a nursing mother to open and close her nursing cup with one hand. An alternative to this is to use a slide hook or a single row hook & eye tape.

PATTERN STYLES

Every pattern change affects the fit of a garment. This can affect where the bra sits on the body and how it covers the breast. Be sure to test each design for fit and functionality.

PADDED BRA

The chapter on padding details how to create a foam insert as well as how to create a padded seamed cup.

An alternative is to purchase a pre-molded and/or padded cup. This type of cup is regularly found in ready-to-wear.

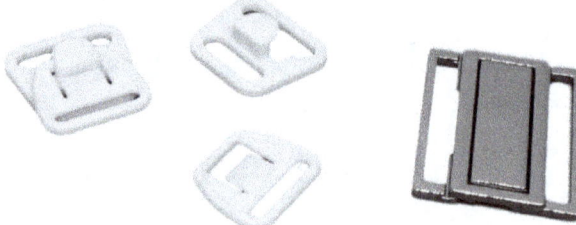

DEMI CUP BRA

A demi bra is a 3/4 coverage bra that dips low in the front. This type of bra is used to enhance the bust or used when the spacing between the breast is too narrow for a full wire. Because the front dips low, this style bra is ideal for a front hook closure.

Demi underwires are generally about 1 1/2" or 38mm shorter than a full coverage wire at the center front. Demi wires can be cut down from a full wire. This allows for more versatility in a custom design.

Other related designs include a semi cup and quarter cup bra. A semi cup is a half cup that generally cuts across the apex. A quarter cup is a bra that contains only half of a lower cup and does not cover the apex. These styles are not covered in this book, but similar modifications can be made to accommodate these styles.

STRAPLESS BRA

The strapless bra varies from the basic bra in that the band covers more of the body. A strapless bra generally has boning and a wider hook & eye closure. There are a variety of strapless designs including backless and plunge.

Backless bras are not entirely backless, but have a long base. These are used for garments with a low cut back. This type of bra will have more boning than an average strapless bra and resembles a bustier or corset.

STYLIZED BRA CUP

The intermediate section introduces changing the style lines of the basic bra. Complex pattern manipulation is covered in the advanced section after creating a custom draft.

In addition to altering the style lines, the design technique of slash & spread is used for adding pintucks and gathering details.

Specialty sewing machine feet can be utilized to help in the construction of both pintucks and gathers.

NURSING BRA

Nursing bras are unique in that they require a cup to partially detach while remaining fully supportive. A nursing bra can be adapted from either a wired or a non-wired bra style.

A non-wired bra design is covered in the advanced chapter.

If a nursing mother chooses to wear an underwire bra, it is very important that the bra fits properly. If the wire does not sit properly under the breast, it can restrict the mammary glands and cause mastitis, a major health issue for nursing women.

MASTECTOMY BRA

Mastectomy bras are usually traditional bras that are altered to add a pocket for a prosthetic. Mastectomy bras can also be underwire or non-wired, although the absence of underwire is more conducive to supporting certain prosthetics.

Prosthetics are available in a variety of shapes and sizes depending on the manufacturer and needs of the customer. When developing a mastectomy bra, it is crucial that the shape and size of the prosthetic is referenced.

CHAPTER 6
PATTERN ADJUSTMENTS FOR FIT

The first section walked through bra construction. This chapter introduces pattern manipulation for fitting a pattern. Most individuals need to sample a variety of bras during the fitting process. The same goes for sewing patterns. Not all patterns are designed to fit every body.

ADJUSTING PATTERNS FOR TORSO SHAPE

There is a very good chance that the bras sewed in the first section of this book may have fit issues. This is very common. As discussed in the first chapter, all patterns are designed around a particular body shape and a set of measurements. There may only be one out of 10 individuals that fit a pattern straight out of the box.

One of the first things to consider when evaluating a pattern for changes is to address the torso size and shape of a pattern versus your measurements. Take a moment to check the following details on all patterns prior to sewing. This involves a little reverse engineering to determine if fit alterations are needed.

1. Review the bridge and frame of the pattern. If the pattern is in two pieces, overlap them on the seam line. Using a straight grid ruler, measure from the center front seam to the side seam (not including seam allowances).

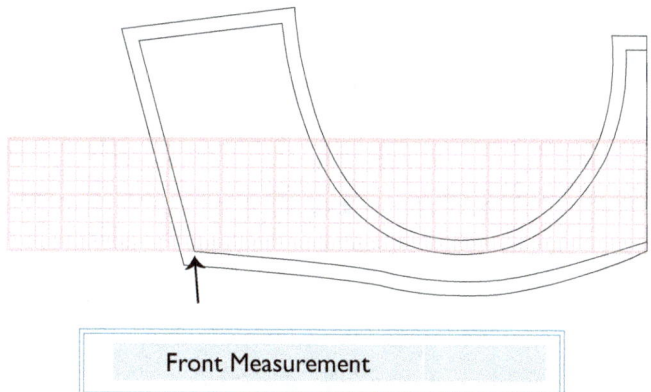

Front Measurement

2. Square a line straight up from the bottom of the side seam, making it parallel to the center front. Measure from the straight line over to the side seam at the top of the seam.

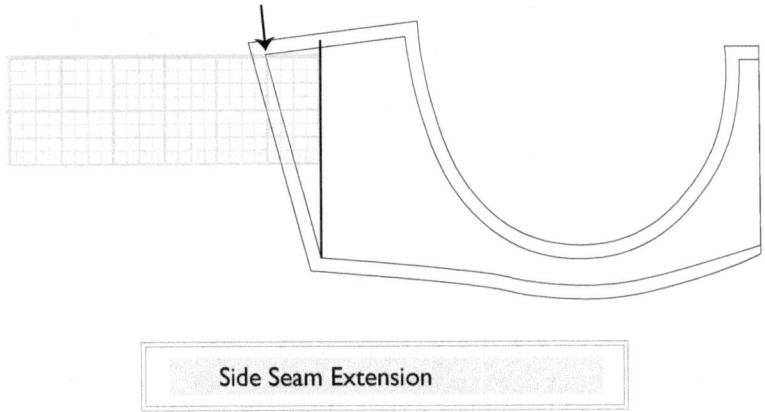

Side Seam Extension

3. Multiply the side seam extension by 4. The result is the difference between the chest and under bust measurements.

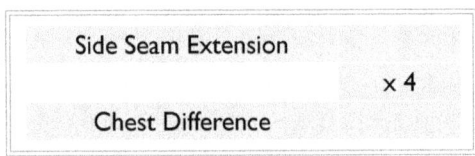

4. The next step is to measure the back band and take into consideration the stretch used for the back. Many pattern makers may opt to keep front bands the same across sister sizes. This means that the back measurement may be approached differently than in a custom draft. Measure the back lower width as demonstrated in Step 1.

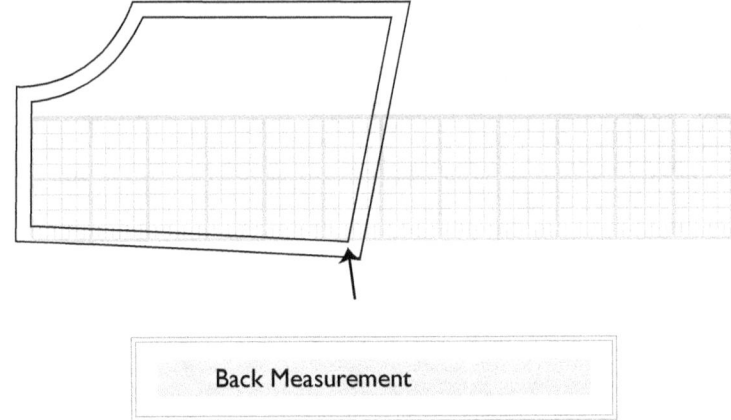

Back Measurement

Intermediate / Pattern Adjustments for Fit | 71

5. Indicate the amount of stretch recommended for fabric by the pattern instructions (if using any of Porcelynne's patterns, the recommended fabric stretch is 50% or 0.5). Multiply the decimal amount by 1.5 to get the percentage that the measurements were reduced by. Divide the reduced back measurement by the pattern stretch reduction to get the original back measurement.

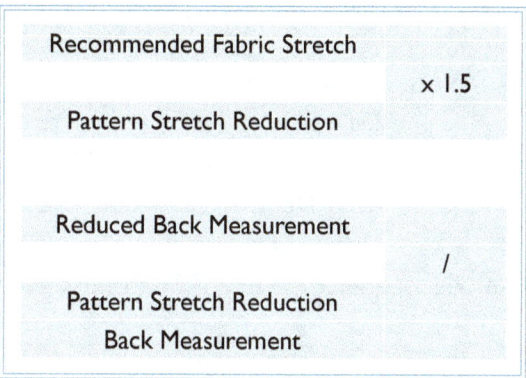

6. To make sure that the band itself will fit you, add the front and back measurements together and multiply by 2. Finally, add 2" for the hook & eye hardware. The total should equal your under bust measurement. If this does not match, an alteration needs to be made to the pattern.

7. All adjustments for the underbust are taken on the front band. The back is not altered. Add or remove one half of the difference between the pattern and your under bust measurements, at the side seam.

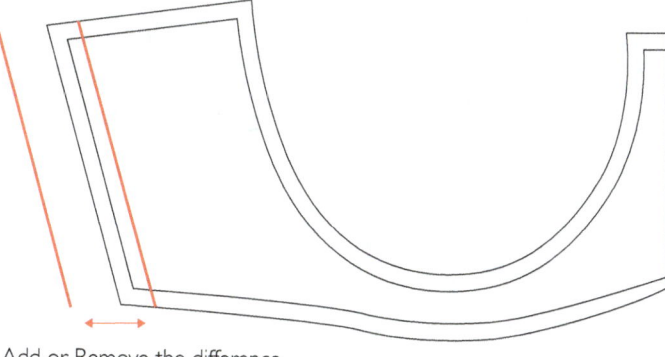

Add or Remove the difference

8. If the chest measurement is incorrect for your shape, take the chest difference from the bra pattern and subtract it from your chest measurement difference. Take that amount and divide it by 4. If your result is a negative number, the top of the side seam needs to be increased. If your result is a positive number, the top of the side seam needs to be decreased.

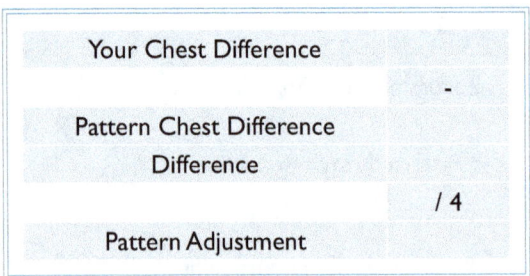

Your Chest Difference	
	-
Pattern Chest Difference	
Difference	
	/ 4
Pattern Adjustment	

9. To adjust the pattern for torso shape, alter the top of the front side seam by the quarter amount.

10. To adjust the back band pattern for the torso shape, multiply the quarter difference by the recommended fabric stretch. This amount will be smaller than the back change, due to the stretch being factored in.

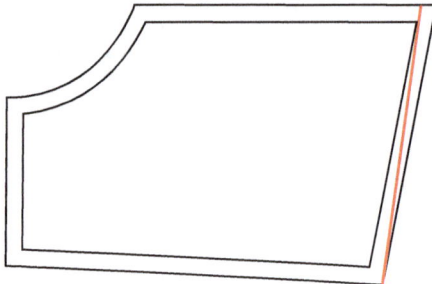

11. On the top cup, draw a line straight from the apex up to the neckline. Slash into the pattern from the top and open (or close) the top of the cup by the 1/4 amount you adjusted the front side seam.

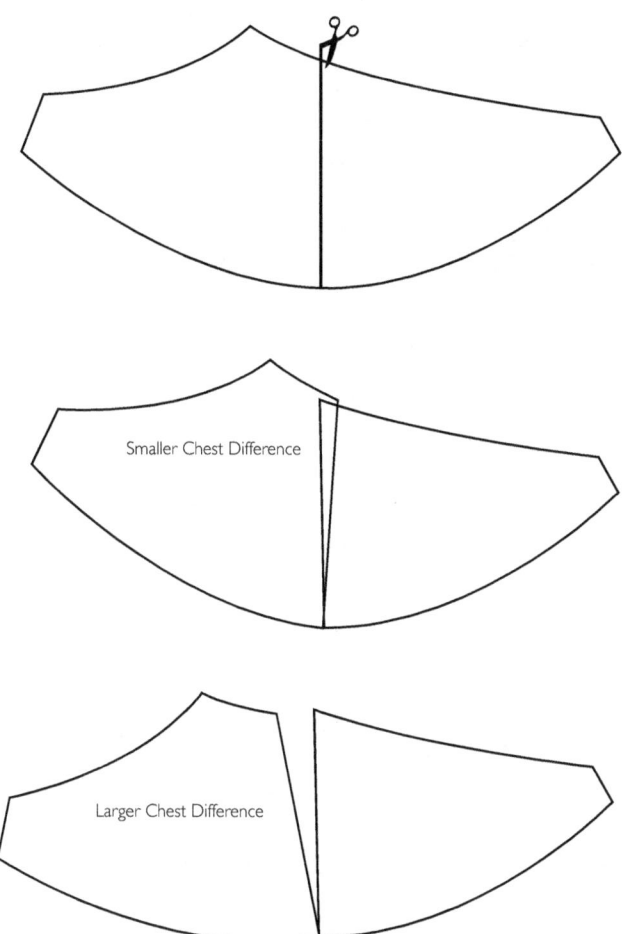

ADJUSTING PATTERNS FOR WIRE SIZE

If you have tested various wires and have decided that a different wire, rather than the recommended wire, fits you better, the band and cup patterns need to be altered.

1. Line up the wire to the frame to compare. Wires grow in width by 5/16" or 8mm. If the wire is one size smaller, move the wire line in by 5/16" or 8mm. If the wire is larger, move the wire line out. Some patterns have wire spring built into them based on the pattern maker's preference. If you remove the wire spring to match the wire, the same alteration needs to be incorporated into the pattern. Wire spring is discussed later in this chapter.

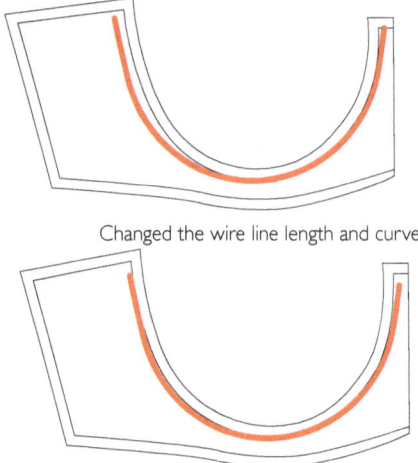

Changed the wire line length and curve

2. The amount removed or added from the band, needs to be removed or added to the cup. If the band was altered for a larger wire, the amount removed from the band is added to the cup in the width. The wire line also needs to be lengthened to match the increase in wire line added to the band.

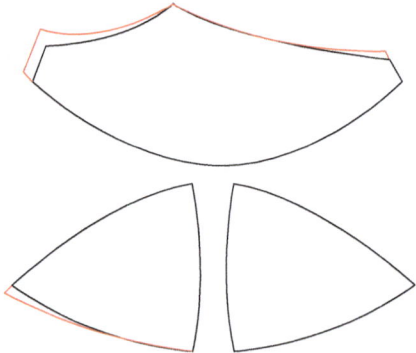

Intermediate / Pattern Adjustments for Fit | 75

ADJUSTING PATTERNS FOR BUST POINT POSITION

The provided patterns in the back of this book place the bust point at the center of the cup both horizontally and vertically. When drafting for a personal fit, the patterns are drafted for the bust depth of the apex, but not for the position horizontally. Some individuals may sit either to the side or to center front.

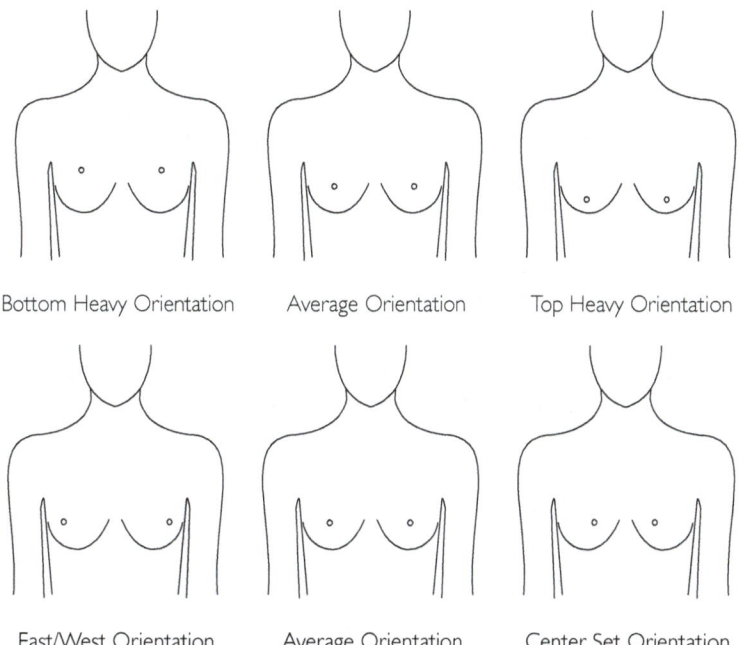

Bottom Heavy Orientation   Average Orientation   Top Heavy Orientation

East/West Orientation   Average Orientation   Center Set Orientation

Most bra patterns are designed to reshape the breasts to sit forward in the cup regardless of the bust shape. When testing the fit of the bra, make note of where your bust point sits in relationship to the sewn sample. Mark on your sample where your bust point is. If you wish to move the high point of the cup, mark on the cup where you wish to place the high point.

CHANGE THE VERTICAL BUST POINT

A depth change in a cup moves the horizontal seam up and down. Complete this change prior to reviewing any horizontal bust point changes.

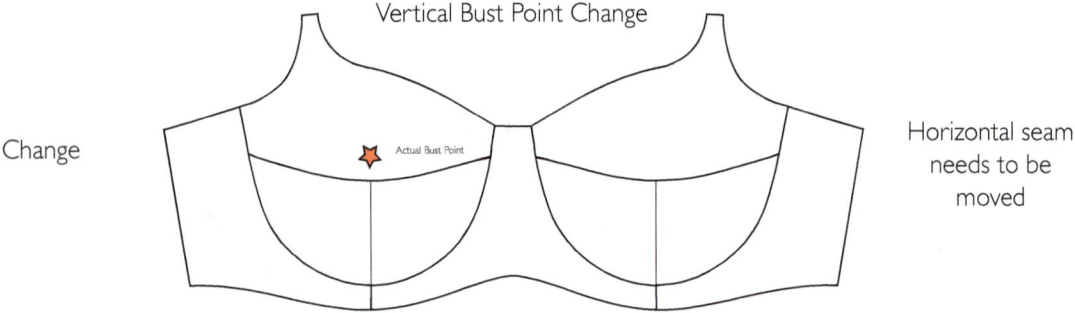

1. To move the bust point vertically on the cup, take the marking from the test cup and make a mark on the cup pattern piece to correspond with the change. Draw in the new curve on the cup.

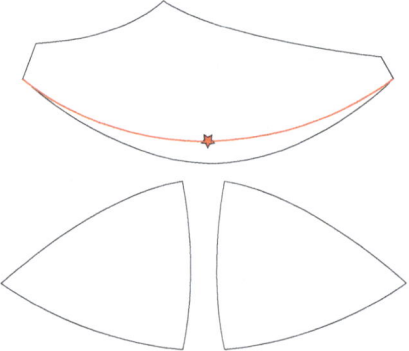

2. When altering one pattern piece, remember that the amount removed from one cup piece, needs to be added to the corresponding pattern pieces.

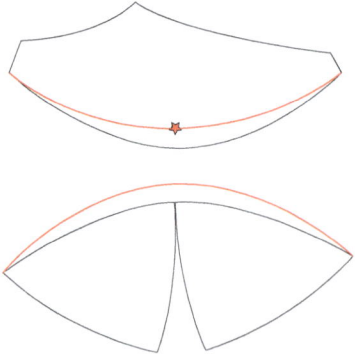

3. Note that the two new seam lines are not the same length. The seam line needs to match the original seam line length. Take the average of the change on each end and alter the seam lines to match both the original length and match each other. Once you have adjusted for the vertical placement, sew a test cup and check for accuracy.

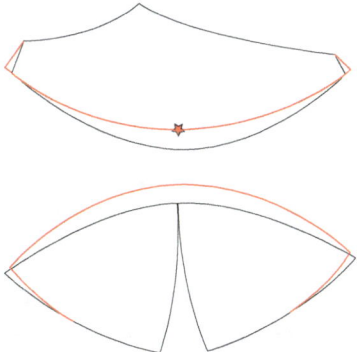

CHANGE THE HORIZONTAL BUST POINT

I do not recommend moving the seam for the bust point horizontally, unless the horizontal point corresponds with a preferred new high point of the bra. These could be the same or completely different based on your shape. This is more likely a change to be made from a self drafted pattern, than an alteration of a pattern already provided for use.

To move the bust point horizontally, follow the same steps as detailed for the vertical bust point change.

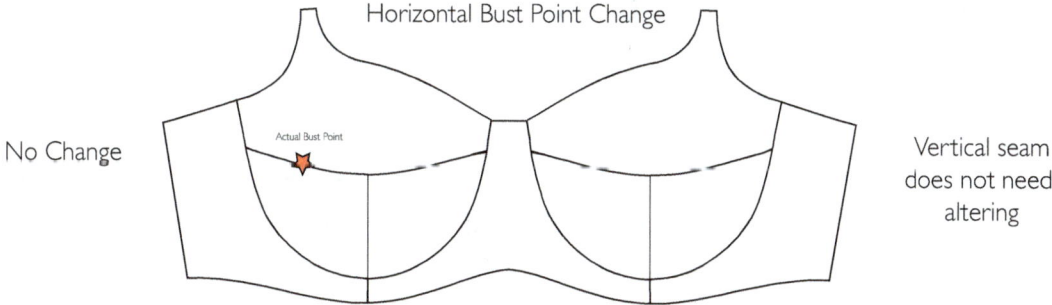

ADJUSTING PATTERNS FOR WIRE SPRING

Some pattern makers build a wire spring into their patterns and some do not. There is no scientific proof that wire spring benefits the fit of a bra. A well drafted pattern does not need to build in wire spring.

In commercial bras, wire spring is built into a bra, in order to fit a wide variety of body shapes and sizes. A great lack of consistency of materials used in manufacturing, cause wires to fail from average daily use. Custom drafted bras do not have this problem. Underwires that are available for bra makers are often a higher quality steel than the wires manufacturers use.

For wire spring to be built into a pattern, the amount of wire spring needs to be determined. Most wires are made of carbon steel alloy. Uncoated wires contain alloys to keep them from rusting, but the alloys used may affect their elasticity. Every alloy of carbon steel has different structural qualities, but this information is never disclosed. Wires can be round or flat, coated or uncoated and can vary in both width and depth. Each variable can affect the amount a wire can spring without failure.

When a wire is sprung, it is considered to be in a state of elasticity. There is a point in a wire's life, when the strain of a wire becomes greater than the stress from wear. This is when a wire reaches a point called plasticity.

The chart below shows the wear and failure of a wire. This chart is called a stress-strain curve. The stress of the wire is the amount of force applied when a wire is worn. The strain is the amount that the wire is pulled from its resting position.

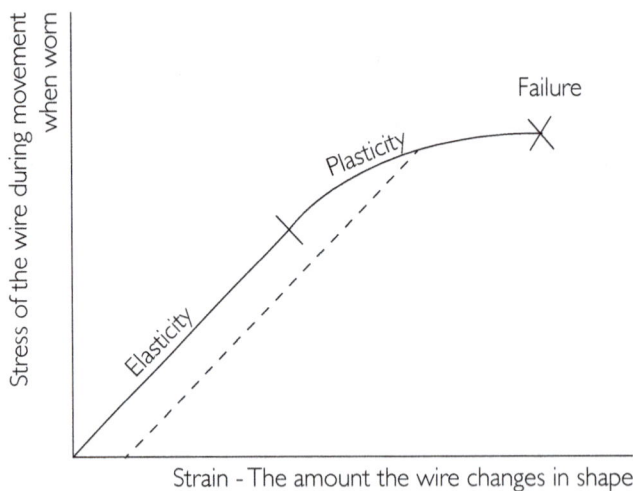

CHART A

In the elasticity phase of a carbon alloy wire, the wire will always return to its original resting position. Once a wire is bent past its elasticity point, the wire reaches the plasticity phase. It is at this phase that the shape of the wire changes.

Dependent on the wire's composition, the new shape becomes either its new permanent shape with limited elasticity or the wire becomes pliable and brittle. If reshaping a wire, I do not recommend building in any wire spring, as once the wire passes into its plasticity phase, the wire can fail with very little force and will snap.

Chart A demonstrates the new elasticity of a wire that has passed into the plasticity phase. This is displayed with the dotted line. The new shape has a very limited ability to spring and not fail.

Chart B demonstrates the difference of a single variable - the carbon content of a wire alloy. High carbon steel wire contains 1% of carbon. This wire can sustain more stress than the low carbon steel of 0.1% carbon. The low carbon steel is more brittle and can not withstand as much wear and tear from the normal stress of wearing a bra. The low carbon steel reaches its plasticity point before the high carbon steel.

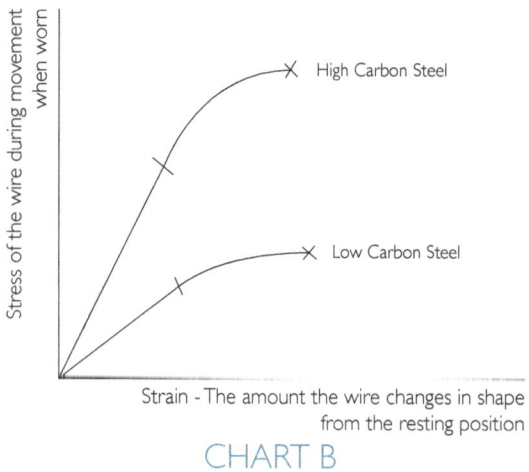

CHART B

Chart B demonstrates how only one factor plays its role in a wire's behavior. How does the addition to various sulfur compositions affect it? How about the thickness of a wire? These are all factors that should be addressed to fully incorporate proper wire spring in a bra.

It is arguable that a bra does not need to have the same structural qualities that is found in a bridge, but some individuals will disagree. While a bra is not life dependent on determining these structural qualities, some science should be factored into the decision making of wire spring.

Commercial bra wires snap because the metal composition, width and depth is not factored into the design, only a uniform wire spring amount. In the commercial bras I tested, wire spring of approximately 1" or 25mm was built in, regardless of the wire size, shape and composition.

The appropriate strain-stress of the wire is not determined when off-shore manufacturing utilizes the cheapest materials available. In a world where all wires' characteristics are factored in, the wear of a wire would resemble Chart A. Chart A shows an equal strain & stress. When the strain out weighs the stress, it fails.

There is a reason that more than 50% of my supply business is in replacement underwires. Either everyone is wearing the wrong size bra, or the bra manufacturers have build in the wrong amount of spring for their wires.

If you are able to determine the stress-strain curve of a wire and wish to add wire spring, follow the instructions for adjusting the wire size on patterns. The same concept applies to altering the wire line of both the band and cup.

CHAPTER 7

PADDED BRA

A padded bra is generally made from preformed molds. As an individual, we are not privy to create our own molds. To create a custom padded cup for an individual, start with an existing pattern that fits. This chapter covers two types of padding. The first is a padded seamed cup. The second is a padded insert which can be added to a cup.

PADDED SEAMED CUP

This bra contains three distinct pattern sets: the lining, the padding and the design fabric. This padded seamed cup is fully lined to encase the padding between the layers.

PART 1: PATTERN MANIPULATION

1. To create the patterns for the foam, trace the cup pieces and draw in the seam allowances of 1/4" or 6mm.

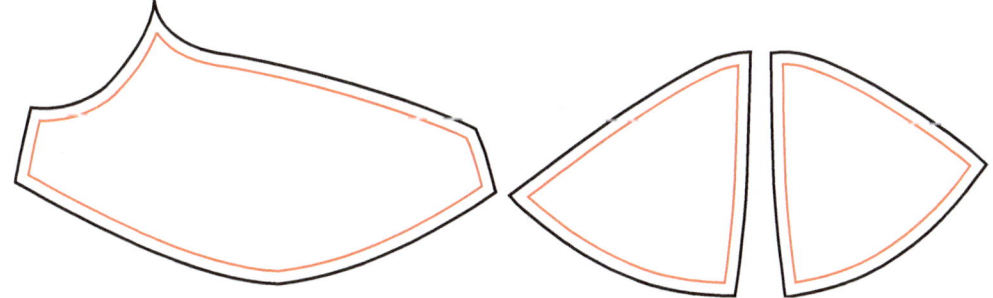

2. Remove the seam allowances and cut these patterns out in a 1/8" or 3mm foam or batting.

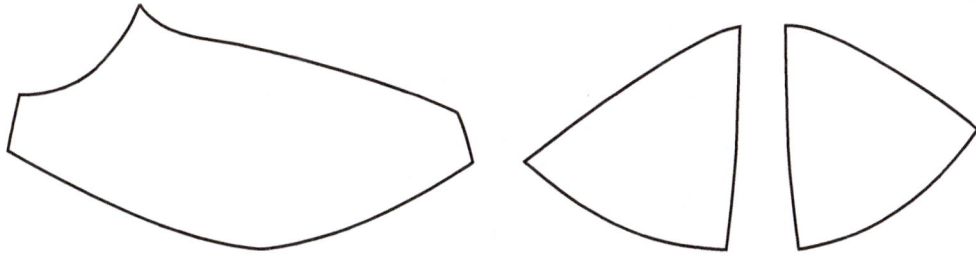

3. To create the pattern for the design fabric, trace the original cup patterns. Add 1/16" or 1.5mm around the outer cup edges. This allows extra room for fitting over the foam batting. If choosing to experiment with different densities and thicknesses of foam or batting, add an amount around the cup equal to 1/2 of the foam thickness.

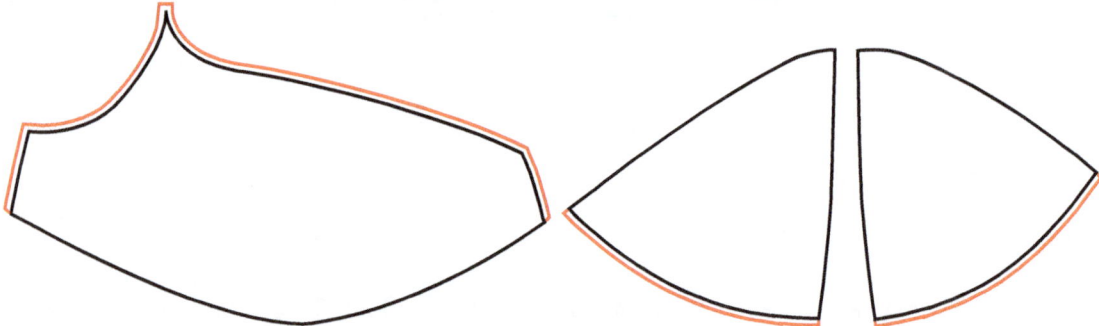

PART 2: CONSTRUCTION METHOD

1. Complete the sewing of the cup design and lining layers as previously demonstrated for a fully lined cup. Attach the foam cups together with a zigzag stitch. The edges should butt against each other. To attach, slowly ease the two edges together through the machine while stitching the two pieces together.

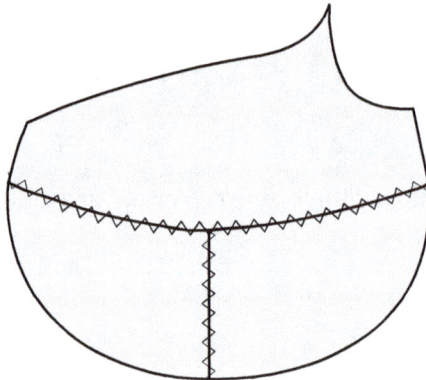

2. Place the elastic of choice on the design fabric's neckline edge. If using a picot or decorative elastic, attach it to the right sides. If using a plain elastic, attach the elastic to the wrong side of the fabric.

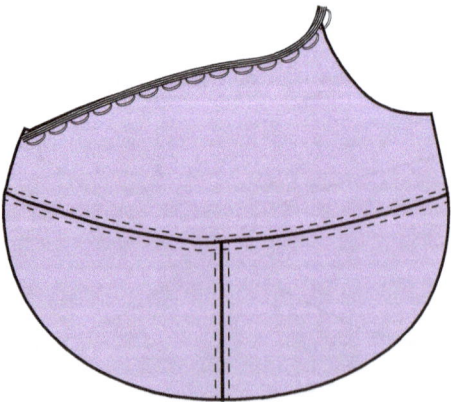

Intermediate / Padded Bra | 83

3. With the right side of the lining facing the right side of the design fabric, stitch together at the neckline.

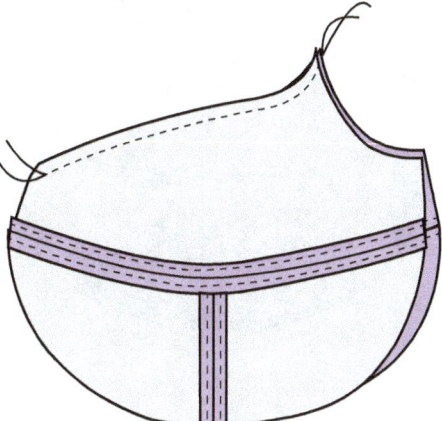

4. Flip the cup right side out and under-stitch the neckline. An under-stitch is when the seam allowance is stitched to the side of the lining. An under-stitch is generally placed right on the edge of the seam at 1/16" or 1.5mm away from the seam line.

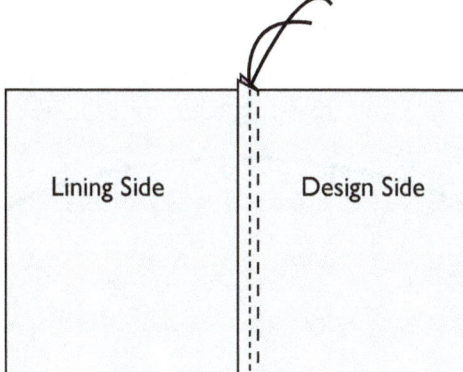

5. Place the foam between the layers of the lining and design fabric. Where the center seam touches the foam, hand tack the center of the seam allowance to the foam. This will keep the cup pieces in place.

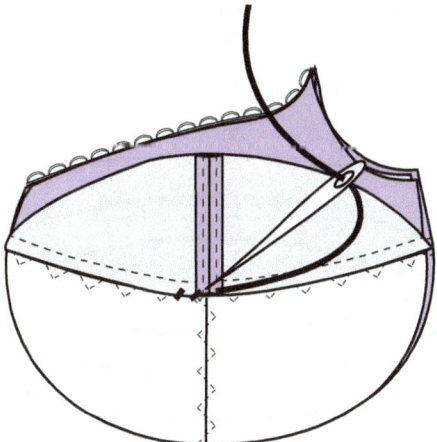

6. Baste stitch the remaining edges together and complete as previously demonstrated.

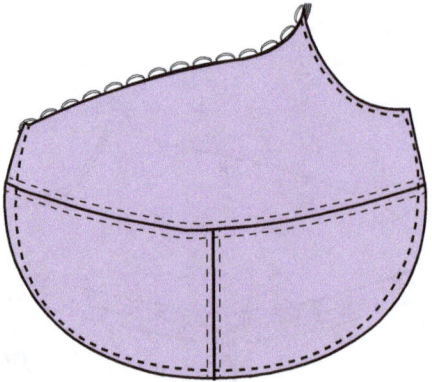

PADDED INSERTS

An alternative to a fully padded cup is to create a padded insert. The insert can be placed in a finished cup, or can be attached between layers in a lined cup.

PART 1: PATTERN MANIPULATION

1. Create the desired shape of the insert. They are generally oval shaped to sit under the bust. This can be used to pad a single side for breast asymmetry or can be used as a push up pad.

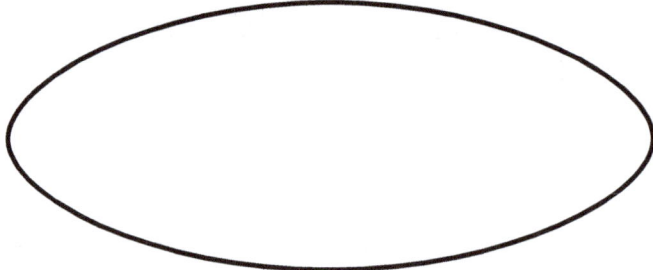

2. Draw in a smaller oval, approximately 1/2" or 12.5mm smaller inside the cup. And another one inside that one, at about 1/2" or 12.5mm. Each of the circles represent a different pattern piece for the batting. For the outer layer, use a thin 1/8" or 3mm batting, for each interior shape vary the thicknesses of batting for graduated padding.

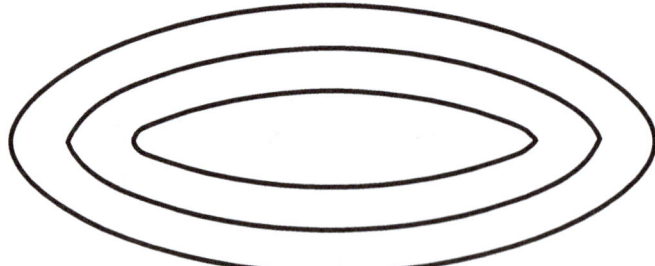

Intermediate / Padded Bra | 85

PART 2: CONSTRUCTION METHOD

A pad can be added loosely inside a cup. To secure the pad between layers of the bra, follow a similar method to securing the full padded cup.

1. Cut out two layers of the two largest circles and one of the inner layer. Layer the pieces together, top, middle, center, middle, top. To secure each layer, use a fabric adhesive or tack the layers together with a hand stitch. When assembly of the insert is complete, stitch around the edges.

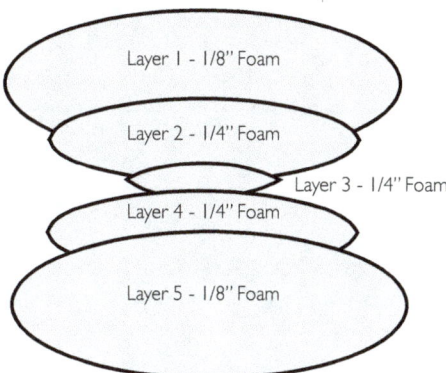

2. Place the pad so it does not fall in the seam allowance of the cup. The pad should not be sewn into the seam attaching the cup to the band. Tack down the pad edges at the center seam in the seam allowance.

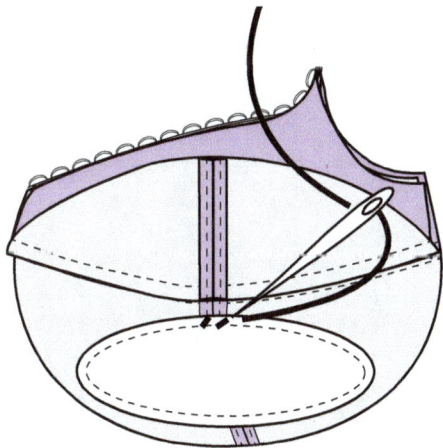

CHAPTER 8
FRONT CLOSURE DEMI BRA

These exercises alter the neckline of the cup and band to create a demi style bra. A shorter wire and front clip closure are used. There are two methods one can take to approach a demi style alteration. The first method uses a demi underwire. The second method designs around a custom cut wire.

METHOD 1: DEMI UNDERWIRE

1. Place the front band and bridge together, lining up the pieces at the joining seam allowances of 1/4" or 6mm.

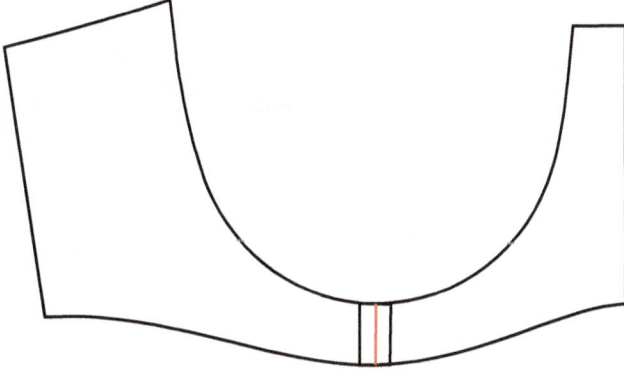

2. Line up the demi underwire under the arm 1/2" or 12.5mm away from the top of the side cup. This allows room for the elastic attachment and wire movement ease.

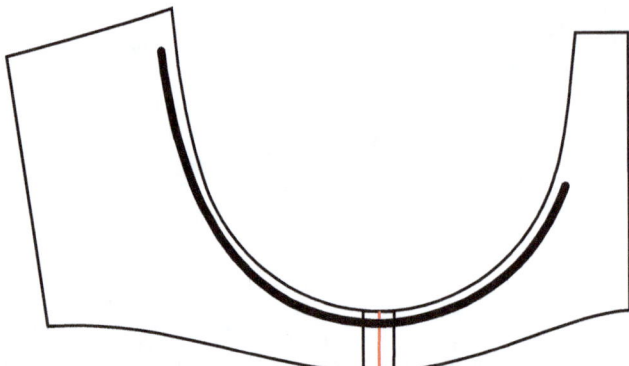

3. Mark on the front neckline where the wire ends. Measure past this point 1/2" or 12.5mm for seam allowance and wire movement. If the pattern being altered does not contain seam allowance, only mark at 1/4" or 6mm. 1/4" or 6mm of this amount is reserved for seam allowance.

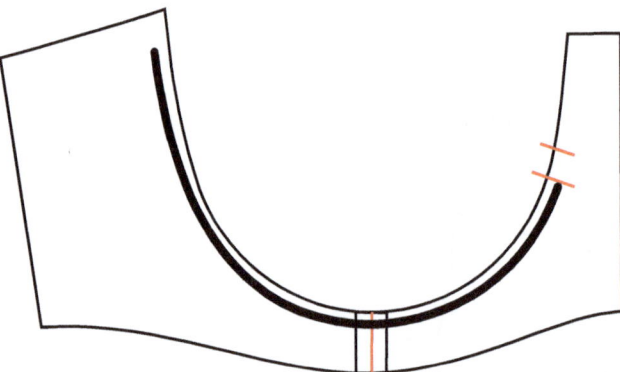

4. Use the following template and sketch the new design. Alter the cup design to meet at the center front neckline where the cup ends.

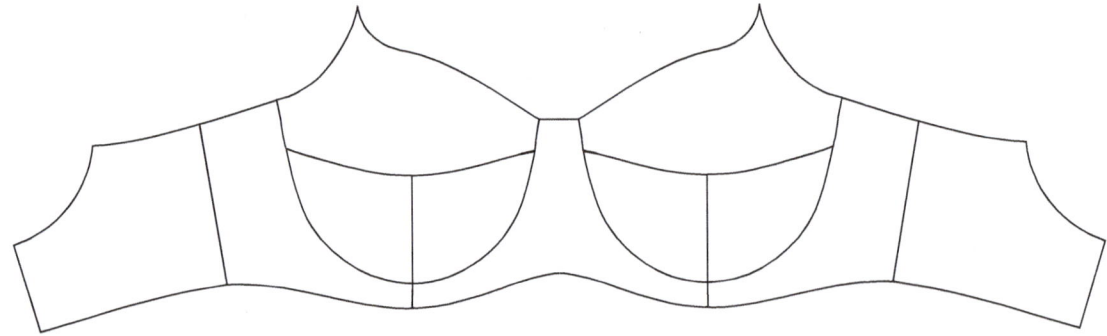

5. The design of this neckline has a descending curve that slopes inwards toward the apex. This neckline shape will show more cleavage and appears as a push up bra, whether or not padding is added.

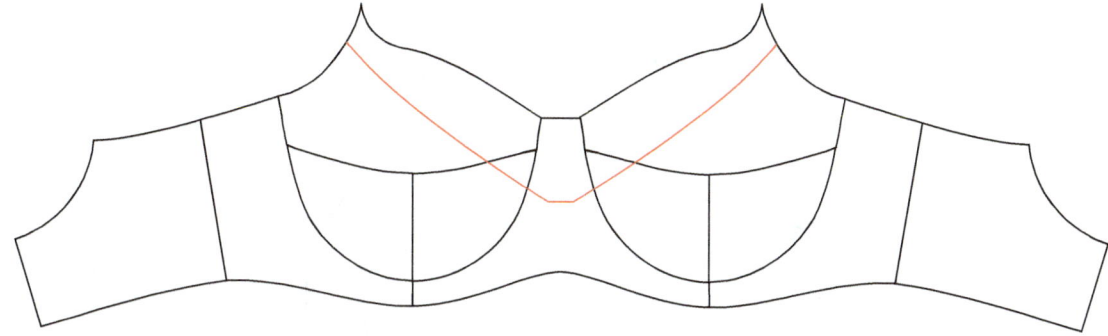

6. a. Select the size of the clasp for the front. The clasp used in this design is 3/4" or 20mm tall. Add 1/4" or 6mm for each seam allowance on the top and bottom. The total amount required for the bridge height is 1 1/4" or 32mm. Notate all measurements on your sketch.

   b. The straight edge across the middle measures the width of the clasp which is 3/4" or 20mm.

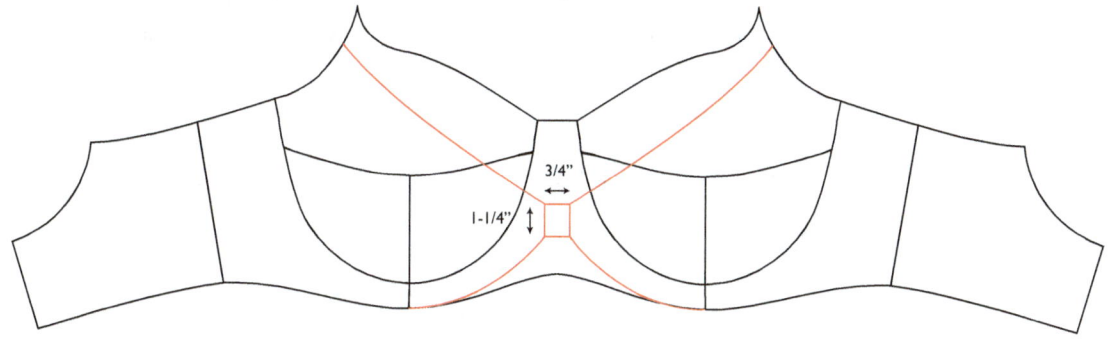

7. Draw in the seam lines for all joining seams on the cup and band.

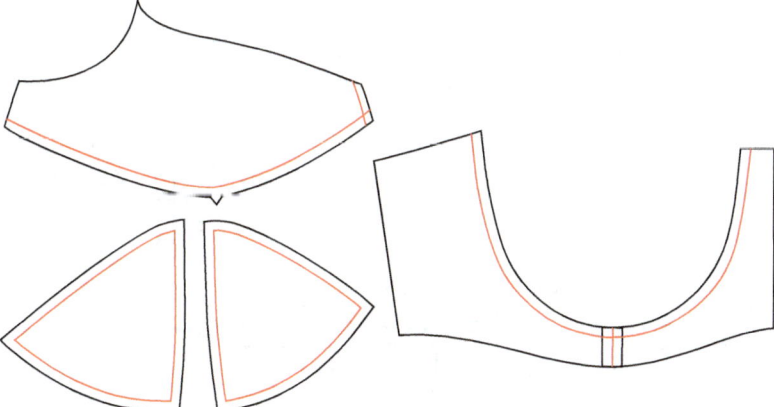

8. Line each of the pattern pieces up at the joining seam lines meeting at the center front.

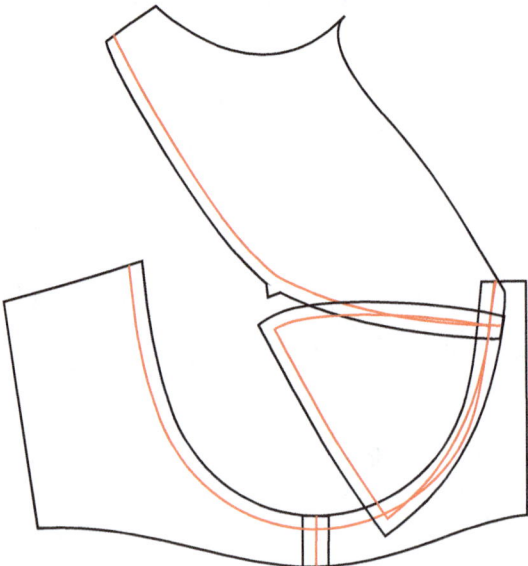

9. Alter the cup and band pattern pieces to meet the specs determined in Step 6. Make sure to match the seam lines of the pattern pieces after separating them and be sure they fit together properly. All joining seam lines need to match in length.

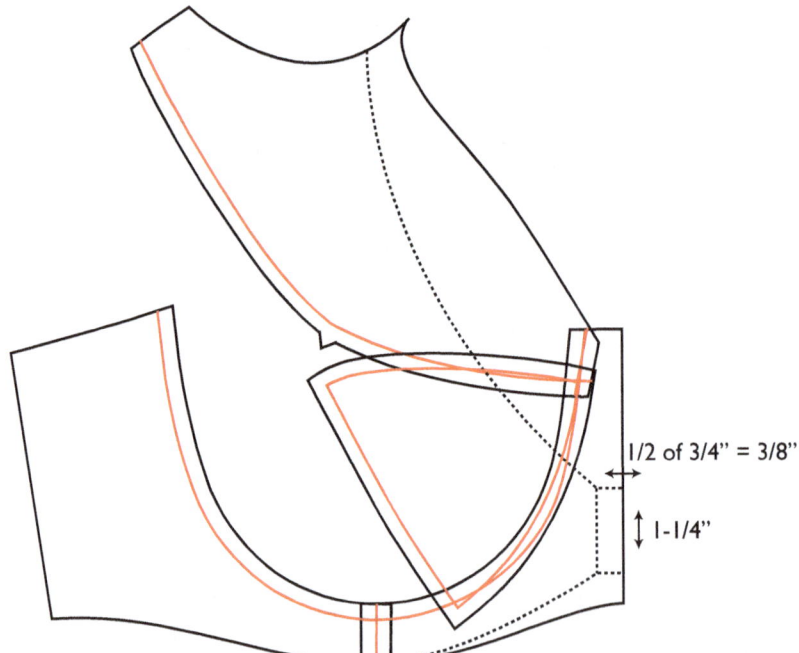

Intermediate / Front Closure Demi Bra | 91

10. Sewing allowance needs to be added to the center front for the front closure. The front pattern was previously designed to be cut on the fold. To attach the front to a closure, the front bridge pattern needs to be altered. Half of the width of the closure needs to be removed from the front.

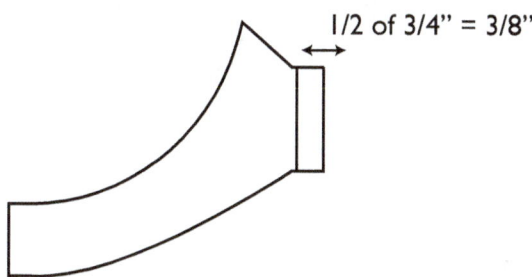

11. The most appropriate finish is a fully lined bridge on both sides of the closure. The new center front should be cut on the fold for both the stabilizer and fabric. Be sure to cut two of both on the fold for each side of the bra.

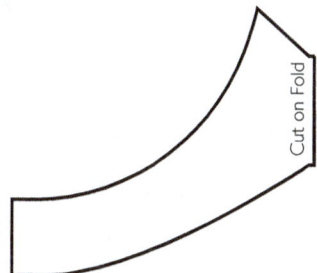

METHOD 2: CUSTOM CUT WIRE

1. This design differs in that the neckline is sloped upwards for more coverage. This cup's neckline is designed to work as a demi cup on a larger bust size. The clasp for this cup measures 1" or 25mm tall. Including seam allowance, the center bridge is 1 1/2" or 38mm. The width of the clasp is 1" or 25mm.

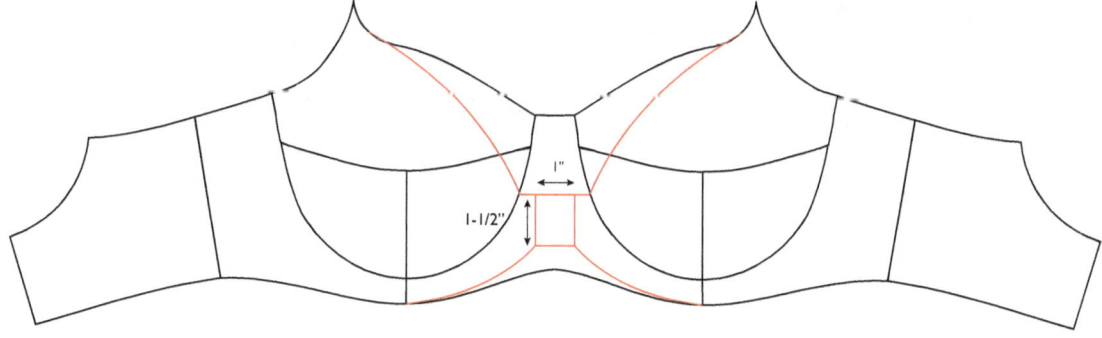

2. Line the bridge and cup pieces at their seam lines and alter the pattern to the specifications of the design.

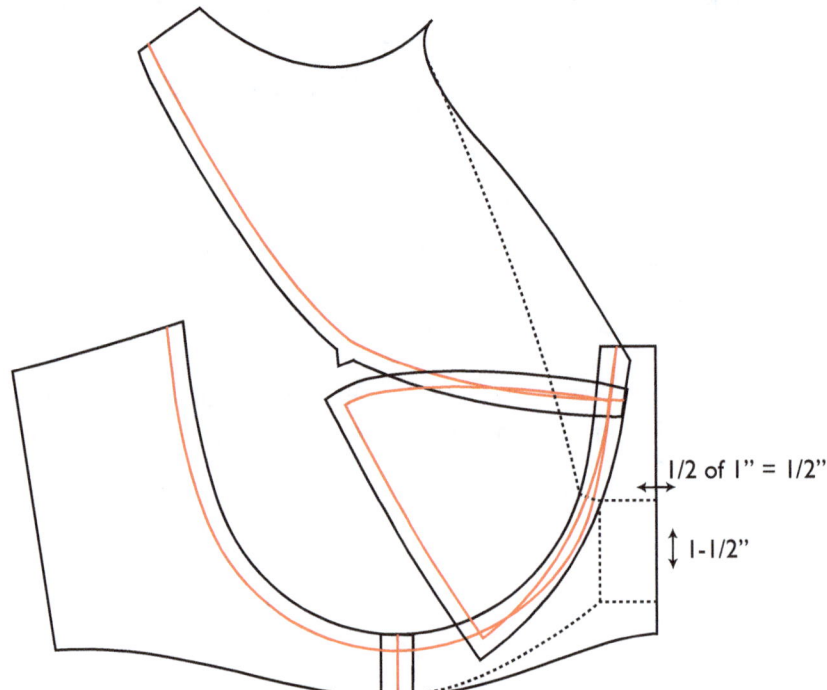

3. Line up the uncut underwire to the band leaving 1/2" or 12.5mm spacing at the under arm for seam allowance and wire movement. Mark on the underwire where the neckline of the band ends. Shorten the underwire by an additional 1/2" or 12.5mm at the center neckline. Adjust the center front of the bridge as demonstrated on the previous page.

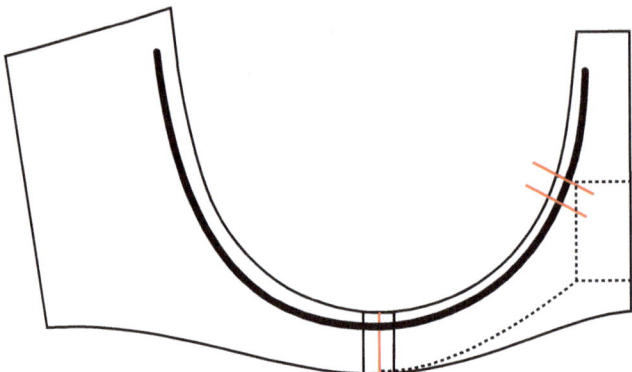

CHAPTER 9
STRAPLESS BRA

This chapter demonstrates two variations of a strapless bra. The first creates a basic strapless design, while the second creates a backless style. Both styles may need additional support in the cups. If this is the case, the recommendation is to create a seamed padded cup following the steps from Chapter 7.

PART 1: PATTERN MANIPULATION

VARIATION 1: BASIC STRAPLESS BRA

1. Trace the top cup of the basic bra.

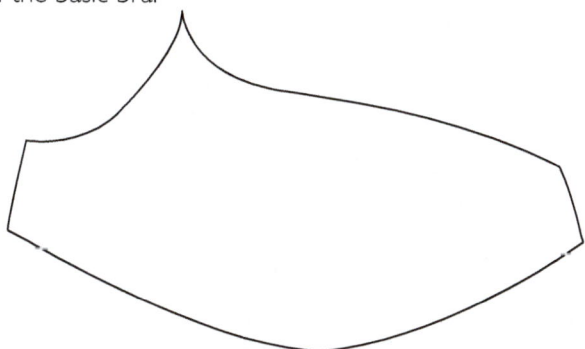

2. Curve the top of the cup as pictured or to a design of preference.

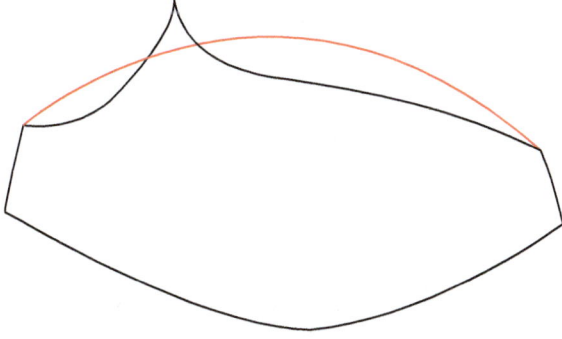

3. Trace the side and back band pattern pieces. These directions can be modified for most band shapes. Draw in the 1/4" or 6mm seam line at the side seams.

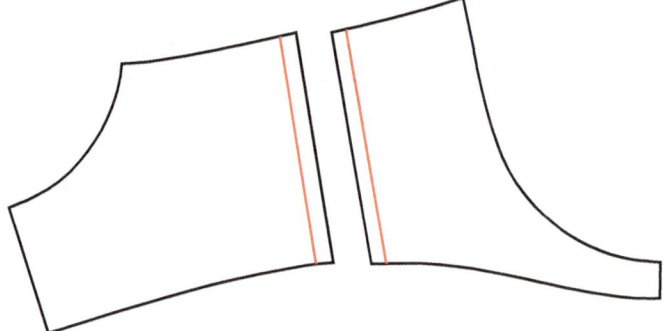

4. Combine each of the seams, overlapping them at the seam lines.

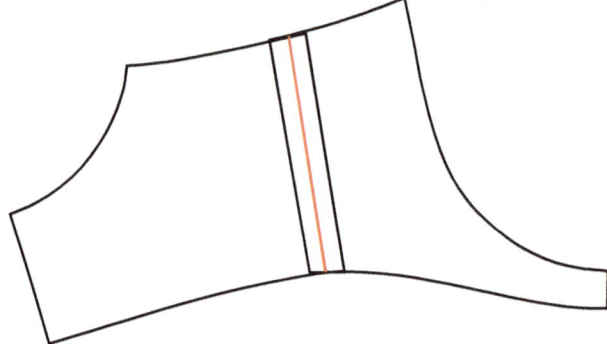

5. A strapless bra hugs the body without the use of a strap. Extend the center back up to accommodate a wider hook & eye closure to support the bra.

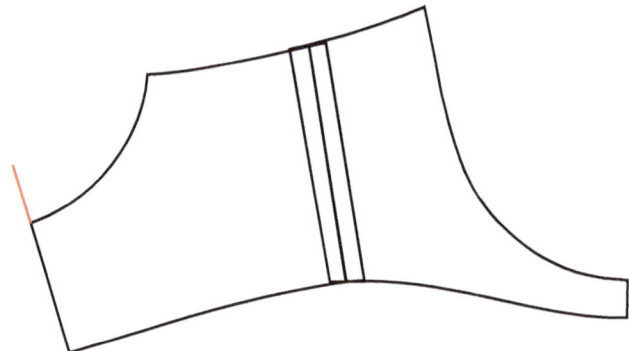

6. Reshape the back neckline.

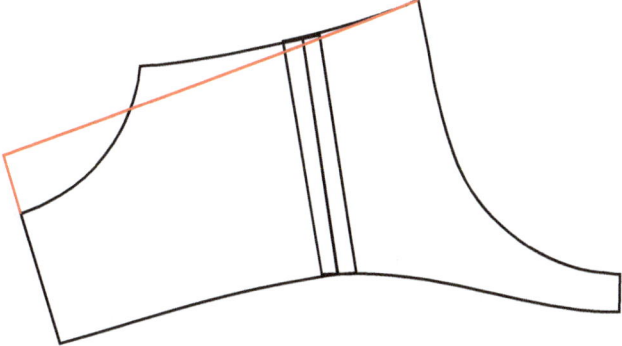

VARIATION 2: BACKLESS STRAPLESS BRA

For backless strapless bra designs, a few additional measurements are needed for development. Similar to the instruction on taking measurements in the beginner section, take two ribbons and tie one below the bust and one at the natural waistline. The natural waistline is the narrowest point of the body, generally several inches above the navel.

1. Take the measurement of the waistline and the measurement of the distance from the under bust ribbon to the waistline ribbon, down the center front of the body.

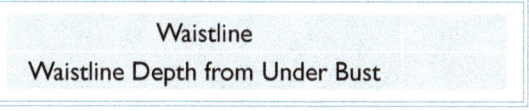

Follow the steps in the previous variation to reshape the top cup and line up the back and side front bands. For this style, a longer band or base is required.

2. Add the bridge in the same manner as the band by lining up the seam lines. Draw in the center back seam allowance.

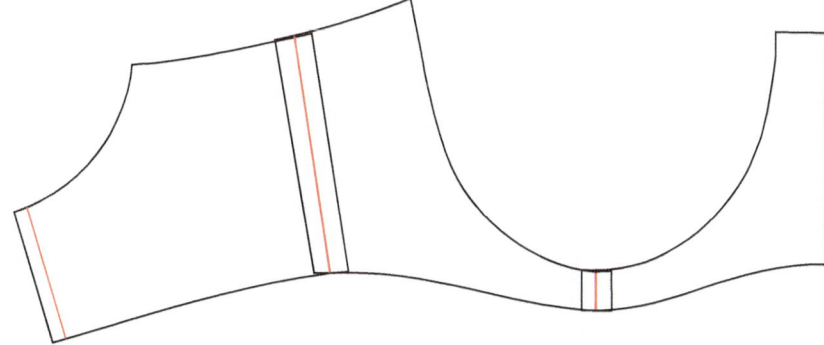

3. Square a line across from the bottom of the center of the cup to the center front.

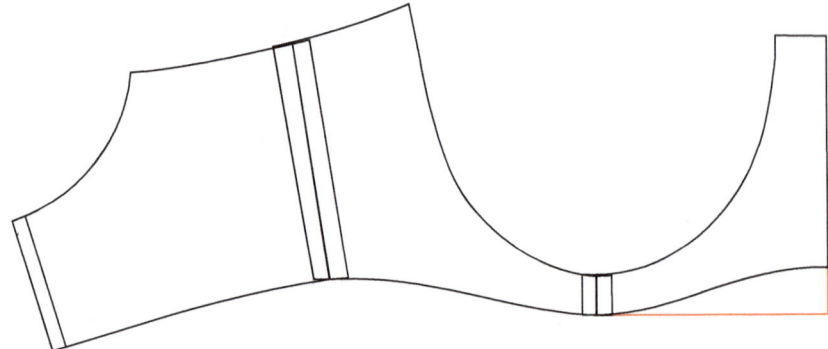

4. Determine the quarter waistline amount by dividing the waistline into 4.

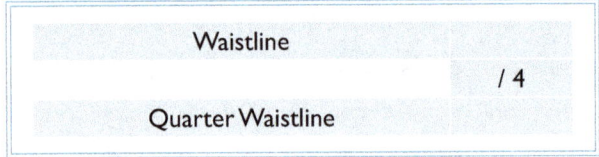

5. From the new horizontal line at center front, measure down the waistline depth. At the depth, square a line across 1/4 of the waistline measurement. This will mark the bottom of the side seam. Draw a line from the top of the side seam to the side of the waistline.

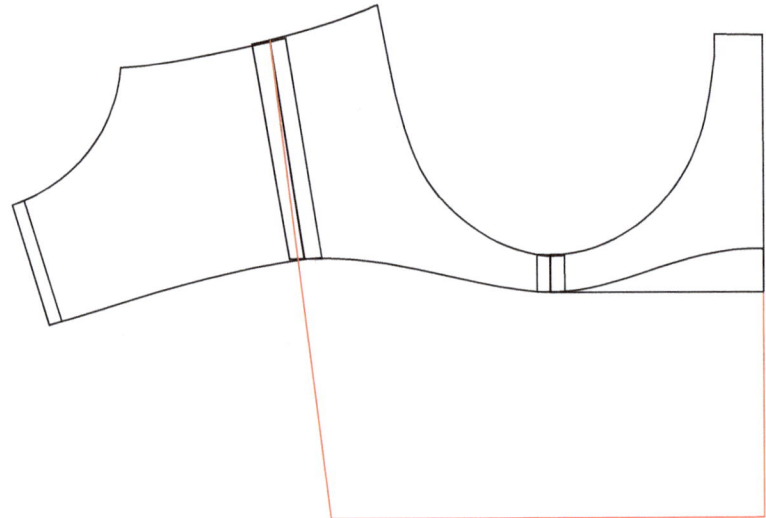

6. The back of a bra is designed for stretch. The back of the bra also contains a hook & eye closure. Because of this, the 1/4 waistline measurement must be altered. Subtract 1" or 25mm from the quarter waistline measurement for the hook & eye. Multiply the result by 0.75 for fabric with a 50% stretch. Select a reduction from Chapter 14 in the advanced section for a fabric with a different stretch.

1/4 Waistline	
	- 1" or 25mm
1/4 Waistline - Hook & Eye	
Stretch Reduction	x 0.75
Reduced Back Waistline	

7. Square a line across from the side seam towards the back, the reduced back measurement amount.

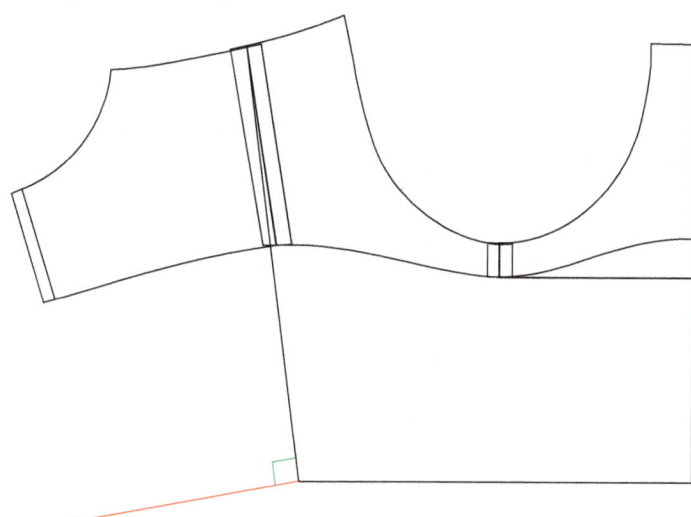

8. From the top of the center back pattern (not including seam allowance), draw a line down to the back of the waistline.

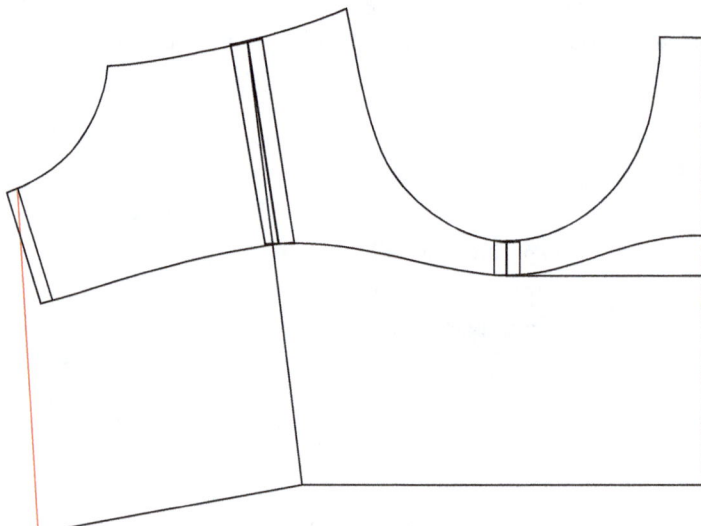

9. Drop the center back to accommodate the hook & eye tape. For this example, 3 1/4" or 8.3cm is used for a five row hook & eye closure. Shape the back neckline and curve the waistline to remove the sharp angles of the draft.

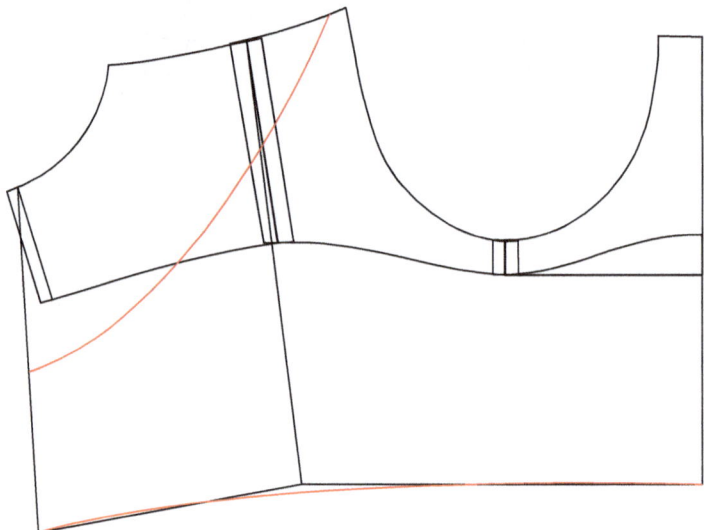

10. Add seam allowance to the center back and to the side seam.

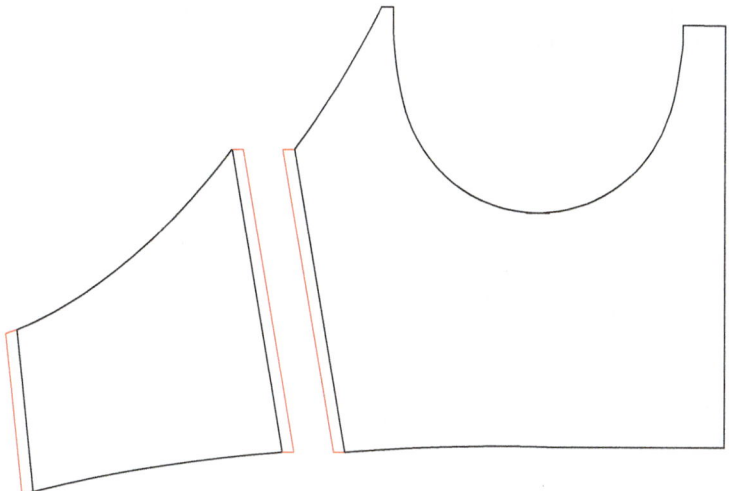

11. The last step is to determine where boning needs to be placed. This can vary based on how low the back is. All boning must be placed in a straight line due to its rigid nature.

    a. Boning Placement - For this example, four boning pieces are added to the front and two on the back. An additional piece of boning is placed at the side seam. Boning pieces can be angled or in a straight line. The angled layout will provide for more comfort when seated. This quantity of boning is not always necessary, as it depends on the support needed by the wearer.

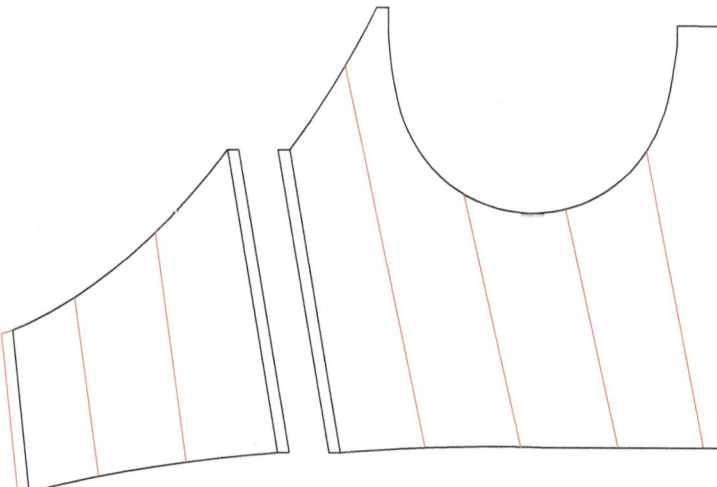

b. To mark where the boning placement goes on the pattern, place notches at the beginning and end of each boning piece. These notches can be inward or outward facing, depending on preference. Inward notches are placed with a notcher. Outward notches are triangle outward facing shapes that are traditionally seen in commercial patterns.

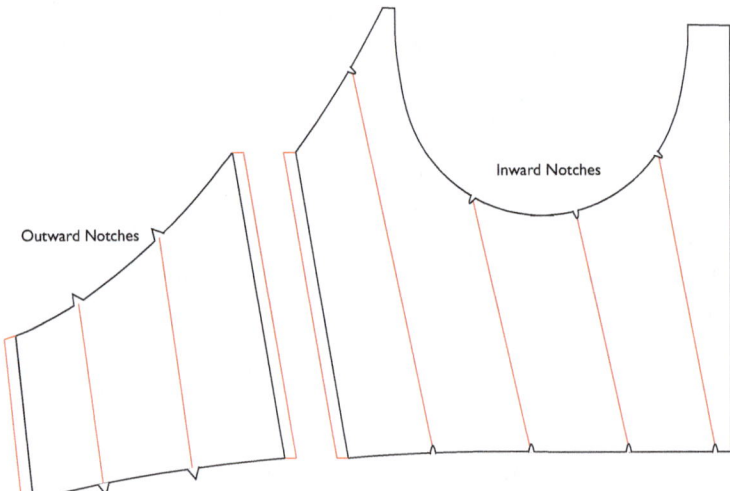

c. Indicate the length of boning and casing needed for in each location. Remove 1/4" or 6mm seam allowance off both ends of the casing for seam allowance and elastic edge finishing. Boning length is shortened by an additional 1/2" or 12.5mm.

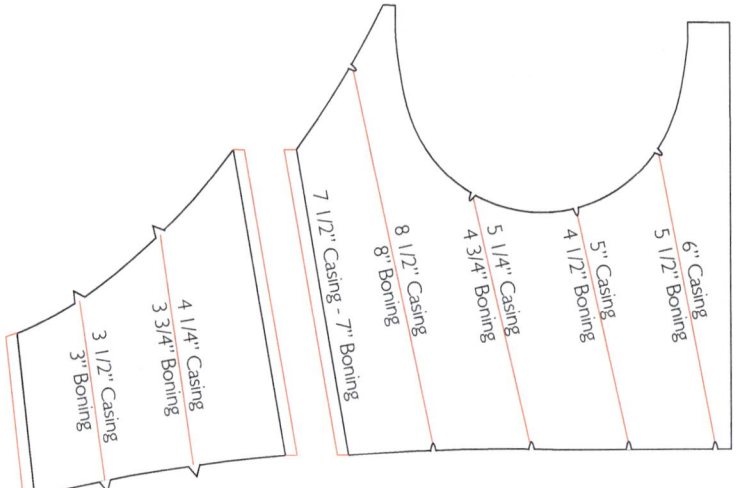

PART 2: CONSTRUCTION METHOD

Follow the construction steps previously demonstrated for the strapless bra, but with the following inclusion. Attach the boning to the side seam as previously demonstrated. Stitch both sides of the casing for each boning placement on the band leaving a 1/4" or 6mm gap at the top and bottom for elastic attachment and seam allowance. Use the pattern markings as guides for layout. Complete the cup, channeling, elastic and hook & eye as previously demonstrated.

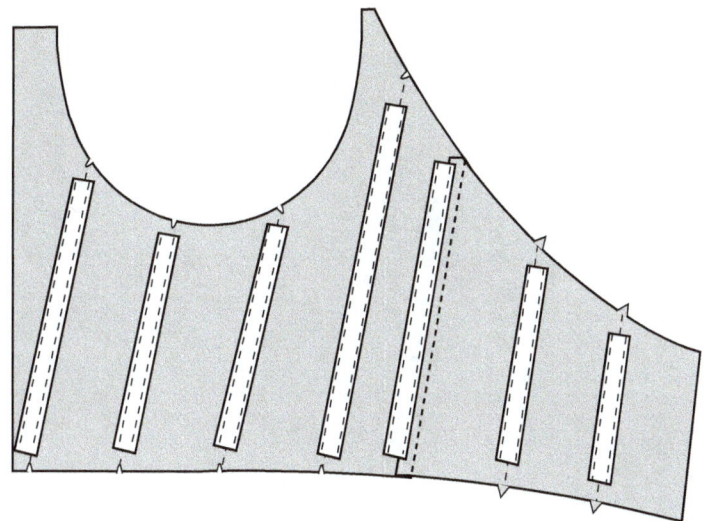

CHAPTER 10
STYLIZING A BRA: SEAM LINES

There are endless possibilities for the style lines one can create. This chapter explores a simple method to achieve a seam line change. The advanced section covers complex style line changes.

CHANGING STYLE LINES

1. Trace the three piece cup. Next to the traced pattern pieces, sketch a stylized cup. For example purposes, the three piece cup will be modified to the design pictured.

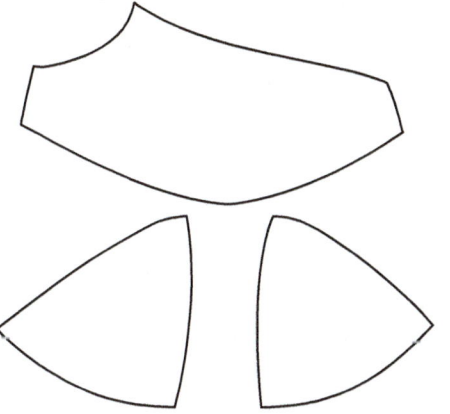 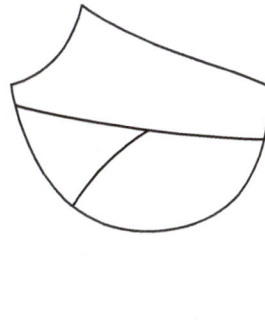

2. List all cup modifications. These alterations apply to this design.
   a. The left side of the upper cup is narrower.
   b. The lower left cup height is increased, while the bottom of the cup is decreased.
   c. The lower right cup has increased in width.

3. Mark the estimated changes on the upper cup.

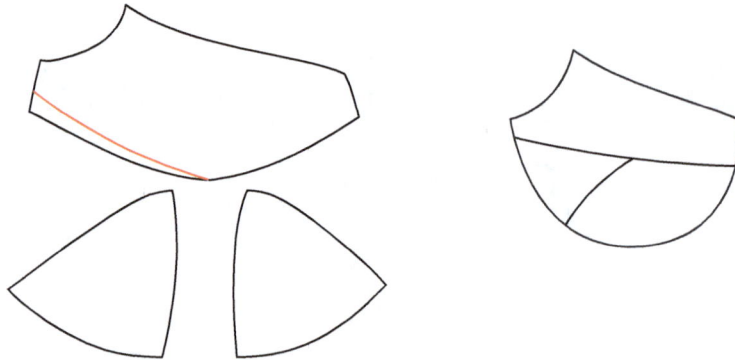

4. Measure the amounts of change on the upper cup and make the corresponding changes to the lower cup. This means where an amount is taken away from one cup piece, it is added to the adjacent cup piece.

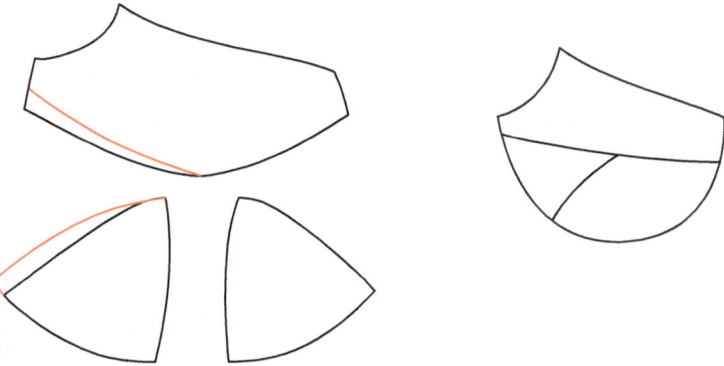

5. The next change is to modify the style lines of the lower cups. Draw in the lower left cup change. Note that even though the style line is curved upwards in the sketch, the curve is in a downward slope on the pattern. These types of changes will need to be sewn to determine if the style line sits where desired.

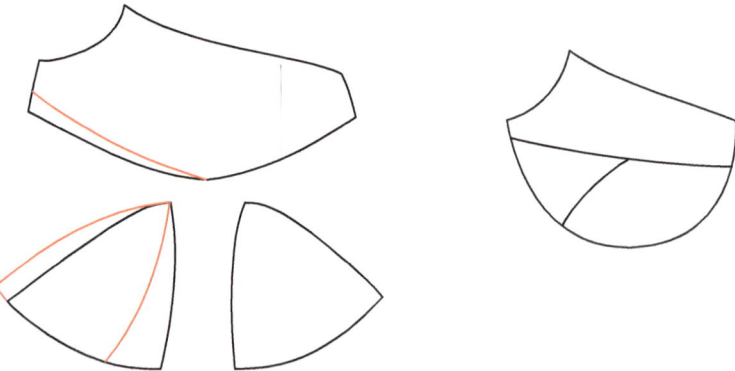

6. Measure and move the style line of the lower right cup. Be sure to measure all new seam lines to make sure each corresponding seam matches in length.

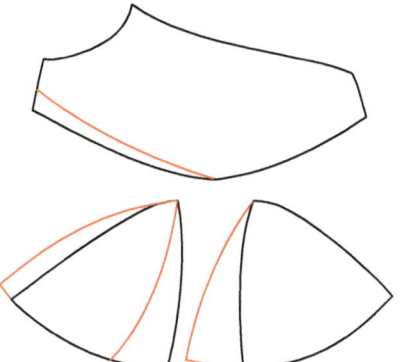
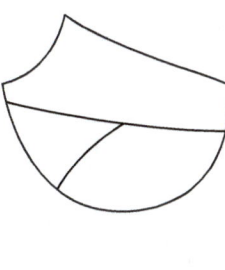

CHAPTER 11
STYLIZING A BRA: SLASH AND SPREAD

Gathering and pintucking details can be added to any cup. The following steps are simple changes that utilize the concept of slash and spread.

GATHERS

Decide on the amount of gathers preferred. These steps utilize a two to one gathering ratio, meaning there will be twice as much fabric that will be gathered into the actual shape.

PART 1: PATTERN MANIPULATION

1. Take the pattern piece and draw a variety of evenly spaced lines across the pattern in the direction in which to span the gathers. Draw a line across the cup. This line will be used to line up the cup pieces in the next step.

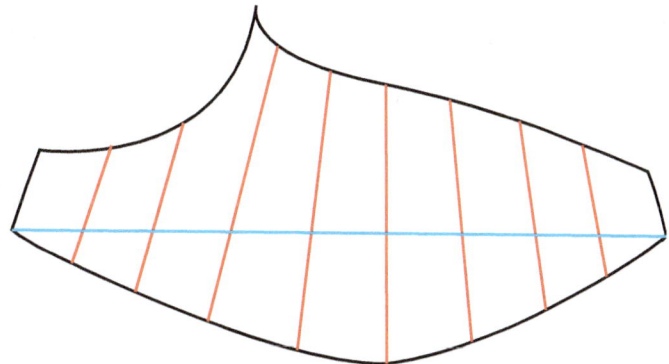

2. Draw a line across another piece of paper. Cut the pieces apart and space them equally apart keeping each divided line parallel to the next. Line up the lines of the cup pieces to the line drawn on the paper below. The total amount of the new pattern is twice the original pattern.

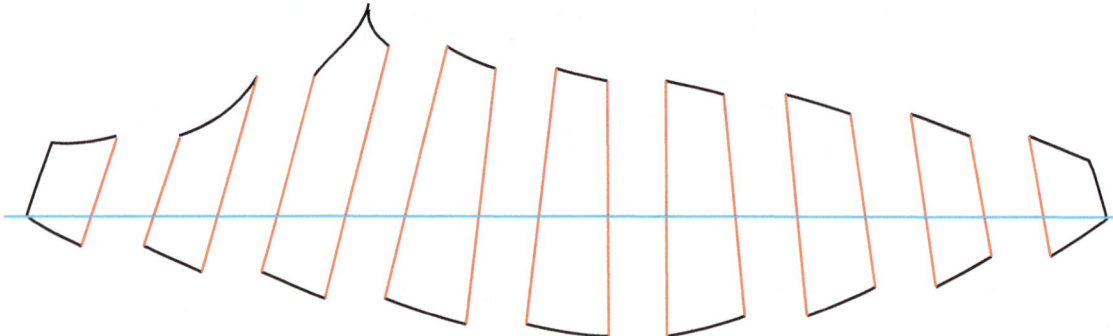

3. Draw in the new seam lines, averaging each point as pictured.

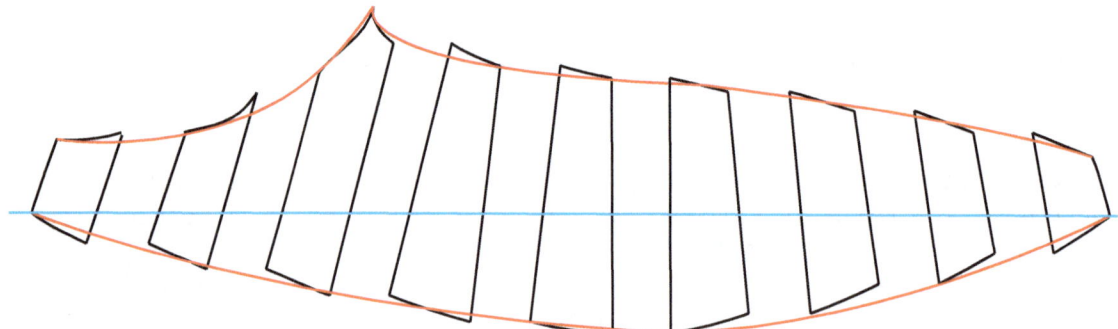

Intermediate / Stylizing a Bra: Slash and Spread | 109

PART 2: CONSTRUCTION METHOD

1. Cut out the original pattern piece and the gathered pattern piece. The original piece can be cut out of tricot lining to reduce bulk. The two layers will be treated as one when constructing the cup.

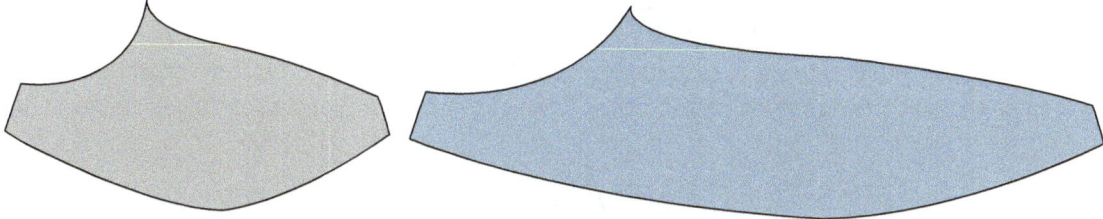

2. Run a basting stitch on the larger pattern piece at 1/8" or 3mm on each section that is gathered. This can be done by machine or by hand.

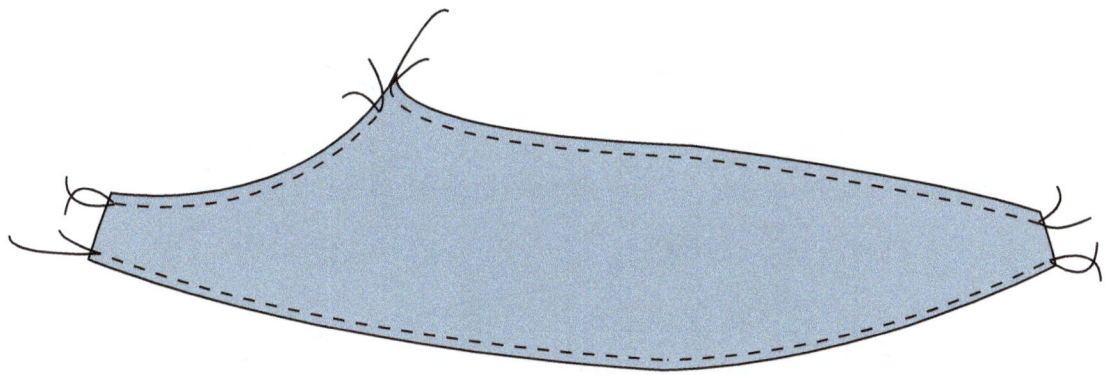

3. Pull the gathering stitches and match the gathered piece to the lining piece. Once they are pulled equally, baste stitch the gathered cup to the flat cup at 1/8" or 3mm and continue constructing the cup as previously demonstrated.

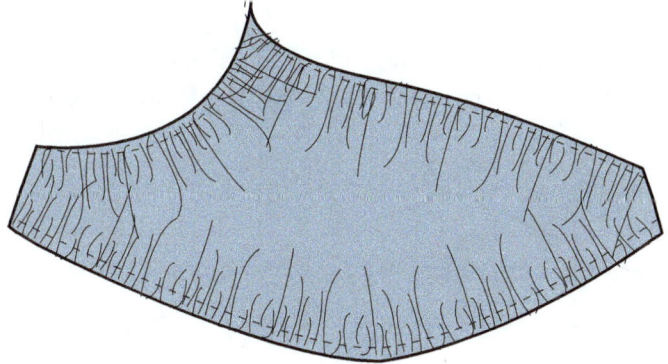

PINTUCKS

Determine the size and spacing of the pintucks. For this example, place 1/8" or 3mm pintucks, 1" or 25mm apart.

PART 1: PATTERN MANIPULATION

1. Take the pattern piece and draw straight lines parallel to each other 1" or 25mm apart across the pattern piece. A similar line drawn across the pattern can be repeated for this exercise. This example excludes that line.

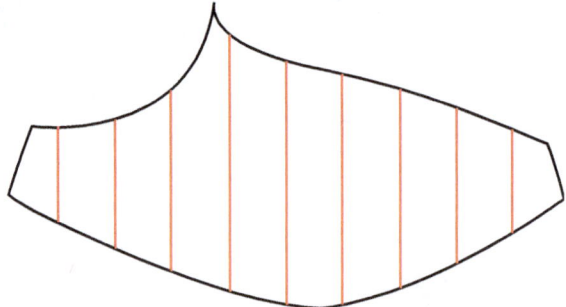

2. Because the pintucks are 1/8" or 3mm when stitched, they are 1/4" or 6mm before stitching. Cut each piece apart and space them 1/4" or 6mm apart, parallel to each other.

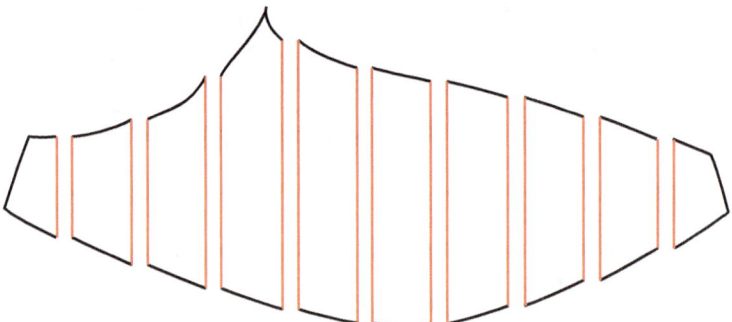

3. Determine which direction the pintucks will lay when fully constructed. For this example, fold the pintucks away from the center front. This information is needed to create the shape of the space in between each pintuck. To create the pattern shape, fold the two edges of the pintuck together then fold towards the side seam. Cut on the original seam lines when folded. This will create the pattern edges of the pintucks.

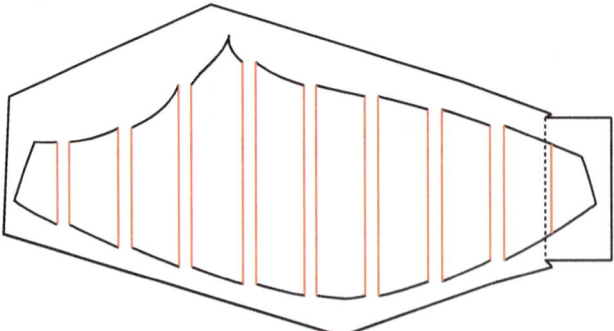

PART 2: CONSTRUCTION METHOD

1. Fold the fabric at the beginning and end of each pintuck and stitch at the pintuck size. A backstitch is not necessary.

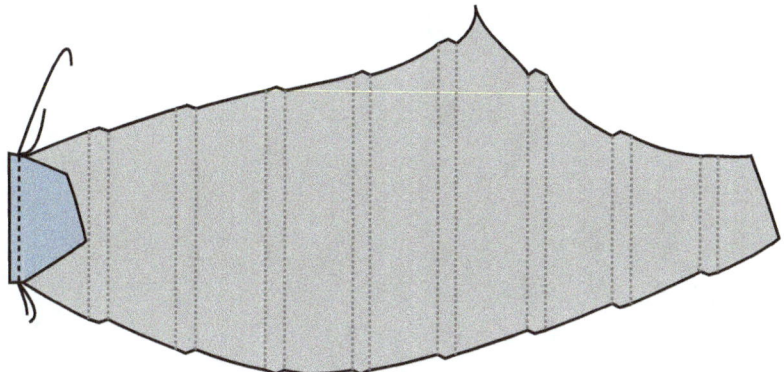

2. After completing all the pintucks, press them to the side indicated by the pattern and stitch in place around the edges. Construct the remainder of the cup as previously demonstrated.

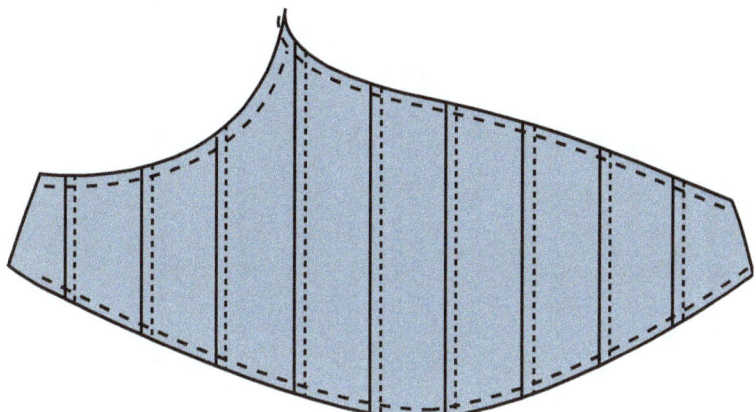

CHAPTER 12
NURSING BRA

This chapter demonstrates a design of a nursing bra with a top cup frame. The frame holds the bra in place when detaching the cup for nursing. Not all nursing bras are created with a frame. An alternative that is often used is to connect the nursing clip directly to the strap with a piece of elastic attached to the side of the bra. The alternative method is not demonstrated.

PART 1: PATTERN MANIPULATION

1. Using the basic pattern, line up the cups at the side seam at the seam lines. The first stage is to create the partial under cup frame to hold up the breast when the outer cup is unlatched for nursing. At the underarm portion of the cup, temporarily connect the lower cup to the upper cup as pictured, overlapping at the seam allowance.

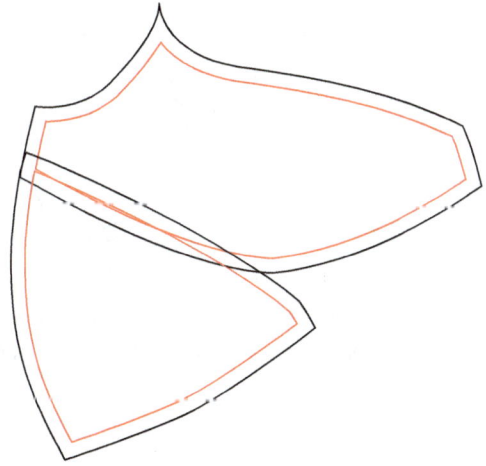

2. From the strap point, measure to the right 1" or 25mm on the neckline towards the center front. On the wire curve, measure down 2" to 3" (5cm to 7.5cm). This can vary based on the cup size. Add a notch to this position on the cup.

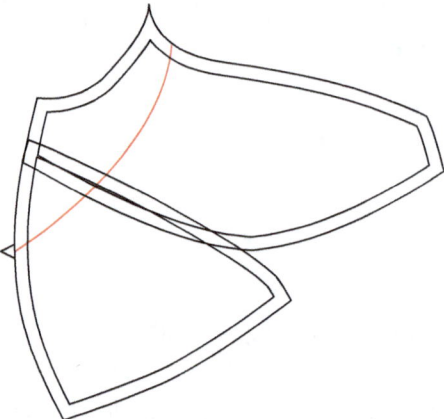

3. Line up the top of the remaining cup piece at the center front of the cup, overlapping at the seam allowance. Mark 1" or 25mm down from the strap point to 2" to 3" (5cm to 7.5cm) on the center front wire curve. Trace the new shape. Add a notch to this position on the cup.

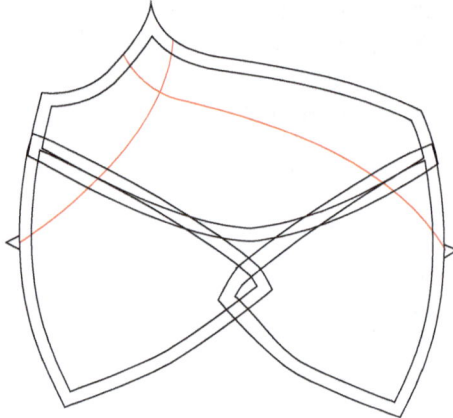

4. Create a pattern piece for the top frame of the cup, combining both markings as shown below. At the inner angle, blend out the point with a curve. This will aid in sewing.

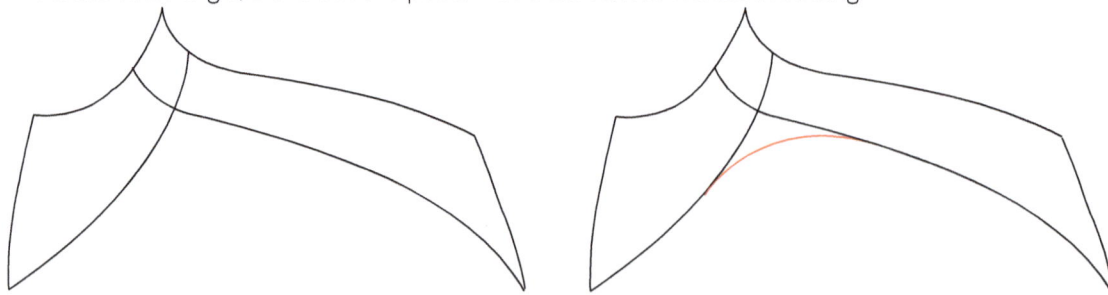

5. The detachable portion of the cup is shortened by 1/2" or 12.5mm on the top of the cup, at the strap point, center front and side.

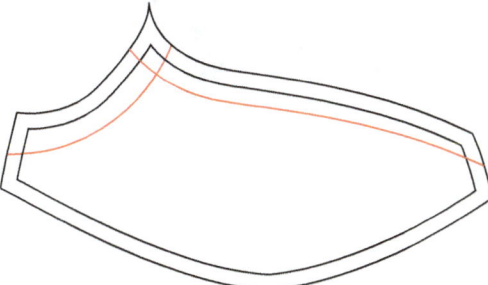

6. Remove the top of the cup. This alteration provides a 1/2" or 12.5mm overlap of the frame.

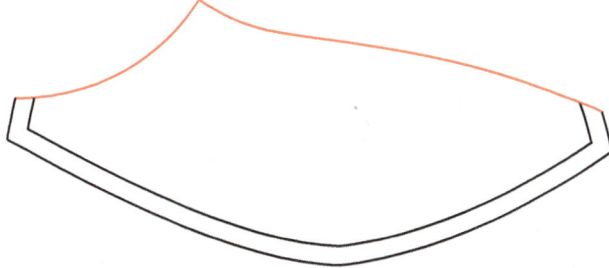

PART 2: CONSTRUCTION METHOD

1. Follow the cup construction techniques previously demonstrated. On the upper cup, complete the remaining side of the neckline by attaching elastic to the neckline.

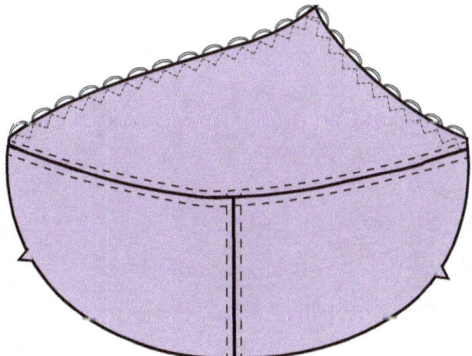

2. On the under cup, attach the elastic to the center front neckline only.

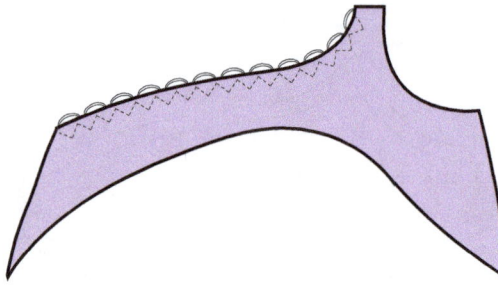

3. On the interior curve on the under cup, either overlock the edge or cover the raw edge with a soft seam tape to avoid irritation. Pictured is an overlock stitch finish.

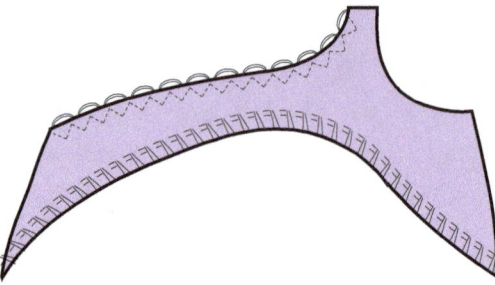

4. Place the top cup frame beneath the upper cup and line up the under cup to the notches. Baste stitch the wire line in place at 1/8" or 3mm. Complete sewing of the band and cup as previously demonstrated. Attach the back neckline and armhole elastic, but leave the front strap unattached.

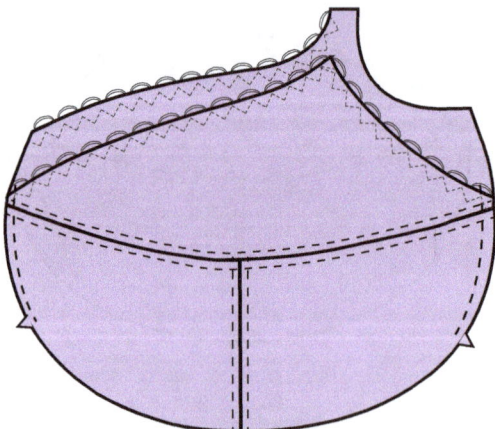

Intermediate / Nursing Bra | 117

VARIATION A: NURSING CLIP

A.1. Before attaching the strap to the under cup, take a small strip of elastic and thread it through the top and bottom of the hook side of the nursing clip and baste stitch in place. Attach the strap clean finishing one end of the elastic and bar tack in place at the top and bottom of the looped elastic.

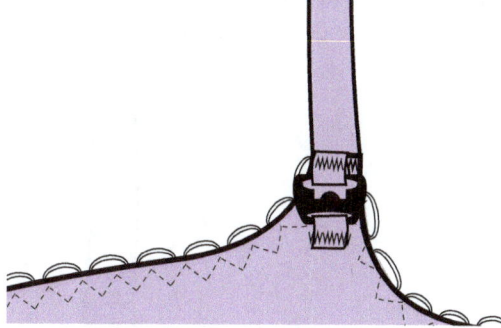

A.2. Attach a loop of fabric with the other side of the nursing clip to the outer cup and secure with a bar tack.

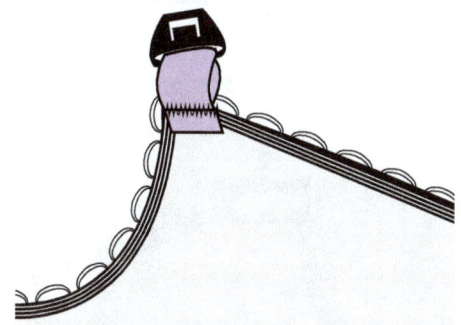

VARIATION B: ADJUSTABLE HOOK & EYE

For greater versatility, use a hook and eye tape in place of a nursing clip. This will allow for three eyes in adjusting the cup as the breast size fluctuates.

B.1. Before attaching the strap to the under cup, place the eye side of the tape to the strap point. Sandwich the tape between the strap and the cup, stitch in place, then fully secure the strap and eye tape with a bar tack.

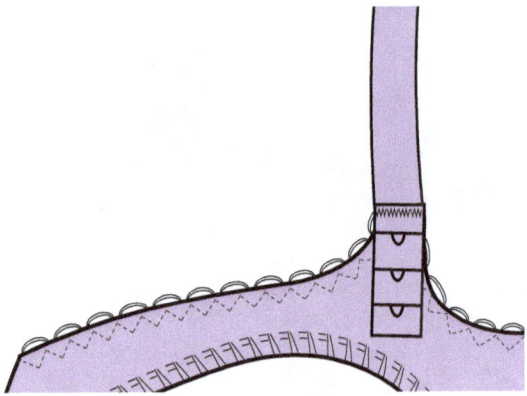

B.2. Attach the hook side of the tape to the upper cup.

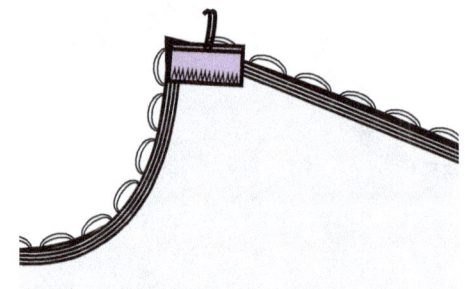

CHAPTER 13
MASTECTOMY BRA

Mastectomy bras are regular bras with a pocket for a prosthesis. Depending on whether the individual had a lumpectomy or a full mastectomy, requirements for mastectomy bras will vary. Prosthetics come in a variety of shapes, sizes and coverage. Before designing a bra for mastectomy purposes, determine what shape is required for the pocket. The directions in this chapter demonstrate a full mastectomy pocket.

PART 1: PATTERN MANIPULATION

FITTING INTO A CUP

Determine the size, shape and where the prosthesis sits on the body in proportion to the bra. Some may extend under the arm and some may sit fully in the bra cup. Modify the following directions to accommodate the specific shape of the prosthesis.

The first consideration is to determine if the prosthesis will fit in the bra fully. For a prosthesis that is larger and may tend to need a full coverage cup, the bra cup neckline will need to be altered to accommodate this shape. Pictured here is the altered neckline shape to cover a prosthesis.

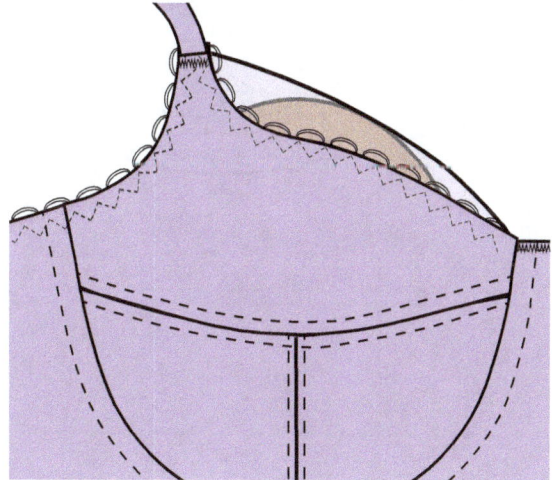

DESIGNING THE POCKET

For a full prosthesis, make a flat interior pocket to provide the best support for the prosthesis and the bra. The pocket should be constructed of a soft jersey.

1. Trace the cup and band pieces shown below. Draw in the 1/4" or 6mm seam allowance as pictured.

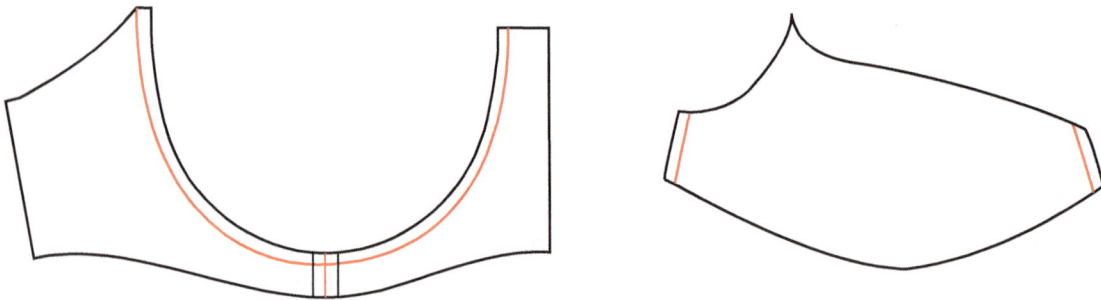

2. Line up the cup top into the band piece at the center front, matching the seam lines.

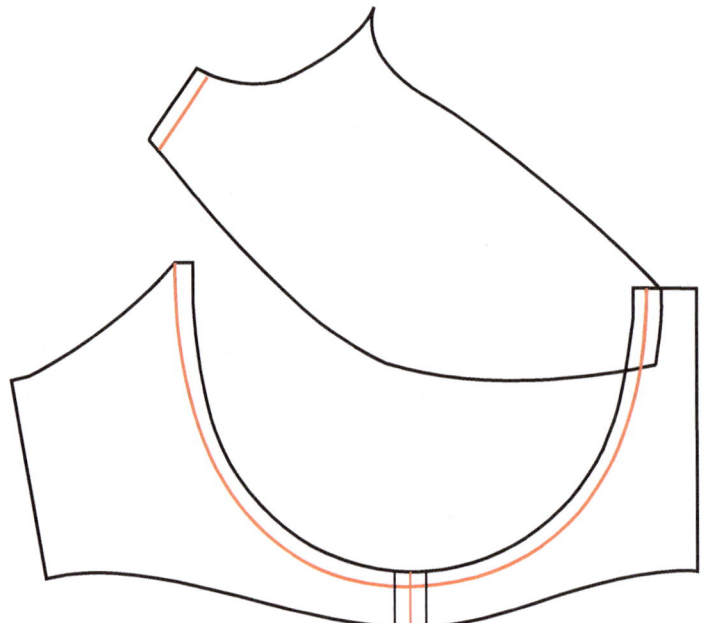

3. Take the left side of the cup and match it to the left side overlapping at the seam lines. This will force the upper cup to take up a dart. Try to keep the exterior lines flat on the table.

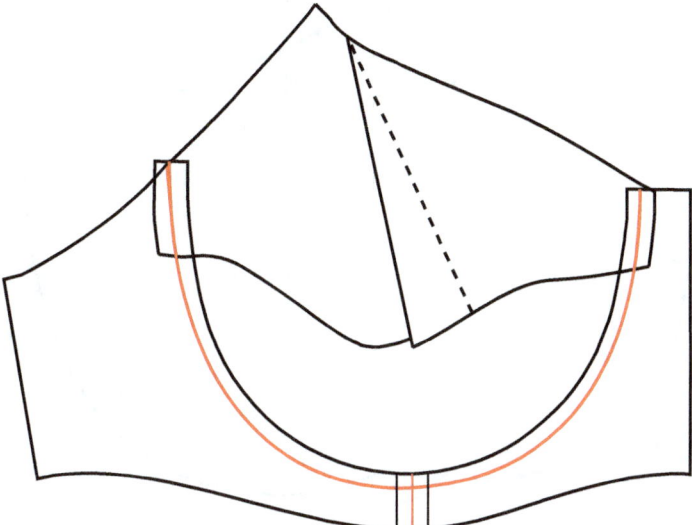

4. Copy the new shape of the neckline, half of the underwire curve (plus the seam allowance of 1/4" or 6mm) and the side seam as pictured.

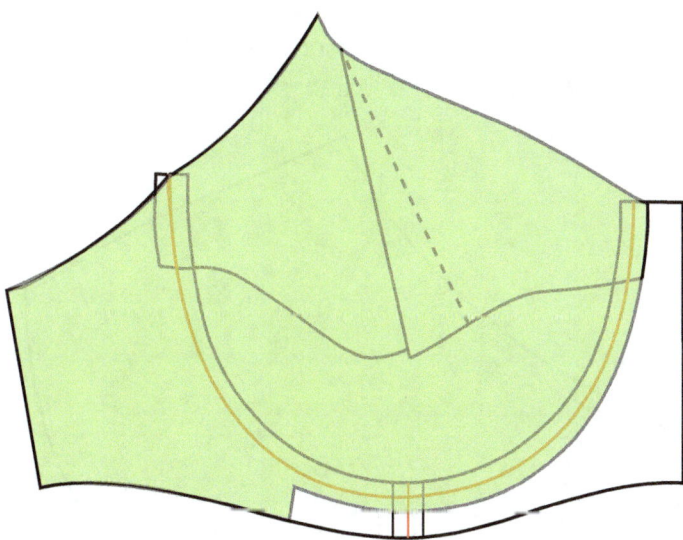

5. Take the pocket pattern piece and remove 1" or 25mm from the armhole. This will be the area where the prosthesis is inserted.

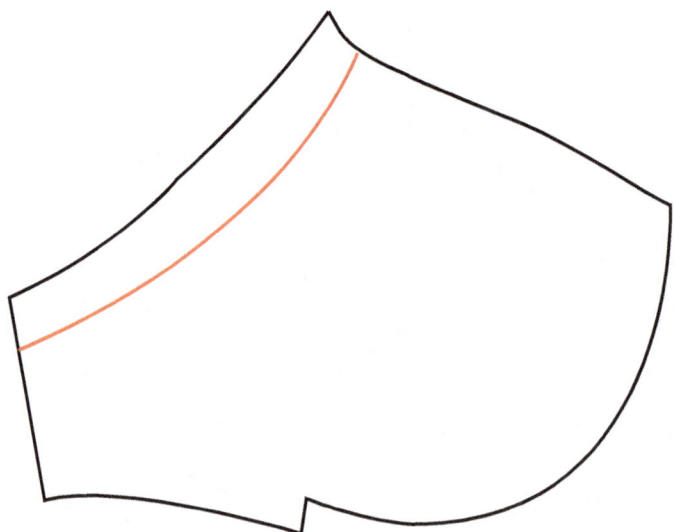

PART 2: CONSTRUCTION METHOD

The construction steps for including the pocket have a few variations from basic bra construction.

1. Finish the pocket opening with an overlock stitch or cover with a seam tape to keep the cut fabric from stretching out of shape or unraveling.

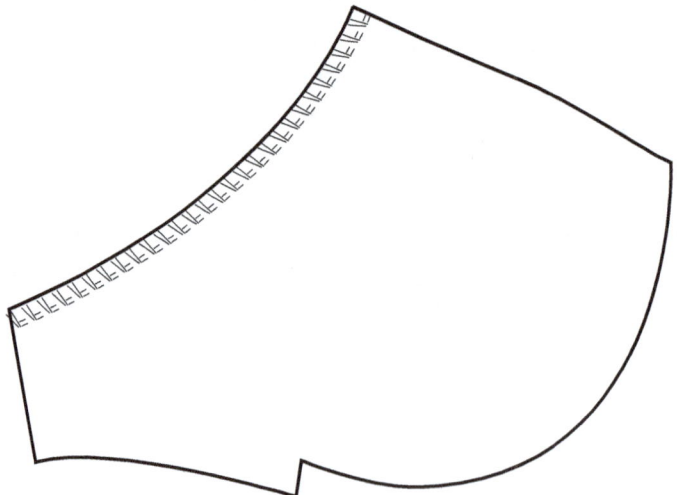

2. Construct the cup seams as previously demonstrated for the bra design. Line up the pocket to the neckline and curve of the cup, baste stitch along the edge to secure.

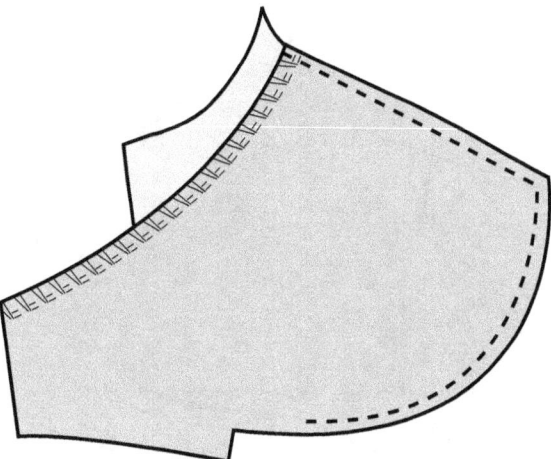

3. Construct the front band as previously demonstrated. Attaching the cup is tricky. It is attached it in two sections because of the overlapped pocket. Stitch the wire curved portion of the pocket into the wire curve of the band. Leave a 1" or 25mm gap at the end of the curve.

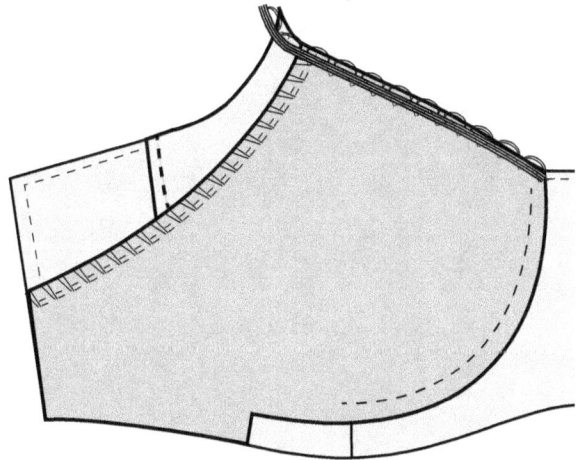

4. Attach the underwire casing carefully, then secure the open end of the pocket to the side seam of the front and secure the lower portion to the waistband. Complete the bra construction as previously demonstrated.

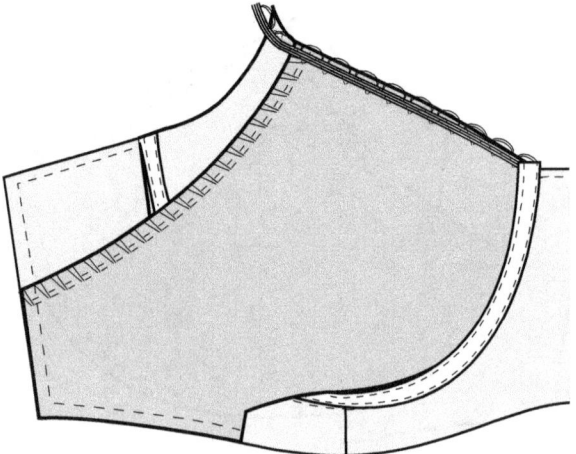

ADVANCED

Chapter 14: Introduction to Pattern Drafting and Grading 127

Chapter 15: Bra Band Pattern Drafting 141

Chapter 16: Bra Cup Drafting: Porcelynne Pattern Drafting Method 165

Chapter 17: Pattern Directions 189

Chapter 18: Create a Sloper: Porcelynne Pattern Manipulation Method 195

Chapter 19: Porcelynne Pattern Manipulation Method 203

Chapter 20: Pattern Manipulation: Bralette 209

Chapter 21: Pattern Manipulation: Non-Wired Soft Bra 215

Chapter 22: Bra Band Grading 219

Chapter 23: Bra Cup Grading 237

CHAPTER 14
INTRODUCTION TO PATTERN DRAFTING AND GRADING

The beginner and intermediate sections of this book have introduced several construction and pattern manipulation concepts.

The advanced section guides one through the process of drafting a basic bra pattern, creating final sewing patterns, making a bra sloper for alterations, designing custom bras and grading patterns into various band and cup sizes.

This section is mathematical in nature. Keep an open mind while entering into the world of engineering math for bra making.

TOOLS

Compass - A compass is a two pronged mathematical device that creates a perfect circle. It will be necessary in drafting both the cup and the band by hand.

Calculator - Having a basic calculator handy is a must when dealing with the intricacies of the bra draft.

Flexible Ruler - This is a flexible/bendable ruler that is used to measure curves. This is used when measuring the cup for accuracy.

Oaktag, Manila or Hard tag paper - Depending on where one is in the world, this may have different names. This paper is thick like poster board and generally manila in color. It is used to finalize patterns and is used for creating slopers. Alternately, use poster board if there is no access to tag paper.

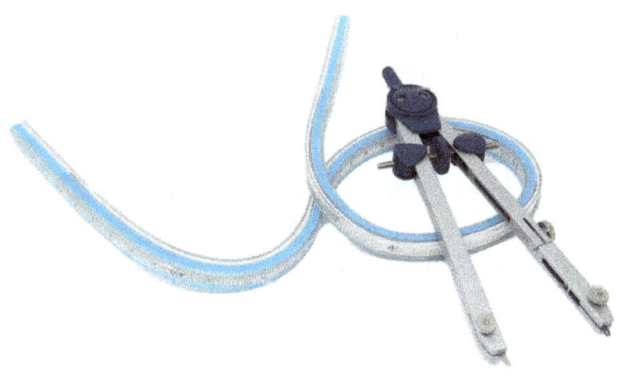

TERMINOLOGY

Grading - The process of creating graduated sizes for a range of sizes.

Slopers - A sloper (or block pattern) is a basic pattern shape used in creating designs. It does not have seam allowance and is created for the sample size. This is a drafting term used in the fashion industry.

FABRICS, ELASTICS AND STRETCH

For cups and the front band, it is recommended to use fabric without stretch. Fabric with stretch can be stabilized with a lining. A mechanical stretch is acceptable as long as the patterns are cut in the correct direction.

The back band contains stretch. The draft for the back is created based on the stretch for the chosen fabrics and elastics.

Test both the fabric and elastic for stretch, in the same manner as stated in the beginner section.

Fabric and elastic should not be reduced by its full amount of stretch, but only by half of its stretch. The chart on the next page is used by multiplying the body's measurements by the reduced measurement multiplier.

Advanced / Introduction to Pattern Drafting and Grading | 129

If the chosen elastic is firmer than the fabric, utilize the stretch reduction for the elastic of the back pattern. If the fabric is firmer than the elastic, use the stretch reduction for the fabric for the back pattern.

Based on how much the fabric and elastic stretch from 5" or 10cm, use the stretch reduction chart below.

It is common to have multiple back drafts for a variety of stretches.

STRETCH REDUCTION CHART FOR FABRIC

Amount Stretched from 5" (Inches - Imperial)	Amount Stretched from 10cm (Centimeters - Metric)	Stretch Ratio	Reduced Measurement Multiplier
5 1/4	10.5	5%	0.9750
5 1/2	11.0	10%	0.9500
5 3/4	11.5	15%	0.9250
6	12.0	20%	0.9000
6 1/4	12.5	25%	0.8750
6 1/2	13.0	30%	0.8500
6 3/4	13.5	35%	0.8250
7	14.0	40%	0.8000
7 1/4	14.5	45%	0.7750
7 1/2	15.0	50%	0.7500
7 3/4	15.5	55%	0.7250
8	16.0	60%	0.7000
8 1/4	16.5	65%	0.6750
8 1/2	17.0	70%	0.6500
8 3/4	17.5	75%	0.6250
9	18.0	80%	0.6000
9 1/4	18.5	85%	0.5750
9 1/2	19.0	90%	0.5500
9 3/4	19.5	95%	0.5250
10	20.0	100%	0.5000
10 1/4	20.5	105%	0.4750
10 1/2	21.0	110%	0.4500
10 3/4	21.5	115%	0.4250
11	22.0	120%	0.4000
11 1/4	22.5	125%	0.3750
11 1/2	23.0	130%	0.3500
11 3/4	23.5	135%	0.3250
12	24.0	140%	0.3000
12 1/4	24.5	145%	0.2750
12 1/2	25.0	150%	0.2500
12 3/4	25.5	155%	0.2250
13	26.0	160%	0.2000

WIRE SELECTION

For drafting a bra, it is best to select the perfect wire for the body being drafted for. The recommendation is to create a wire trace of the breast and align the trace to various wire charts to match the best wire shape.

To create a wire trace, mold the flexible ruler around the breast and carefully transfer the shape to a piece of paper. Alternative options use craft wire or pipe cleaners to get the shape.

Start with the suggested wire from Chapter 1. Place the wire around the bust (without a bra on). Does the wire fully encompass the breast tissue? If it does not fit comfortably, try the next wire up. If there is plenty of room beside the wire and the breast tissue, try smaller wires until a wire is selected that fits around the bust.

REGULAR WIRE
SHORT REGULAR WIRE*
LONG REGULAR WIRE*
DIAMETER CHART
Porcelynne.com
Top Spread 1/2" or 12.5mm

Wire Size	Wire Diameter (Imperial)	Wire Diameter (Metric)
28	4	10.2
30	4 5/16	11
32	4 5/8	11.8
34	4 15/16	12.6
36	5 1/4	13.4
38	5 9/16	14.2
40	5 7/8	15
42	6 1/4	15.8
44	6 9/16	16.6
46	6 7/8	17.4
48	7 3/16	18.2
50	7 1/2	19
52	7 13/16	19.8
54	8 1/8	20.6
56	8 7/16	21.4
58	8 3/4	22.2
60	9 1/16	23

*Porcelynne.com does not currently carry these wire styles.

VERTICAL WIRE
LONG VERTICAL WIRE
SHORT VERTICAL WIRE
DEMI WIRE
DIAMETER CHART
Porcelynne.com
No Top Spread

Wire Size	Wire Diameter (Imperial)	Wire Diameter (Metric)
36	4 1/2	11.4
38	4 13/16	12.2
40	5 1/8	13
42	5 7/16	13.8
44	5 3/4	14.6
46	6 1/16	15.4
48	6 3/8	16.2
50	6 11/16	17
52	7	17.8
54	7 5/16	18.6
56	7 5/8	19.4
58	7 15/16	20.2
60	8 5/16	21

Evaluate how the wire lands on the body. Does either end of the wire poke into the rib cage? It is an indicator that the wire is not the perfect wire for the breast or body shape.

Location dependent, different wires are available. Find a couple wires prior to drafting. If ordering wires from Porcelynne, the charts below can be used for the band and cup drafting details prior to receiving them.

Please compare the chosen wires to Porcelynne's wire charts to get the closest match. Porcelynne's wire charts can be downloaded on Porcelynne.com under each wire style. The charts on these pages can then be referenced for the draft.

Wire sizes vary in both width and length. In the following chapter, reference these wire charts for determining the diameter of the wire chosen for the draft. The width measurements of nearly all manufacturers increase by 5/16" or 8mm. Check with the specific manufacturer of the chosen underwire for differences.

The regular wire has a top spread amount that is fairly standard. If choosing not to use these charts for comparison, please subtract 1/2" or 12.5mm from the tip-to-tip measurement of a regular wire.

WIDE FLAT VERTICAL WIRE DIAMETER CHART
Porcelynne.com
No Top Spread

Wire Size	Wire Diameter (Imperial)	Wire Diameter (Metric)
44	5 7/16	13.8
46	5 3/4	14.6
48	6 1/16	15.4
50	6 3/8	16.2
52	6 11/16	17
54	7	17.8
56	7 5/16	18.6
58	7 5/8	19.4
60	7 15/16	20.2
62	8 5/16	21
64	8 15/16	21.8

REGULAR WIRE LENGTH CHART
Porcelynne.com Regular Wires
Wire Growth 1/2" or 12.5mm*

Wire Size	Wire Length (Imperial)	Wire Length (Metric)
28	6 7/8	17.5
30	7 3/8	18.7
32	7 7/8	20
34	8 11/32	21.2
36	8 27/32	22.4
38	9 5/16	23.7
40	9 13/16	24.9
42	10 9/32	26.1
44	10 25/32	27.4
46	11 5/16	28.5
48	11 3/4	29.9
50	12 1/4	31.1
52	12 3/4	32.3
54	13 7/32	33.6
56	13 11/16	34.8
58	14 3/16	36
60	14 11/16	37.3

*Approximately

If using a short or long regular wire, the top spread might vary. The recommendation is to use a compass and create a circle using the amount in the chart as a guide. This will help determine the actual shape change of your wires.

The vertical wire chart has no top spread as the ends point straight up. This is important to note when drafting.

Not all sizes are available in all styles. In these charts, the regular wires are available in sizes 28-60 and the vertical wires are available in 36-60. Short and long vertical wires have the same diameter, just as short and long regular wires do. Demi wires have the same base wire diameter as a vertical wire.

Each wire manufacturer has their own specifications, check wires against Porcelynne's wire charts to accurately use the charts below.

In addition to knowing the width, it is also important to know the length of the wire. The wire needs to fit in the casing. The charts on these pages are the corresponding length charts to the width charts provided on the previous pages.

VERTICAL WIRE LENGTH CHART

Porcelynne.com Vertical Wires
Wire Growth 5/8" or 15mm

Wire Size	Wire Length (Imperial)	Wire Length (Metric)
36	9 5/16	23.7
38	9 29/32	25.1
40	10 15/32	26.7
42	11 1/16	28.3
44	11 21/32	29.6
46	12 1/4	31
48	12 13/16	32.5
50	13 1/2	34.3
52	14 5/32	36
54	14 27/32	37.8
56	15 17/32	39.5
58	16 3/16	41.1
60	16 7/8	43

SHORT VERTICAL WIRE LENGTH CHART

Porcelynne.com Short Vertical Wires
Wire Growth 5/8" or 15mm

Wire Size	Wire Length (Imperial)	Wire Length (Metric)
36	8 1/16	20.5
38	8 21/32	22
40	9 1/4	23.5
42	9 27/32	25
44	10 7/16	26.5
46	11 1/32	28
48	11 19/32	29.5
50	12 3/16	31
52	12 25/32	32.5
54	13 3/8	34
56	14 3/4	37.5
58	15 11/32	39
60	15 15/32	40.5

Advanced / Introduction to Pattern Drafting and Grading | 133

Wire lengths can grow in a variety of different amounts. The regular wires in the chart below grow in length by 1/2" or 12.5mm. In comparison, the vertical wires grow by 5/8" or 15mm in length.

Each wire shape caters to a different shaped breast. Different styles may need to be tested to determine the most appropriate wire.

WIDE FLAT VERTICAL WIRE LENGTH CHART

Porcelynne.com Wide Flat Vertical Wires
Wire Growth 5/8" or 15mm

Wire Size	Wire Length (Imperial)	Wire Length (Metric)
44	9 7/16	24
46	10 1/32	25.5
48	10 5/8	27
50	11 7/32	28.5
52	11 13/16	30
54	12 13/32	31.5
56	13	33
58	13 19/32	34.5
60	14 5/32	36
62	14 3/4	37.5
64	15 11/32	39

LONG VERTICAL WIRE LENGTH CHART

Porcelynne.com Long Vertical Wires
Wire Growth 5/8" or 15mm

Wire Size	Wire Length (Imperial)	Wire Length (Metric)
36	11 13/32	29
38	12 1/32	30.5
40	12 17/32	32
42	13 3/16	33.5
44	13 25/32	35
46	14 3/8	36.5
48	14 31/32	38
50	15 9/16	39.5
52	16 1/8	41
54	16 23/32	42.5
56	17 5/16	44
58	17 29/32	45.5
60	18 1/2	47

DEMI VERTICAL WIRE LENGTH CHART

Porcelynne.com Demi Vertical Wires
Wire Growth 5/8" or 15mm

Wire Size	Wire Length (Imperial)	Wire Length (Metric)
36	7 1/2	19
38	8 1/16	20.5
40	8 11/16	22
42	9 1/4	23.5
44	9 15/16	25
46	10 7/16	26.5
48	11 1/32	28
50	11 5/8	29.5
52	12 3/16	31
54	12 13/16	32.5
56	13 3/8	34
58	13 31/32	35.5
60	14 9/16	37

MEASUREMENTS FOR THE PORCELYNNE PATTERN DRAFTING METHOD

Based on the wire charts on these pages, record the information for the chosen wire. Be sure to include the wire style, size, width and length.

Wire Style
Wire Size
Wire Width
Wire Length

Not everyone wears a wire and not everyone needs one. For the drafting directions, a wire is required. Once a sloper is created, a non-wired bra can be drafted following the directions in Chapter 21.

DRAFTING MEASUREMENTS

In the months of research for the third edition, I ventured out to create a mathematical calculation to make drafting for oneself more precise and less reliant on taking horizontal and vertical bust measurements.

The general feedback was that taking those specific measurements on saggy breasts were very difficult and were not very accurate.

After four months on one single mathematical calculation to determine the horizontal measurement, I have concluded my findings. This new method for drafting and manipulation is referred to as the Porcelynne Pattern Drafting and Manipulation Method. The calculation is based on five factors.

The first factor is the wire width, which was discussed on the previous pages.

The second through the 4th measurements should be taken sans bra (without a bra and on bare skin).

Take two lengths of string, yarn or ribbon and tie one at the under bust. Take the second one and tie it at the chest (over the bust and above the breast tissue). Measure the chest height between the two strings in the center of the body between the breasts for the second measurement. This measurement is referred to as the chest height.

Take the measurements where both strings are tied for the 3rd and 4th measurements.

For the 5th and final measurement, wear a well fitting bra. This can be a sports bra if that is the best fit available.

If the bra is not very supportive and the breasts fall lower than they should, enlist the assistance of a friend or family member. Have them take the full bust measurement while elevating the breasts manually to an acceptable level.

Record the full bust measurement as the final measurement.

Wire Width
Chest Height
Chest Measurement
Under Bust Measurement
Full Bust Measurement

Advanced / Introduction to Pattern Drafting and Grading | 135

ALL THE MATH I DID

This part is not for the faint of heart. I detail this information to explain how and why I came up with this particular mathematical calculation.

If you do not wish to know how and why I came up with this math, skip to the next heading for instructions on how to do the math. If you prefer to cheat, go to the web page *https://blog.porcelynne.com/porcelynne-pattern-drafting-and-manipulation-method-bra-making-calculator/* to plug in measurements for an automatic output of these calculations.

To determine how much of the full bust measurement is actually dedicated to breast tissue, I first needed to determine the circumference of the body where the breasts are, but without breasts.

This was a simple average of the chest and under bust measurements.

I then quartered the body to determine the bust (no bust) area for one side of the front. I divided the previous average by four.

Next, I determined the percentage of the quarter of the body in which the wire encompasses. This is determined by dividing the wire width by the 1/4 of the body from the previous step.

I then determined the amount of each breast. This I determined to be the full bust measurement minus the average body size. This part took a number of terrible illustrations for me to visualize.

The reason why the amount is not divided by two is, if you measure the circumference of the body, then measure the same circumference with one hill on it, versus the same circumference with two hills on it, you will have the same measurement difference.

The reason one or two breasts would be the same amount is that you are still measuring the up and down, but the up on one hill and the down on the second hill. The center is not measured separately, as that is part of the actual body circumference.

The final math step creates the horizontal amount for the cup. Take the calculated percentage of wire-to-body and multiply that by the bust amount in the previous step. Finally, add the wire width for the horizontal measurement.

The vertical measurement was slightly more challenging for me to determine, I enlisted my husband to help me figure it out. I tried this calculation several times, but it did not work for all of my testers, only one or two. He took one look and within 15 minutes, we scrambled the original calculation I created and came up with one that worked for all my testers. I had all the parts I needed, they were just in the wrong order.

To calculate the vertical measurement, I added the bust measurement (calculated during the horizontal calculation) to the chest height. I then multiplied that sum by the percentage calculated by the wire-to-body ratio.

Of course, there may be exceptions to this calculation, but of my testers, this was the most accurate way to calculate the horizontal and vertical measurements without taking tedious measurements of each breast.

These measurement calculations account for both the torso shape and height, which are just a little closer to custom than I had in previous editions.

The last calculation we created is the position for the front strap on the cup. If the cup is wide and extends under the arm, the strap placement should not be over as far as an individual with a narrow frame would have.

To determine the strap position, I took half of the wire width, since the position is between the half way point and the side cup. I subtracted the full wire width from the quarter of the body (without breast). I multiplied the half wire by that result to create the position off the center of the cup in which the strap should be placed.

THE CALCULATION

To make this a little easier to follow than my explanation. Record the measurements where applicable.

In this first step, add the chest and under bust measurements together and divide by 2 to get the average.

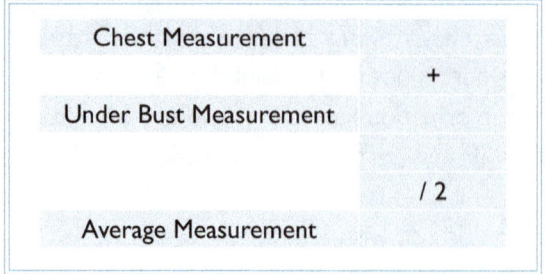

Next, divide the average measurement by 4.

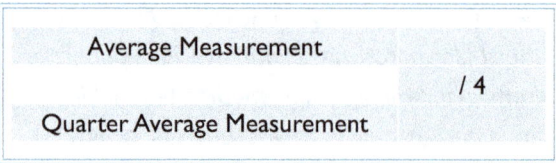

Divide the wire width by the quarter average measurement.

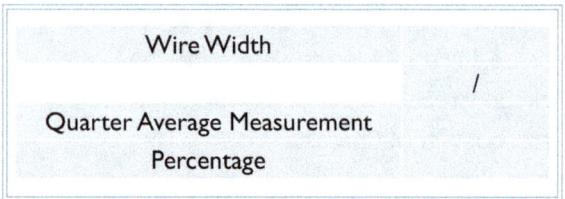

Subtract the average measurement from the full bust measurement.

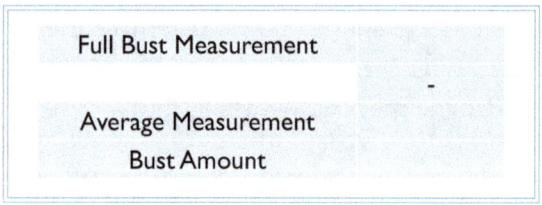

Multiply the bust amount by the percentage then add the wire width for the horizontal measurement.

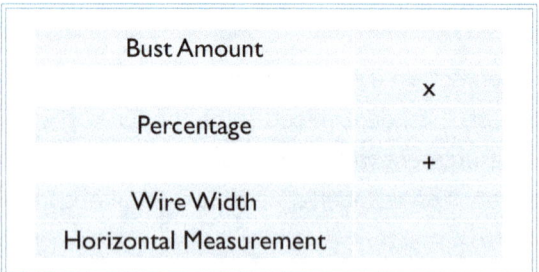

Add the chest height to the bust amount, then multiply the result by the percentage for the vertical measurement.

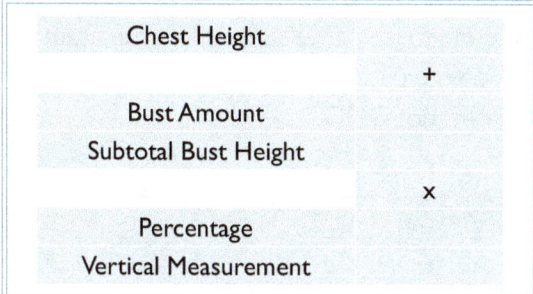

For the strap position movement off the center of the cup, subtract the wire width from the quarter average measurement. Divide the wire width by 2, then divide this result by the quarter average measurement. Multiply the two results for the strap position.

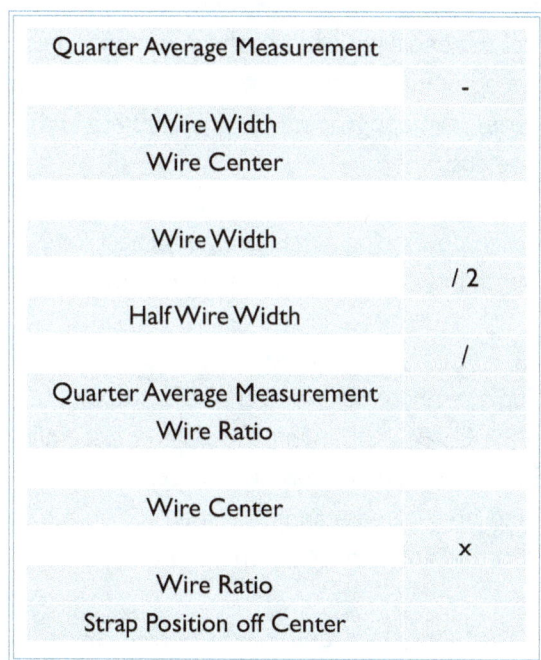

ADJUSTMENT FOR BREAST ASYMMETRY

The calculations created assume breast symmetry. To account for asymmetry, two separate drafts should be completed, one for each size.

For a single size difference in cups, subtract half the cup grade amount (1/4" or 6mm) from one side and add the half cup grade amount (1/4" or 6mm) to the measurement of the other side.

For more extreme size differences, create multiple drafts to determine the best fit for each side. A two size difference will require adding a single grade amount (1/2" or 12.5mm) to one cup, while removing it from the second cup.

The idea is that the horizontal measurement creates two equal cups. Making one larger, will require one to be smaller to still fit into the calculations created.

SLOPERS & PATTERN MANIPULATION

Creating the draft is only half the battle. Once a successful fitting draft has been created, a sloper is made to create any design. Prior to creating the sloper, be sure to review the fitting chapter in the intermediate section. The sloper should be created from the final fit.

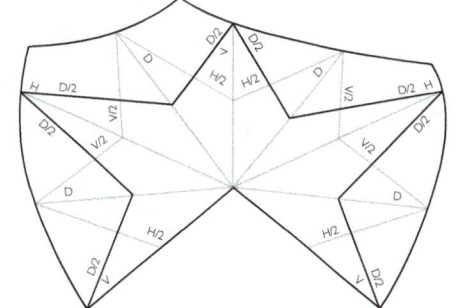

Once the sloper is created, any design can be created. In this section, learn how to use the sloper to create a custom cup design as well as specialty bras, such as bralettes and non-underwired soft bras.

BRALETTE

Bralettes can be used as sleep bras, training bras for teens or for individuals who do not require support of an underwire. This style of bra is generally seen in cups A through F as they may not need the support of an underwire.

NON-WIRED SOFT BRA

Non-wired soft bras have a variety of different styles. Altering a pattern to remove a wire may need multiple fit samples.

PATTERNS AND LABELING

Patterns are generally labeled with a variety of information including Style Name, Piece Name, Size and Cut Number.

Patterns should be marked with grainlines to indicate the length grain of the pattern for proper orientation. This is different than the direction of greatest stretch (DOGS). If choosing to label DOGS, be sure to indicate that on the pattern. The sample below is the grainline, not DOGS.

GRADING & GRADE RULES

Grading is a term that is used in reference to creating a size range. Grading is a very complicated subject and varies depending on the garment.

When beginning a venture into grading, the size chart needs to be defined. The recommendation is to use the information in this book, including the size charts and adapt a size chart appropriate for your country and base customer.

When developing a measurement chart for sizes, a basic grade rule chart is created.

GRADING FOR NONSTRETCH

Cup sizes increase and decrease in size by 1/2" in the US & UK, 1cm in Australia and 1.25cm in Europe and other international countries. Band sizes increase and decrease by 2" in the US & UK and 5cm everywhere else.

	Cup Volume	Band Grade
US/UK	1/2"	2"
Euro	1.25cm	5cm
Australia	1cm	5cm

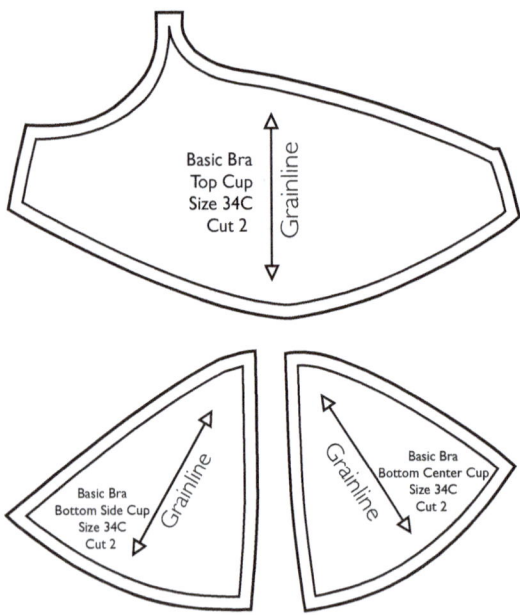

BAND GRADING

There are two methods in which to grade a band: the sister size method and the full grade method.

The sister size grade is easier for pattern makers as the front is graded for the wires, but not the band size. This allows all fronts to be used across separate sister sizes. This method was demonstrated in both the first and second edition of this book.

This method is detailed in the following chapters, but the second method is also demonstrated in this book. One way is not more correct than the other. It is up to the preference of the pattern maker.

The second methods splits the grade between the front and back bands.

After creating the basic woven grade rule for the band and cup, partition out the grade for the quarter of the body for each portion of the draft. The band grade is divided by four for each quarter of the body.

The back grade needs to be reduced based on the materials used for the bra. Therefore, a stretch grade must be developed for the bra back.

For the patterns included in this book, the stretch measurements are based on a medium to heavy weight power netting and elastic that contain a 50% stretch. The use of power net is not required, but a fabric should be used with a similar stretch.

The following stretch grade chart is based on the 50% stretch of a power net and elastic. Since the back pattern encompasses only a quarter of the body, take the quarter grade of the body and multiply it by the stretch reduction chart on page 129.

	Back Band Grade
US/UK	3/8"
Euro	10mm
Australia	10mm

Use the following chart to create a custom grade rule for a specific fabric or elastic.

CUSTOM CHART	
Fabric	Back Band Grade

CHAPTER 15
BRA BAND PATTERN DRAFTING

The directions for the bra band are broken into three main parts: the wire, the front band and the back band. The chapter following this covers drafting of the cup, using the Porcelynne Pattern Drafting Method, based on the band draft. In an effort to work with all users' styles and the ever changing marketplace, an additional set of directions for drafting and grading within Adobe® Illustrator® is provided.

For consistency in drafting, the draft is of one side, with the side seam to the left and the center front seam on the right side.

DRAFTING BY HAND

WIRE DRAFT

1. Use the wire diameter charts from the previous chapter to fill out the following information.

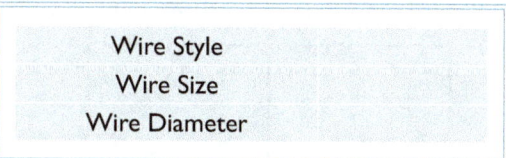

2. Draw a square using the diameter of the underwire as the height and width. Label the right vertical line Center Front.

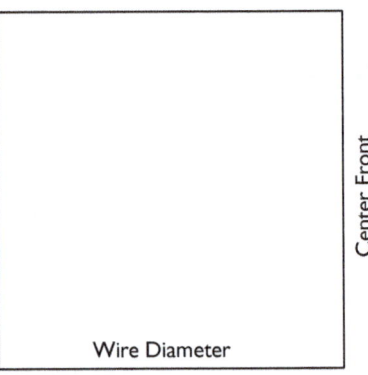

3. Divide the wire diameter in half, both vertically and horizontally.

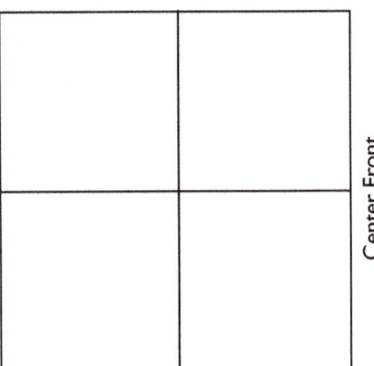

4. Take a compass and line up the point at the center cross point and the pencil up to the center of the bottom line. Make a full circle with the compass. If everything is marked correctly, the edges of the circle should touch the right, left, top and bottom intersections.

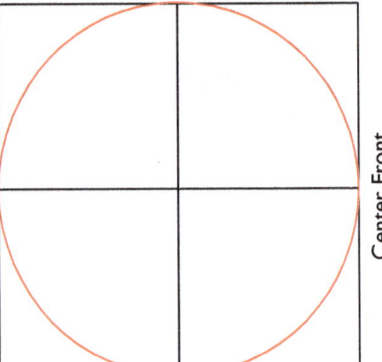

Advanced / Bra Band Pattern Drafting | 143

BREAST SPACING

5. On the right side, draw a line parallel based on the spacing between the breasts. For **wide set breasts**, measure 1/2" or 12.5mm. For **average spaced breasts** measure 3/8" or 10mm. For **narrow set breasts**, measure to the right 1/4" or 6mm. Individuals using a regular wire generally have wider spacing. If unsure of which to start with, use the "average." This can always be altered later when testing the draft for fit.

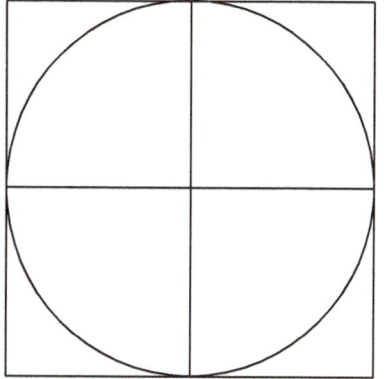

WIRE STYLES

The next steps create the shape of the wire. Please note that wire spring is not done in these steps as explained in Chapter 6. A variety of wires styles are detailed in the following steps. Choose the wire shape draft based on the style. Review the following steps to determine which wire the draft is for.

Regular Wires

A. On the original center front line on the right, measure up 1/2" or 12.5mm and square a line across towards the new right line 1/8" or 3mm.

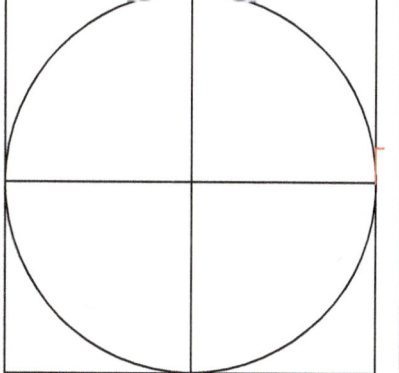

B. Blend the bottom part of the circle to meet the 1/8" or 3mm mark with a slightly curved line.

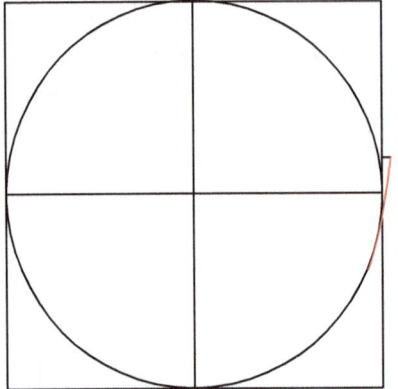

C. For regular wires, on the left side of the center line, measure up 3/4" or 20mm and square out to the left 3/8" or 10mm. This amount, in addition to the 1/8" or 3mm from Step A should equal the top spread amount of the regular wire.

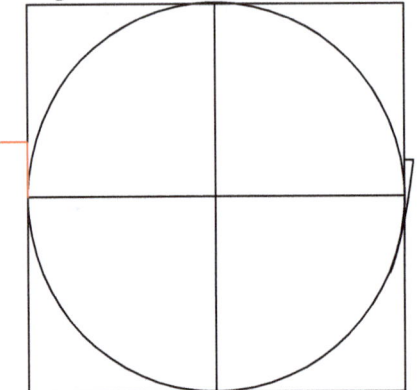

D. Using a slight curve, draw in a line towards the bottom of the wire curve.

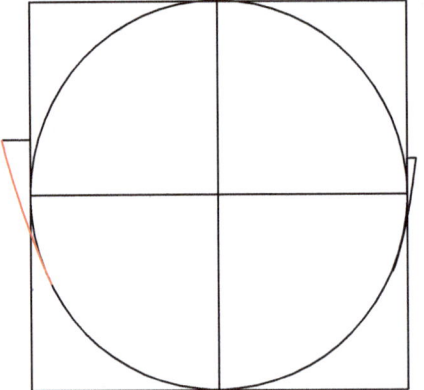

For shorter and longer regular wires, line up your wire to the circle and mark where the wire ends on each end. Porcelynne does not carry either of these wires. I do not feel I can accurately modify these directions for those wires as all manufacturers have their own specs when it comes to longer and shorter wires.

Vertical Wires

A. On the original center front line on the right, measure up 5/8" or 16mm. Do not square a line across any amount as this wire is straight up at the center front. This line will be hard to see, make a small mark at the top of the line.

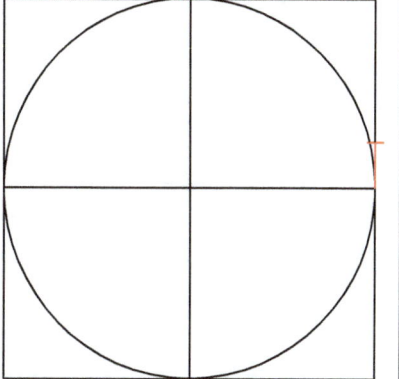

B. From the center line on the left side of the circle, measure up 1 1/2" or 38mm. Do not square a line across any amount as the wire is straight up at the side. This line will be hard to see, make a cross mark at the top of the line.

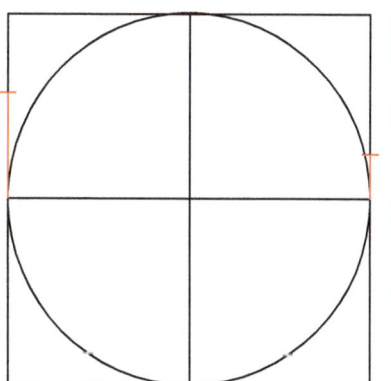

Short Vertical Wires

A. On the original center front line on the right, measure up 1/8" or 3mm. Do not square a line across any amount as this wire is straight up at the center front. This line will be hard to see, make a cross mark at the top of the line.

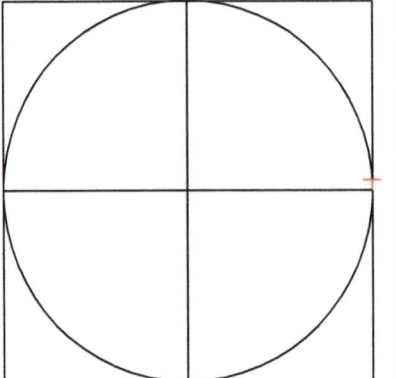

B. From the center line on the left side of the circle, measure up 13/16" or 20mm. Do not square a line across any amount as the wire is straight up at the side. This line will be hard to see, make a cross mark at the top of the line.

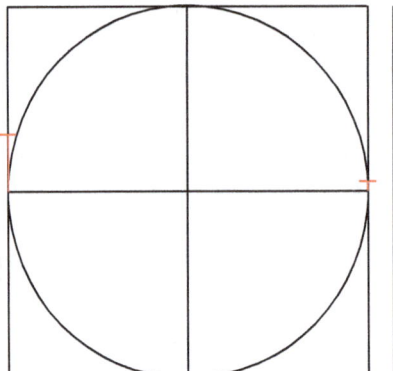

Long Vertical Wires

A. On the original center front line on the right, measure up 1 7/16" or 37mm. Do not square a line across any amount as this wire is straight up at the center front. This line will be hard to see, make a cross mark at the top of the line.

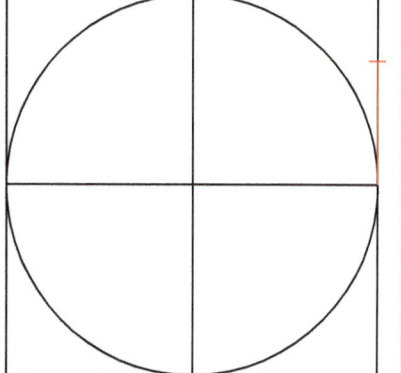

B. From the center line on the left side of the circle, measure up 2 3/4" or 7cm. Do not square a line across any amount as the wire is straight up at the side. This line will be hard to see, make a cross mark at the top of the line.

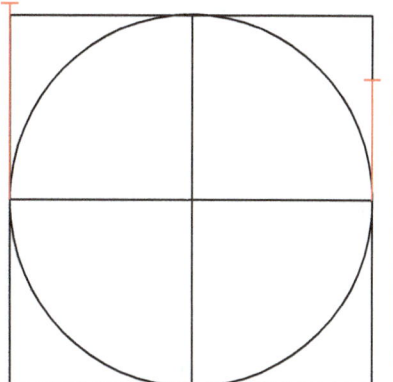

C. Some longer vertical wires vary in shape on the lower curve. Line up the wire used to the draft and modify the wire line appropriately.

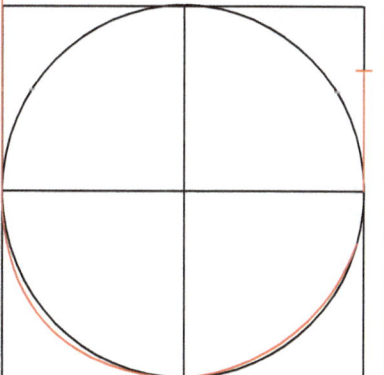

Wide Flat Vertical Wires

A. On the original center front line on the right, measure up 3/16" or 5mm. Do not square a line across any amount as this wire is straight up at the center front. This line will be hard to see, make a cross mark at the top of the line.

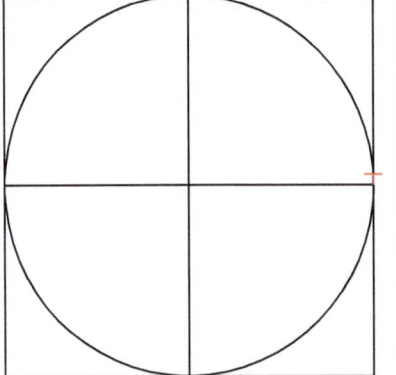

B. From the center line on the left side of the circle, measure up 1 1/32" or 26mm. Do not square a line across any amount as the wire is straight up at the side. This line will be hard to see, make a cross mark at the top of the line.

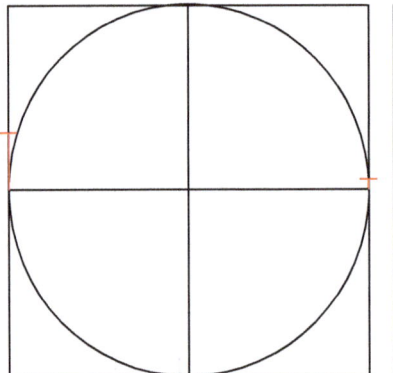

C. At the bottom of the circle, mark up 3/8" or 10mm. Blend the new point into the curve.

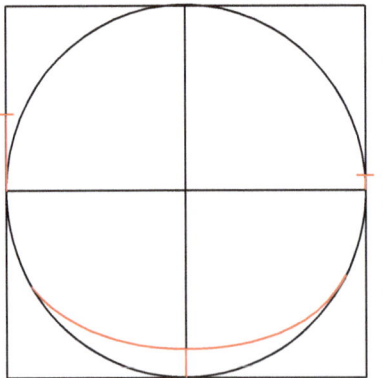

Demi/Plunge Wires

A. On the original center front line on the right, measure down on the curve 1 1/4" or 32mm. This line will be hard to see, make a cross mark at the position of the curve.

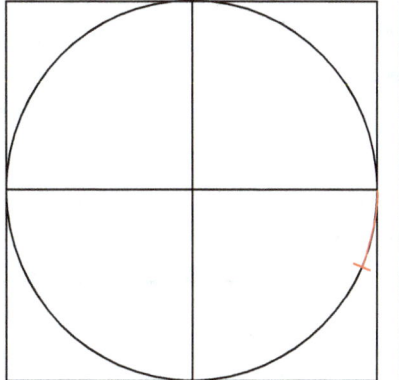

B. From the center line on the left side of the circle, measure up 1 13/16" or 46mm. Do not square a line across any amount as the wire is straight up at the side. This line will be hard to see, make a cross mark at the top of the line.

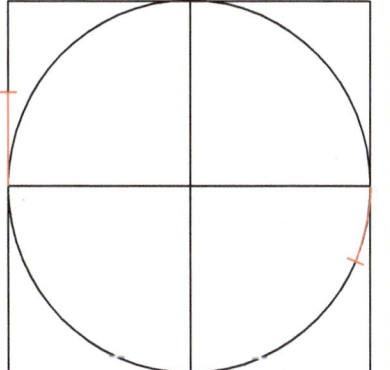

FRONT BAND

6. Record the chest and under bust measurements. Divide each by four to indicate one quarter of the body. Record the chest height from the under bust to the chest at center front.

Chest Measurement	1/4 Chest Measurement
Under Bust Measurement	1/4 Under Bust Measurement
	Chest Height Measurement

7. From the bottom right point, measure up the chest height amount and measure to the left, one quarter of the chest measurement.

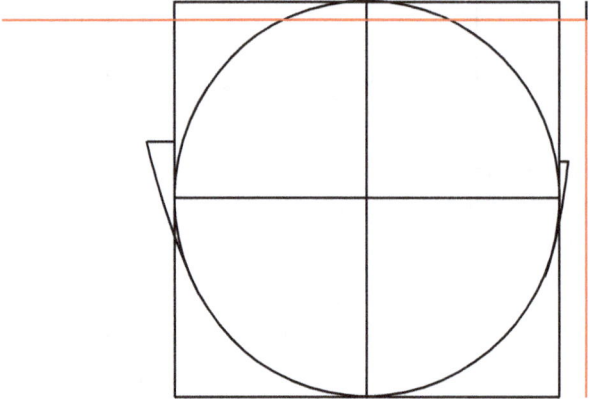

8. From the bottom right point, measure to the left, one quarter of the under bust measurement. Note that this example has the same under bust and chest measurements. This draft is for a tubular shaped body. Each draft will vary based on the measurements used.

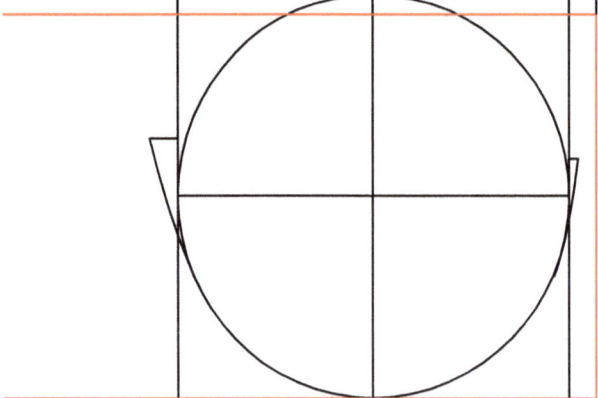

9. Connect the two lines together at the ends to form the side seam. The measurements used in a custom draft may provide an angle and not a straight vertical line.

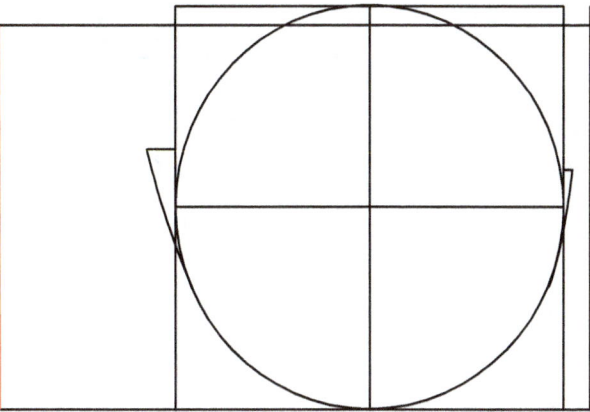

BACK BAND

10. a. For the back of the band, begin by taking one quarter of both the chest and under bust measurements.

Chest Measurement	1/4 of Chest Measurement
Under Bust Measurement	1/4 of Under Bust Measurement

b. Because the back also contains a hook & eye and the hook & eye is not part of the back band pattern piece, remove the amount needed for a hook & eye. At the hook's tightest, it is 1" or 25mm and at its loosest, it is 2" or 5cm. The fit needs to be snug, use the loosest amount, this will help account for fit when elastics begin to stretch out. This draft is for half the body, divide the hook & eye amount by two. 2" becomes 1" (5cm becomes 2.5cm).

Back Chest Bust – Hook & Eye
Back Under Bust – Hook & Eye

c. A snug fit is needed, take the stretch of the fabric and elastics into account. Using the stretch ratio charts found in the previous chapter, reduce the back measurements based on the stretch of the fabric. Take the quarter measurement and multiply it by the reduction chart.

Reduced Back Chest
Reduced Back Under Bust

11. Continue the back band draft on the front draft. At the new side seam line created in Step 9, square a line across at 90 degrees, the reduced chest and under bust measurements in their respective positions.

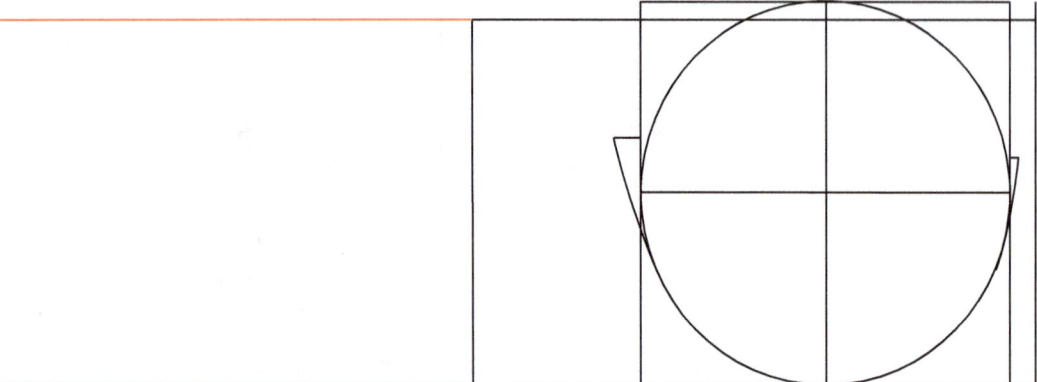

Note that a draft with more extreme measurements will look more like this.

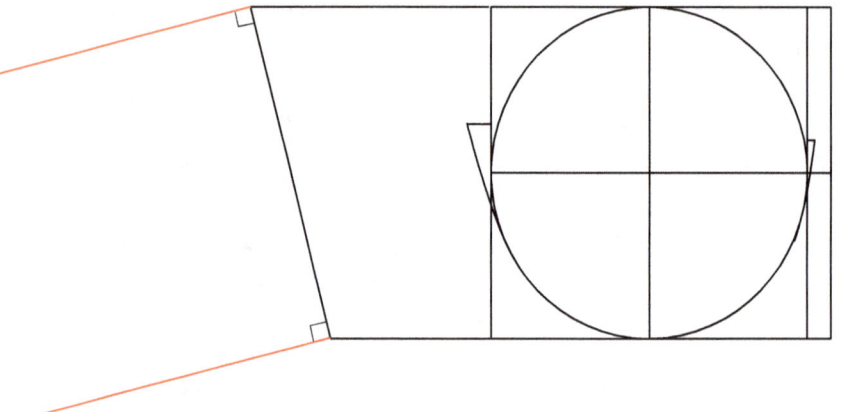

12. Connect the ends of the two lines together with a straight line. This is the center back line.

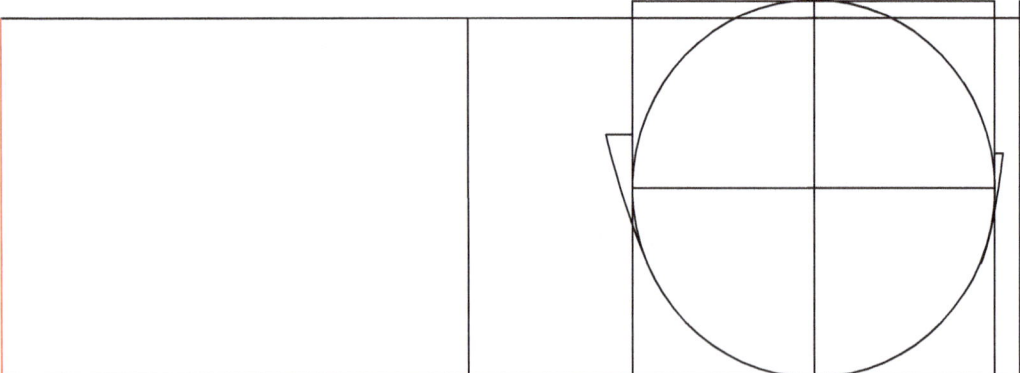

13. At the center back, from the bottom of the line measure up the amount required for the size of hook & eyes chosen. This chart may not reflect all manufacturers. Refer to the hooks being used.

Rows	Inches	Centimeters
1	3/4	1.9
2	1 1/4	3.2
3	1 3/4	4.5
4	2 1/4	5.8
5	2 3/4	7.1
6	3 1/4	8.4

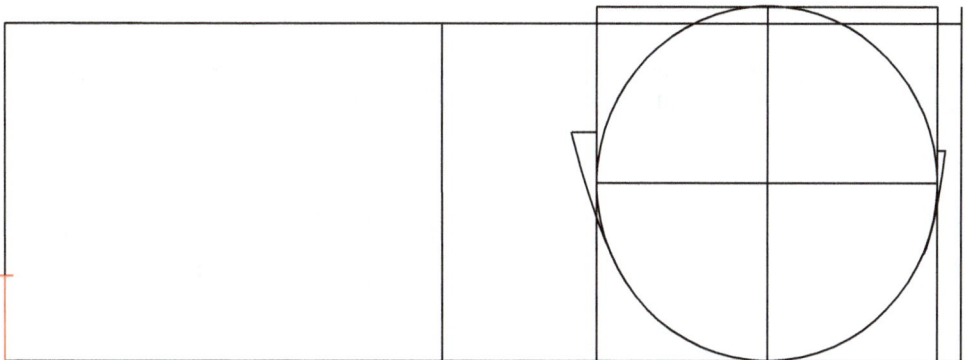

14. Where the front meets the back on the side seam, measure up an amount between 1/8" and 3/4" (3mm and 20mm). This is to help in the shaping of the bra. This amount can be modified to fit design specifications. As pictured, the side is raised by 1/4" or 6mm.

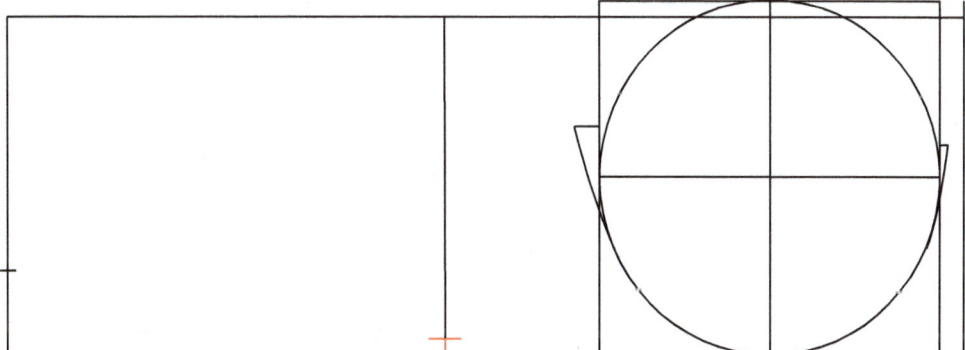

15. At the bottom of the circle, measure down 1/2" or 12.5mm. This too can be modified depending on the design, 1/2" or 12.5mm is the minimum amount of room needed to stitch down the underwire channeling.

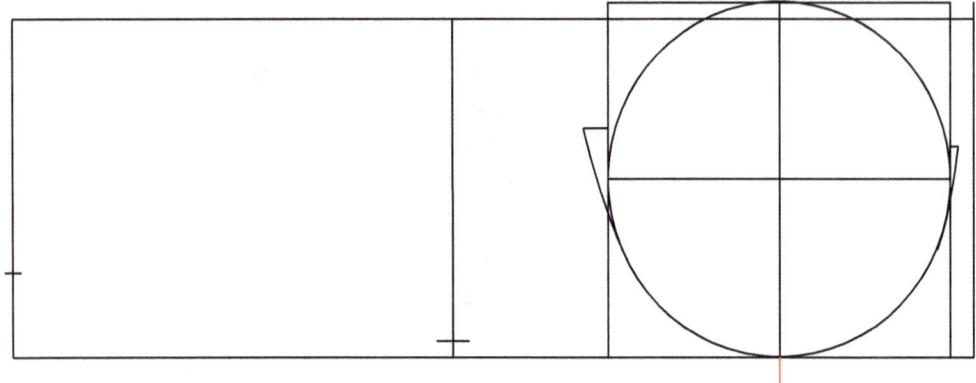

16. At the center front hem, measure up an amount of 1/4" to 3/4" (6mm to 20mm). This amount is variable based on design and helps shape for comfort. This example is raised 1/2" or 12.5mm.

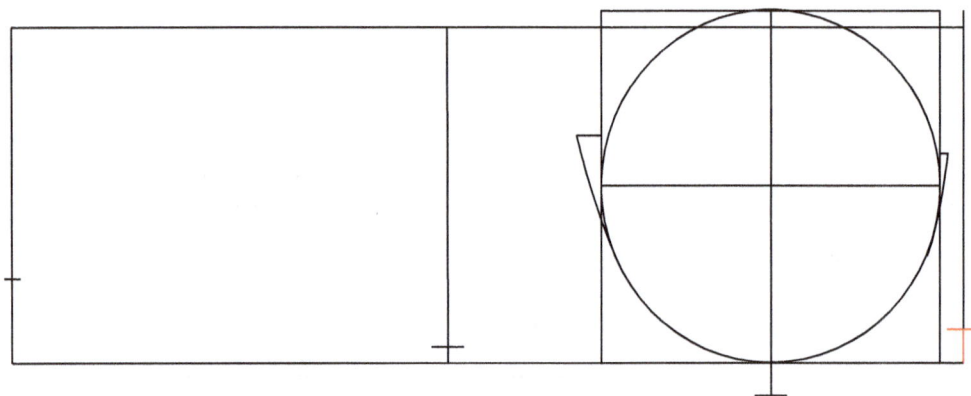

17. Using the hip curve, use a series of curved shapes to shape the hemline, connecting each of the points marked.

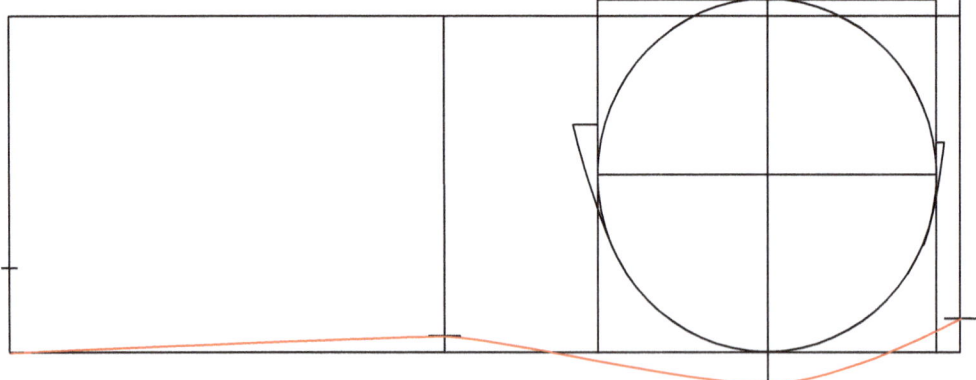

18. Extend the wire lines up 1/4" or 6mm. This amount is needed for wire play. Wire play is an extra amount needed for wire movement throughout the day to prevent the wires from poking out of the casing. This is to allow for sewing room and ease at the ends of the underwire.

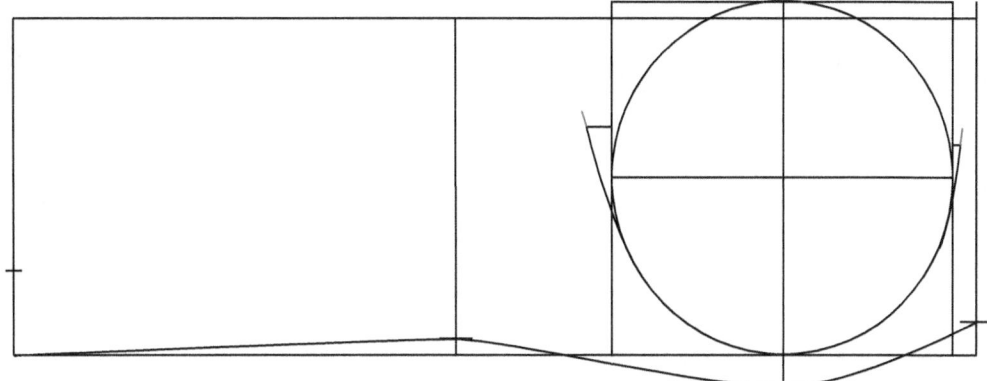

19. Square a line from the top of the front wire, from the center front to the side seam. This will serve as a guide for the side seam height.

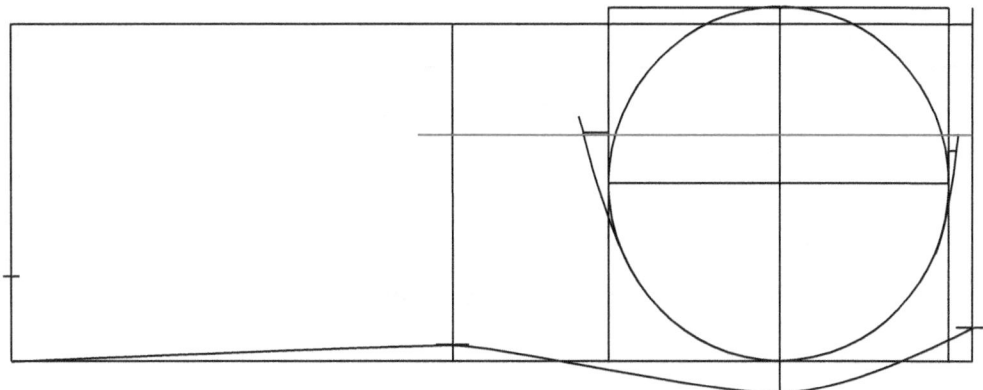

20. For the back, split the back band measurement into three. Mark one third of the amount from the center back and draw in a guideline for strap placement.

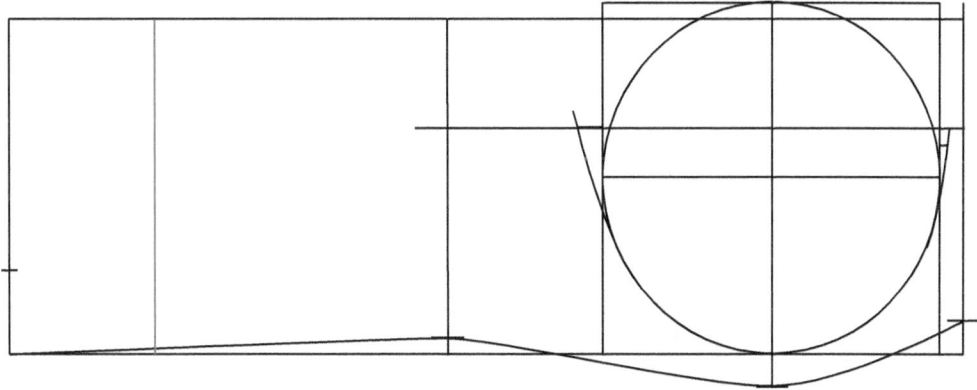

21. Draw a perpendicular line from the side seam height marking to the center back. This will help determine the back strap height.

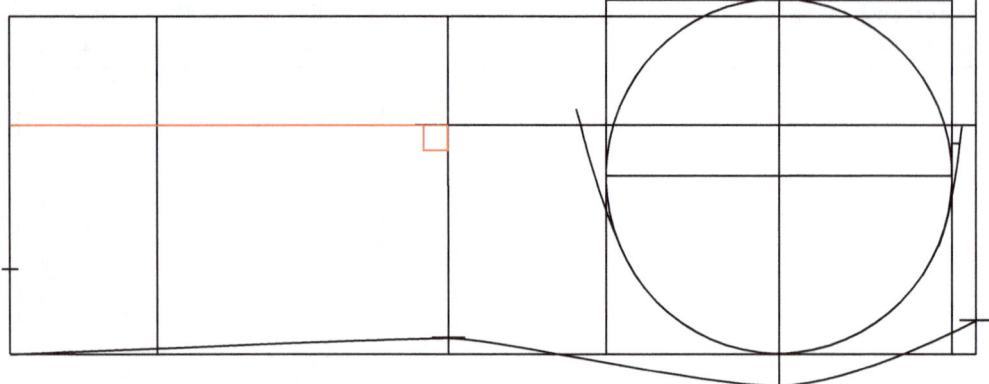

22. Using a curved ruler, blend in the back and front band shape as pictured.

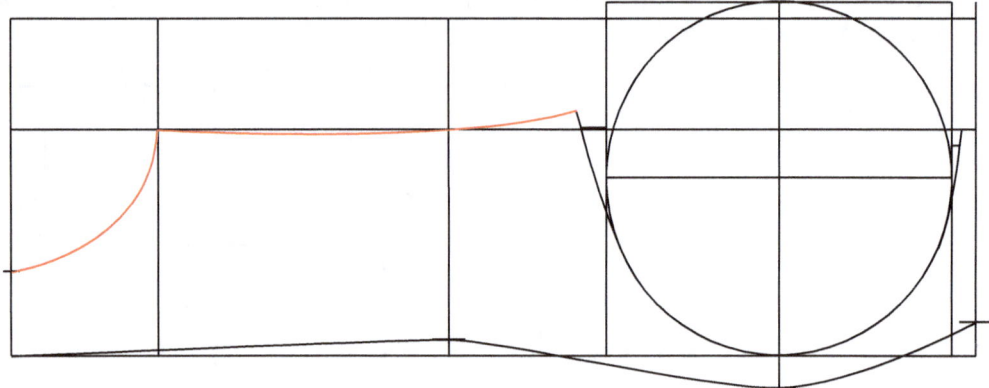

Advanced / Bra Band Pattern Drafting | 157

DRAFTING ON ILLUSTRATION SOFTWARE

Most wire manufacturers provide a wire chart in a PDF format. Most PDF wire charts can be opened in Illustrator® unless they are protected. Many charts include the actual wire lines, but some are photos. One may need to use the vector tools to recreate the wire lines for a particular manufacturer. The pictured wire template is available for download, under the third edition of the book, as a download option on the website Porcelynne.com. They correspond to the wires available on the same website and the ones detailed in this book.

1. Select a wire from a wire template and copy it into a new document. Be sure to select *Smart Guides* under the *View Menu* to see all guides for these steps.

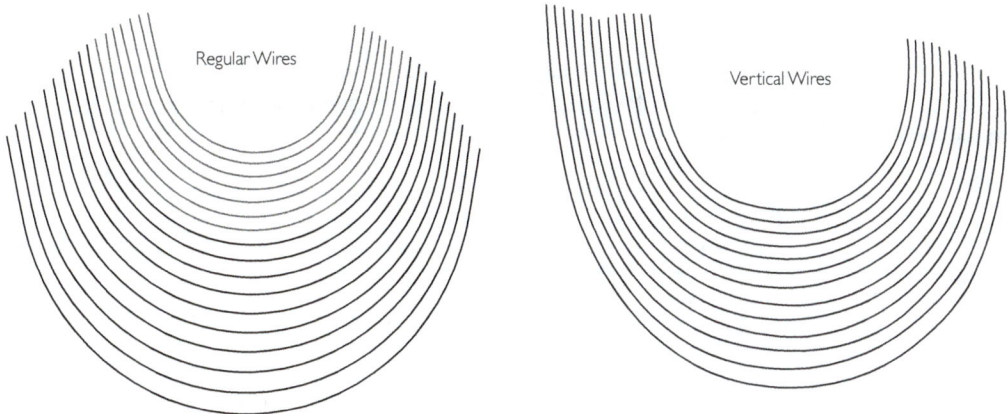

2. At the ends of the curve, use the *Line Segment Tool* and add 1/4" or 6mm.

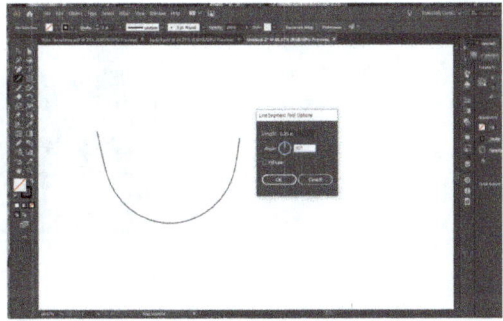

158 | Bare Essentials: Bras

3. At the center front, use the **Line Segment Tool** to draw half the center bridge amount. To determine this amount, refer to step 5 of hand drafting, but remove the portion extended by the top spread on a regular wire style. *For example, we chose 3/8" or 10mm for the bridge, but the wire extended into that area by 1/8" or 3mm. This would mean that the bridge amount would only be 1/4" or 6mm.*

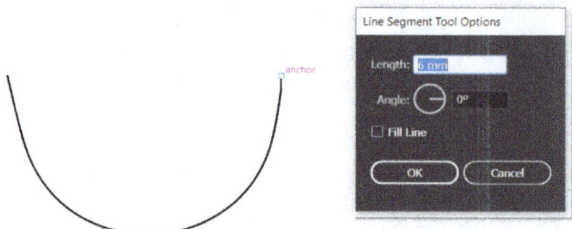

4. With the **Pen Tool** selected, draw a line straight down until it is in the same position as the bottom of the wire curve. Holding the **Shift Key** down while drawing the line will ensure it remains at a 90 degree angle.

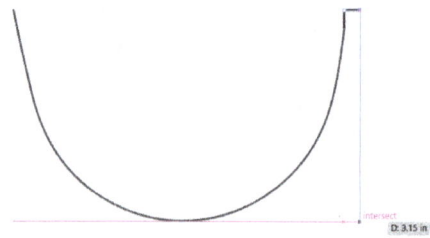

5. Use the **Line Segment Tool**, draw a line to the left side, in the amount of the quarter under bust measurement.

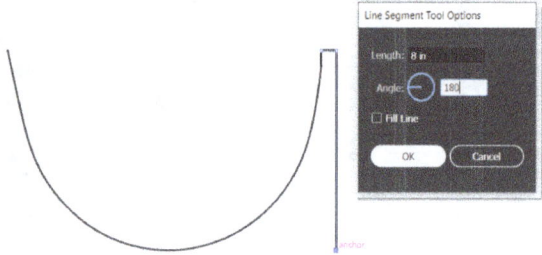

Advanced / Bra Band Pattern Drafting | 159

6. At the end of the under bust measurement, continue to use the **Line Segment Tool** and extend a line up the chest height amount.

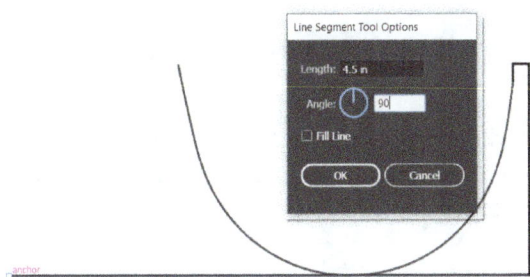

7. At the end of this line, draw a line across to the left, the difference between the quarter chest and quarter under bust measurement.

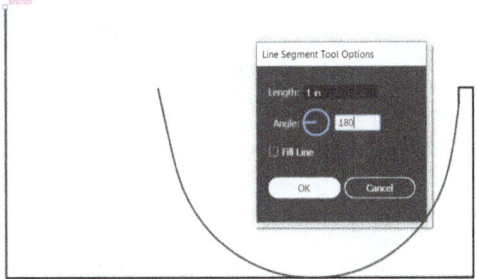

8. With the **Line Segment Tool,** connect the top of the chest measurement line to the lower under bust measurement. Make note of the angle you create. Pictured is 283 degrees.

160 | Bare Essentials: Bras

9. Subtract 90 degrees from the angle in the previous step.

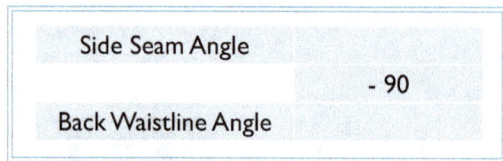

10. Take the stretch adjusted quarter under bust and quarter chest measurements and draw the measurements from the top and bottom of the side seam using the line segment tool and the angle from the previous step.

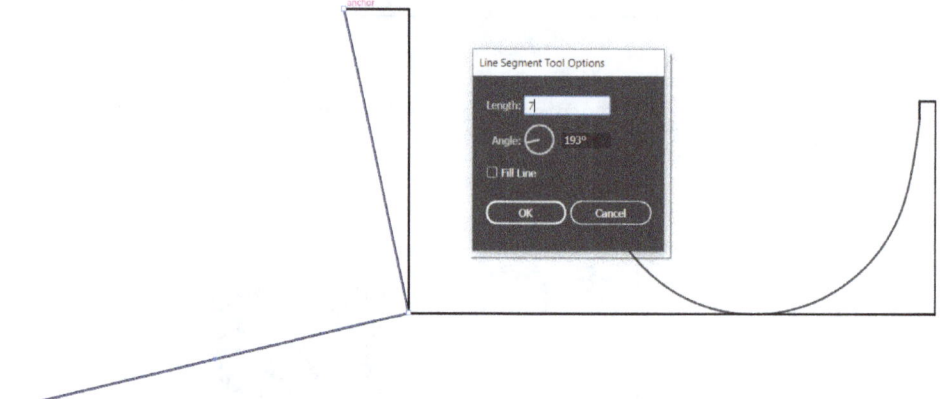

11. Draw the center back line by connecting the ends of the two lines, drawing the line from the bottom up. Record the degree of the angle created. Here it is 114 degrees.

Advanced / Bra Band Pattern Drafting | 161

12. At the center back line from the bottom corner, use the **Line Segment Tool** and type in the amount for the hook & eye height and the degree recorded the previous step. Change the color of this short line segment to stand out.

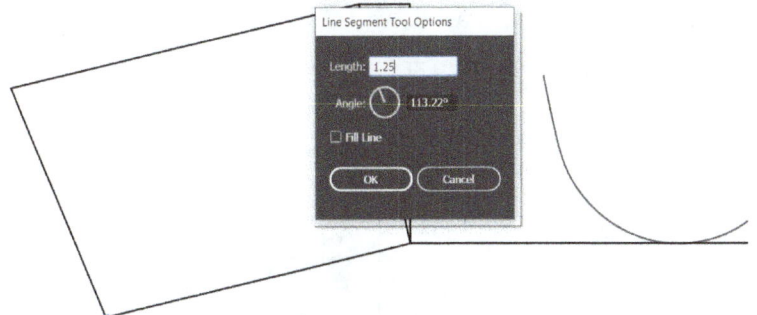

13. Determine a third of the back chest and underbust lines. Select the line and in the transform window on the right, click on the **Constrain Proportion** button and in either the **H** or **W** field, add "/3" behind the amount. This will make the line 1/3 of the original length.

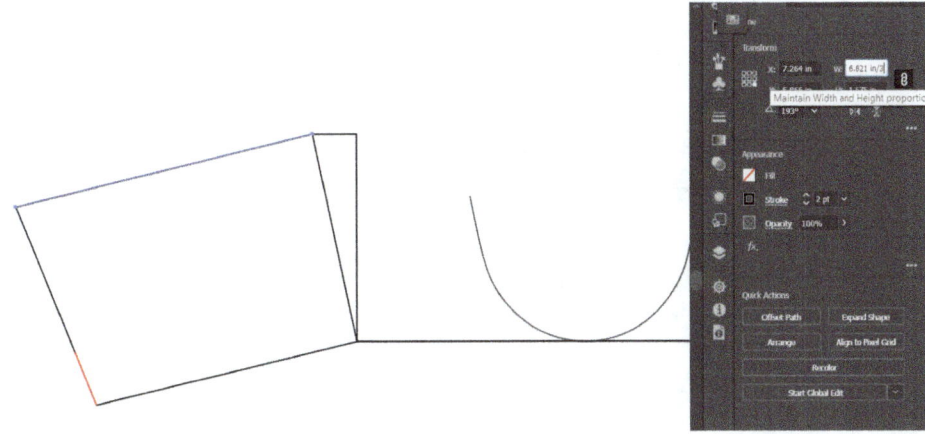

14. Move both third sections and line them up to the center back. Add a line segment connecting the two line segments. This indicates the strap position.

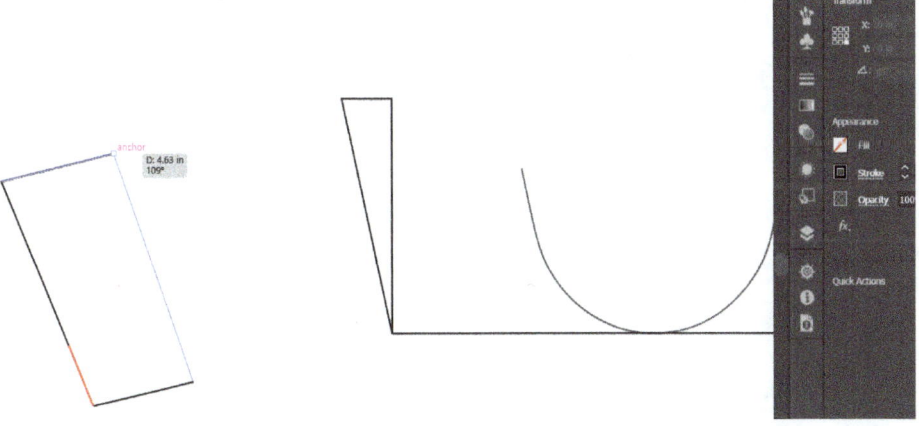

15. Create the following guides, using the **Line Segment Tool**, for the waist curve. Change the line color to help these lines stand out.

  a. For the center front, draw up 1/2" or 12.5mm at 90 degrees.

  b. At the bottom of the wire curve, draw down 1/2" or 12.5mm at 270 degrees.

  c. At the side seam, draw up 1/4" at 6mm at the side seam angle. To get the angle, subtract 180 from the angle noted in step 8.

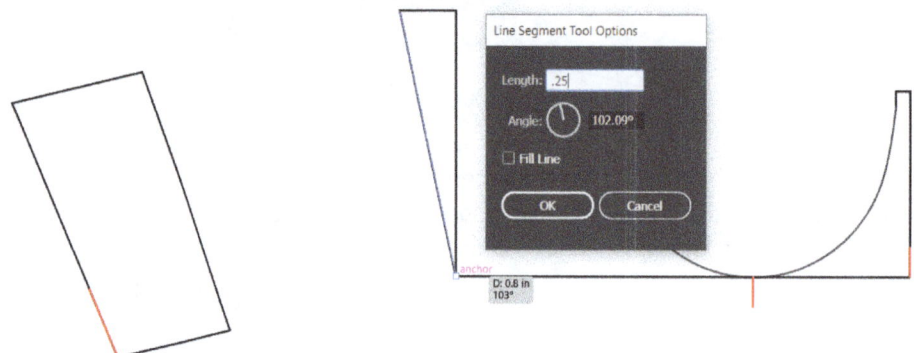

16. a. Lock the layer and create a new layer.

  b. Select the **Pen Tool** and draw in the waistline curve.

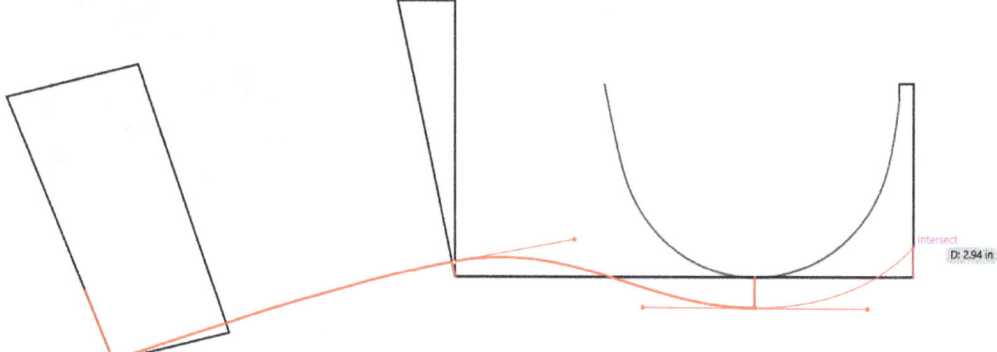

17. Measure the new center front height. On the strap line on the back, draw a line up from where the curve hits the line, in the amount of the new center front height. Use the degree from Step 14 for the back strap height. This can also vary based on design preferences.

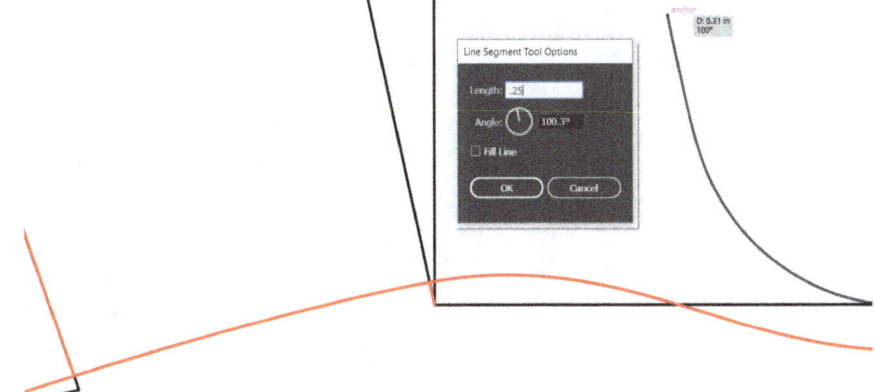

18. a. Lock both the back strap guide and the wire guide, from the previous step, in the layers menu.

   b. Draw in the neckline curve with the Pen Tool.

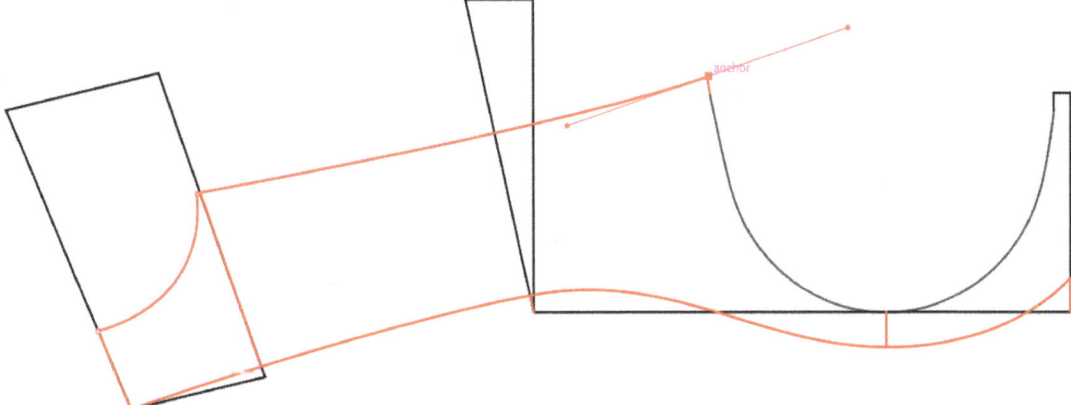

19. a. Unlock the first layer.

    b. Use the scissors tool to separate the front from the back at the side seam. Group or join the line segments to create the front and back patterns.

CHAPTER 16

BRA CUP DRAFTING: PORCELYNNE PATTERN DRAFTING METHOD

In this chapter, a three piece cup is drafted using the Porcelynne Pattern Drafting Method. Reference the band draft in the previous chapter.

DRAFTING BY HAND

WIRE CIRCUMFERENCE

1. Copy the measurements from the calculations in Chapter 14 into the chart below. If you are creating two drafts, one for each bust, indicate the amounts for each side. Indicate the radius of the horizontal diameter. Divide the diameter in half to determine the radius.

	Left	Right
Horizontal Bust Diameter		
Horizontal Bust Radius		
Vertical Bust Diameter		

2. Begin by drawing two intersecting lines, one horizontal and one vertical. From the center point, measure horizontally, the radius of the horizontal bust measurement.

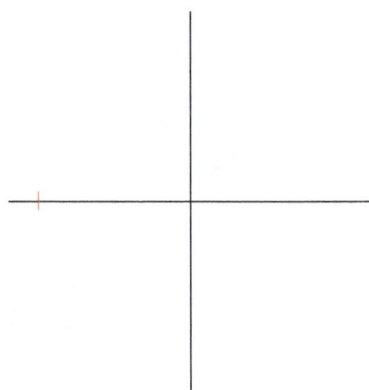

3. Use a compass to draw the circumference around the center point lining the compass point to the radius measurement.

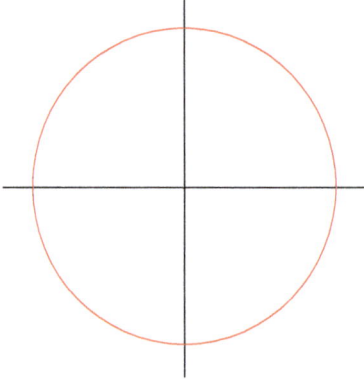

4. Split the cup in half, across the center horizontal line.

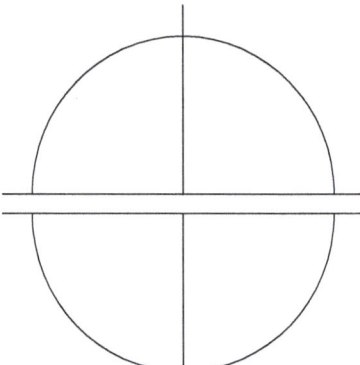

5. The cup must fit into the circumference of the wire. Refer to the wire diameter used in the band draft. Calculate the circumference of the wire by multiplying the wire diameter by Pi (3.141592). Divide the circumference by four. This is to evenly space the cup within the wire curve of the band.

Wire measurement	
	× 3.141592
Circumference of Wire	
	/ 4
Quarter circumference	

6. Take the quarter circumference amount and measure from the center of the bottom of the cup, up the sides of the curve. Repeat for the top cup. Use a flexible ruler to get an accurate measurement. For drafting a cup to fit into the specialty wide flat vertical wire, the bottom half of the wire was shortened by a total of 1/8" or 3mm. Remove 1/16" or 1.5mm off of the bottom halves.

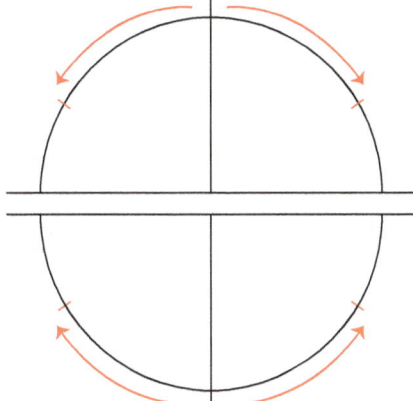

LOWER CUP BUST DEPTH

7. a. The vertical bust point is affected by the depth of the bottom cup. If the bust point is in exactly the center of the breast, the bust point would be considered **average**. If the bottom cup is larger, meaning the bust point is higher than the middle, bottom cup is **deep**. If the top cup is heavier than the bottom cup, meaning the bust point is lower than the average, the bottom cup is **shallow**. The following percentages are starting points to help place the bust point. If unsure which cup depth is appropriate, work on multiple drafts for the bottom cup depth or select average and adjust the depth during fitting.

Shallow Bottom Cup	45%
Average Bottom Cup	50%
Deep Bottom Cup	55%

b. To determine the bust point vertically multiply the vertical bust diameter by the bottom cup depth percentage. To determine the amount for the top cup, subtract the bottom cup bust depth from the vertical bust diameter. The horizontal bust placement is not altered for this draft. Refer to the chapter on fit adjustments in the intermediate section for more details on moving the horizontal bust point.

	Left	Right
Vertical Bust Diameter	x	x
Bottom Cup Percentage		
Bottom Cup Bust Depth		
Vertical Bust Diameter	-	-
Bottom Cup Bust Depth		
Top Cup Bust Height		

8. On the lower cup, mark up from the bottom the amount you determined for the bottom cup bust depth. Repeat for the top cup, using the top cup bust height.

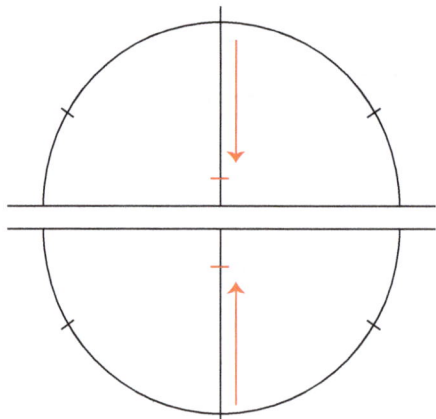

Demi Wire Cup Alteration - For drafting with a demi wire, a few additional markings need to be made. The first step is to divide the quarter wire circumference by two. On the top cup, lower the marking on the right side by the half amount. On the bottom cup, decrease the bottom cup by moving the position towards the center line by the same half amount. Leave the left side of the cups alone. The right side of the draft indicates the center front of the bra where the wire is shorter.

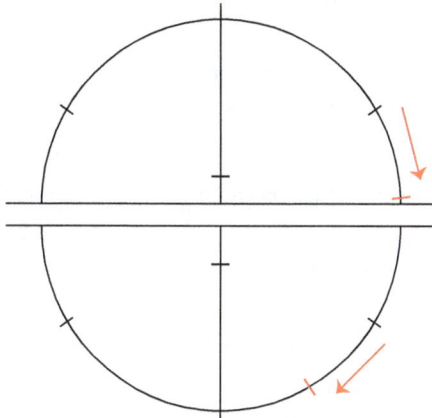

9. Draw lines from the points we created in Steps 6 & 8. Cut on these lines.

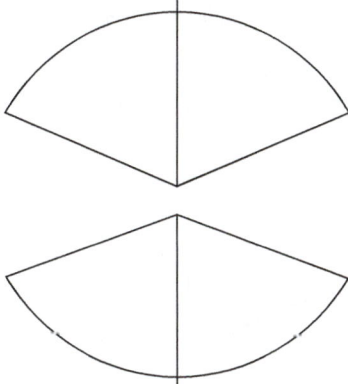

Demi Wire Cup Alteration - The demi wire will look a fair amount different at this point.

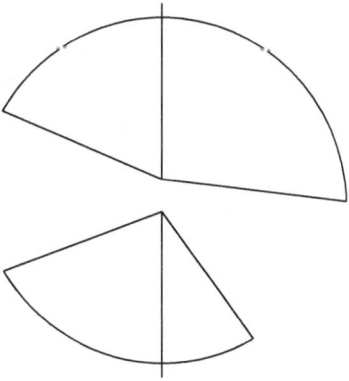

TORSO SHAPE ADJUSTMENT

10. a. The top cup may need additional width based on the difference between the chest and average measurements from Chapter 14. Take the chest measurement and subtract the average measurement to determine the chest difference.

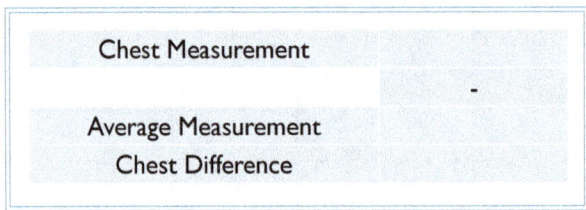

b. The top cup width is determined by subtracting the average measurement from the chest measurement. Divide this amount by 4 to split the volume across the body. This quarter amount is used to increase the top cup.

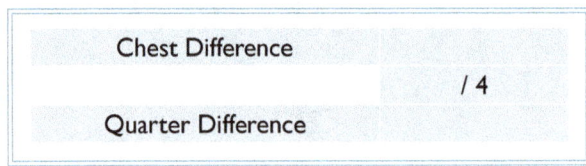

11. Split the top cup on the center line from the top to the tip, but do not separate, if possible. Spread the top of the cup by the quarter difference from the previous step.

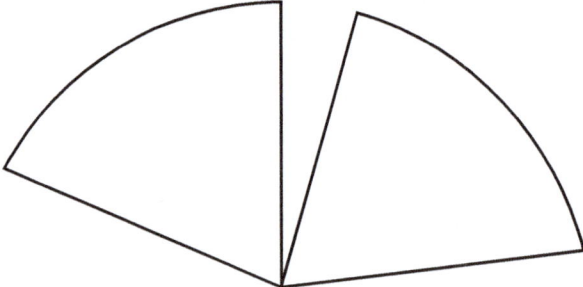

12. Split the bottom cup into two pieces on the center line. If the cup volume places you in a cup size up to an C cup, you may wish to keep the bottom cup in one piece, as the additional volume added to the center of the cup is not significant for a smaller cup size.

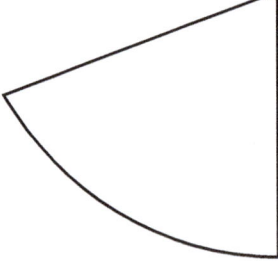 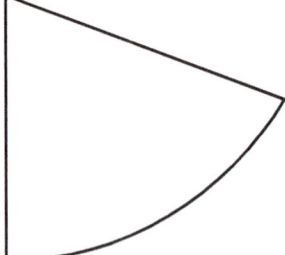

Demi Wire Cup Alteration - The change to the wire line has caused the length of the seam for the right side of the top and bottom cup to be inconsistent. To properly determine the appropriate amount, the diagonal amount needs to be determined.

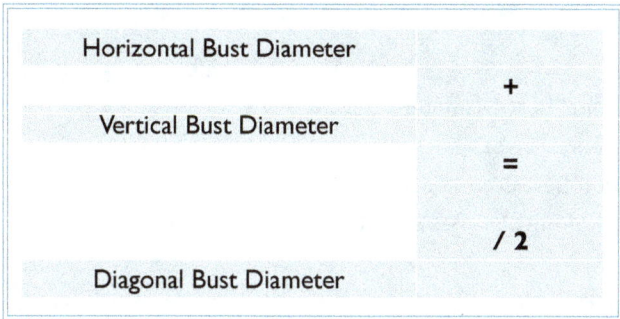

Alter the length of the diagonal lines on the right side of the cup for both the top and bottom cup.

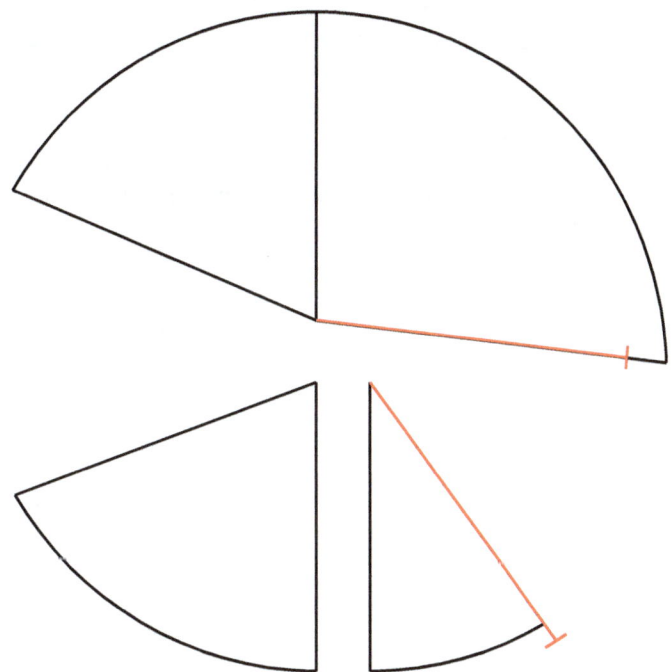

CUP CURVES

13. To make appropriate curves for the cup, determine 2.5% and 5% for both the vertical and horizontal measurement of the cup.

	Left	Right
Horizontal Bust Diameter - 2.5%		
Horizontal Bust Diameter - 5%		
Vertical Bust Diameter - 2.5%		
Vertical Bust Diameter - 5%		

Demi Wire Cup Alteration - To make appropriate curves for the cup on the diagonal seams, determine 5% of the diagonal measurement determined on the previous page.

	Left	Right
Diagonal Bust Diameter - 5%		

14. Alter the pattern curves in the following manner. Measure perpendicular from the indicated division point on each line, in the amount specified. These instructions are only guides, an individual may need to modify these curves to best fit their shape. Three wire styles are detailed. Additional wires style drafts can be modified using these directions.

a. Regular Wire - Find the half way point on each line. The right side of the draft is located towards the center front of the body. The left side of the draft is towards the side seam.

    i. Lower cup vertical seam, measure 2.5% of the vertical bust measurement.

    ii. Horizontal seams, measure 2.5% of the horizontal bust measurement.

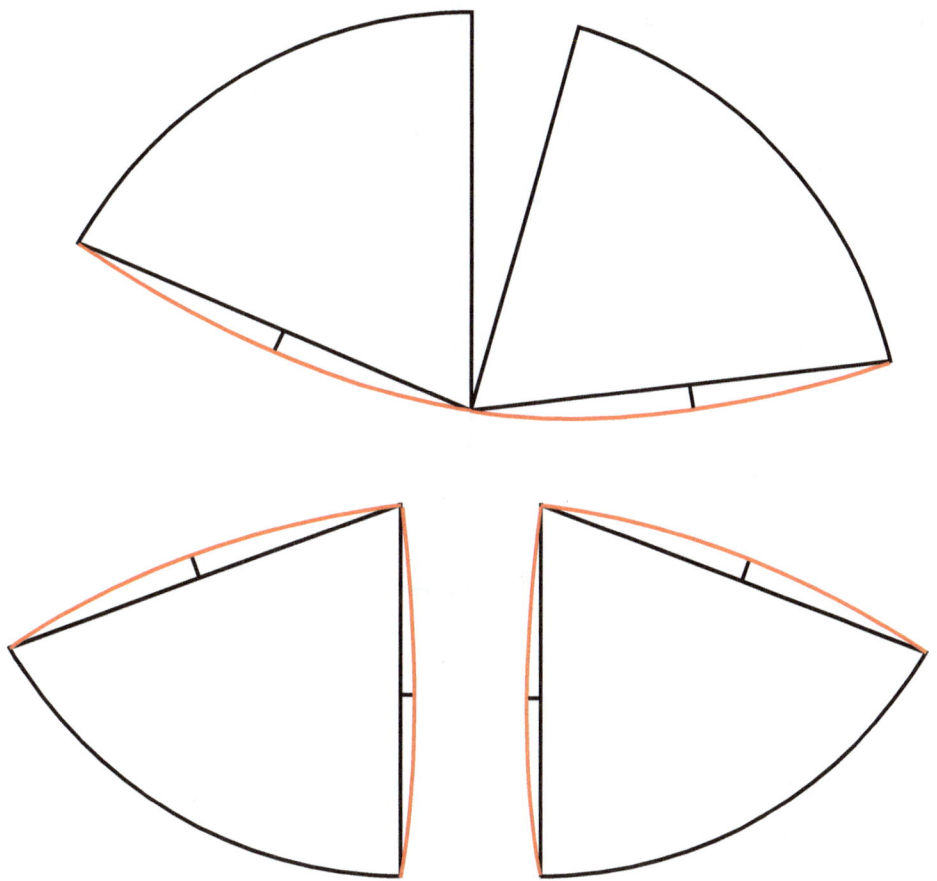

b. Vertical Wire - Find the half way point on the center vertical seam and the left side of the horizontal seam. On the right side of the horizontal seam, mark one third of the way from the apex towards the right side. The right side of the draft is located towards the center front of the body. The left side of the draft is towards the side seam.

   i. Lower cup vertical seam, measure 5% of the vertical bust measurement

   ii. Horizontal seams, measure 5% of the horizontal bust measurement. (To decrease the roundness of the side of the cup, decrease the amount on the side of the cup to 2.5% of the horizontal measurement as pictured.) To keep a smooth curve on the top cup, the apex point may no longer hit the original apex point. A narrower chest may hit the apex, and a wide chest will not.

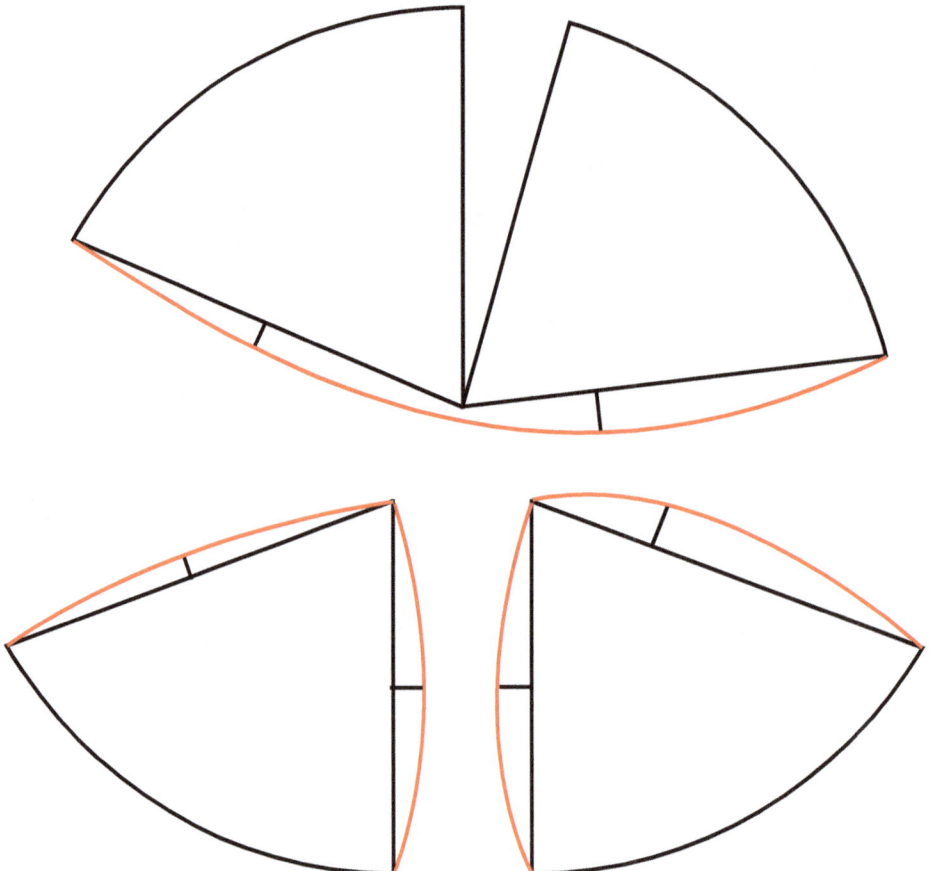

c. Demi Wire - Find the half way points on the vertical seam and the side horizontal seam. Find a third of the line from the apex towards the center front. On the right side of the horizontal seam, mark one third of the way from the apex towards the right side. The right side of the draft is located towards the center front of the body. The left side of the draft is towards the side seam.

    i. Lower cup vertical seam 5% vertical bust measurement

    ii. Left Side horizontal seam 5% horizontal bust measurement. (To decrease the roundness of the side of the cup, decrease the amount on the side of the cup to 2.5% of the horizontal measurement as pictured.)

    iii. Right side diagonal seam 5% diagonal bust measurement.

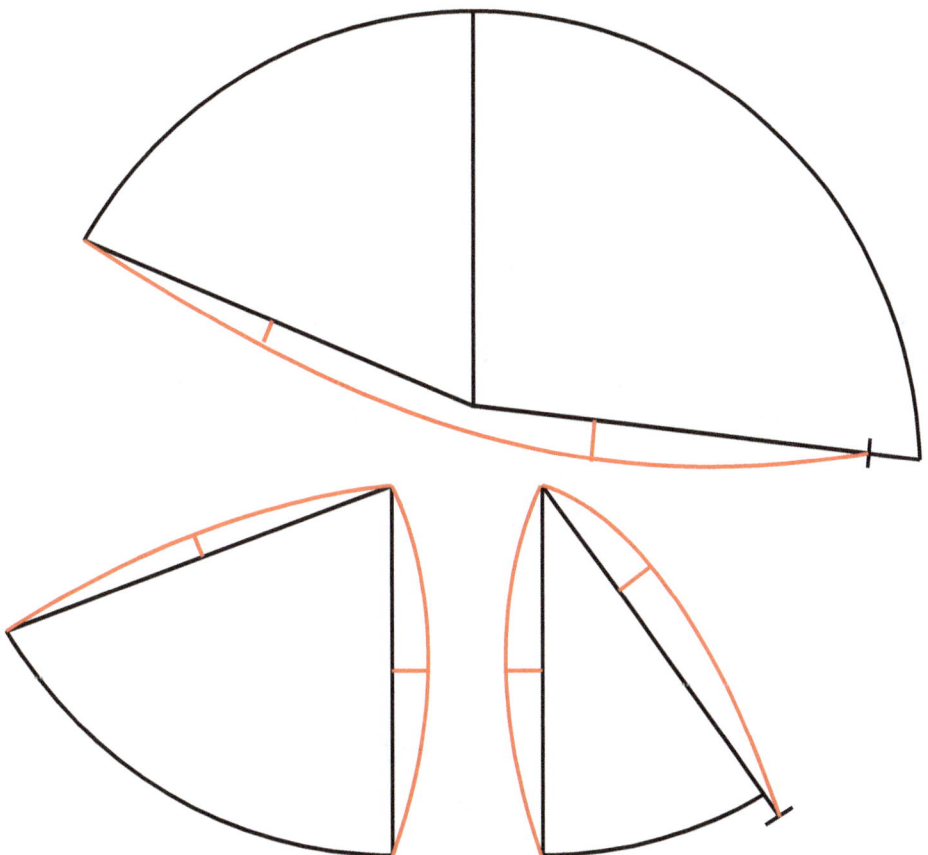

15. Adjust the seam lines of the cups to match the original horizontal and vertical amounts.

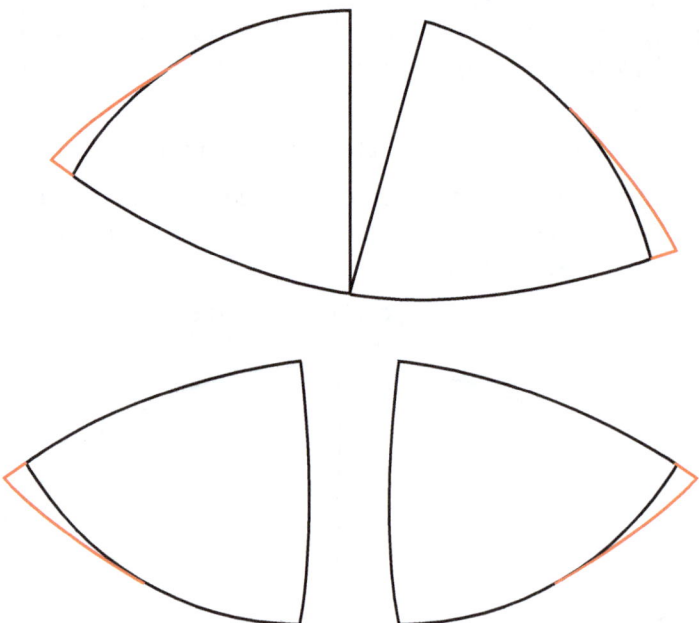

16. Align each cup seam and straighten the seams to remove any concave points. Leave convex points as is (the joining top and bottom cup in this image). These are removed in the next steps. Note that this step may increase the vertical and/or horizontal amounts. Do not readjust for horizontal and vertical amounts from this point and moving on.

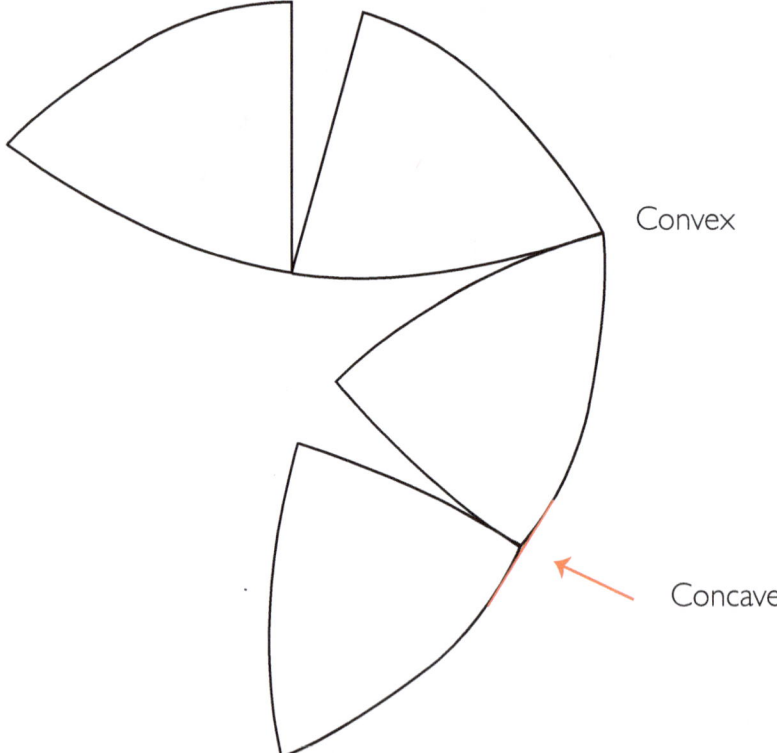

WIRE LINE

17. Take the quarter circumference measurement and measure that amount up from the center of the wire curve on the band in both directions. Double check that the measurement of the bottom cup did not change with the cup adjustments in the previous step. If it did, adjust the cup to the quarter circumference amount. Make both notches square to the curve line, creating a 90 degree angle where the notch intersects the curve.

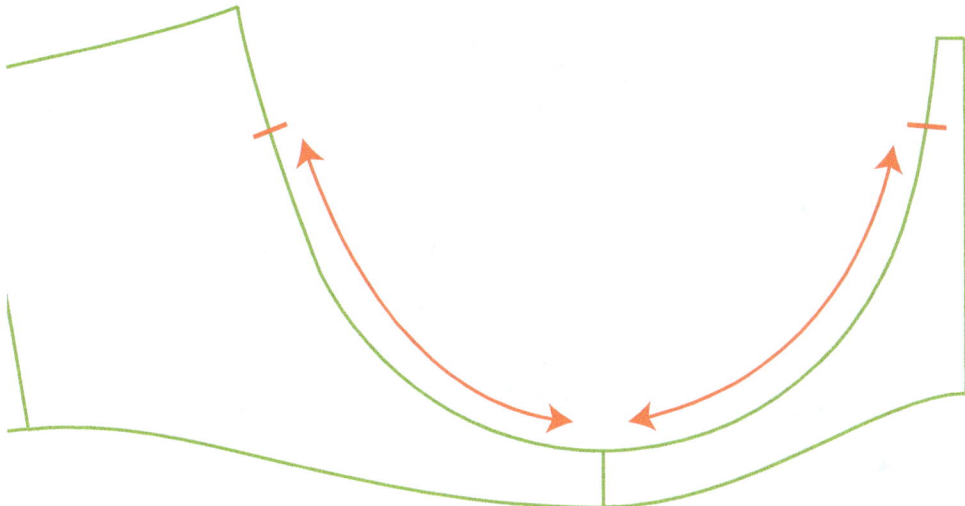

18. The cup draft is currently round and based on the circumference of the wire of the draft. The cup shape needs to be adjusted to fit into the wire curve of the band.

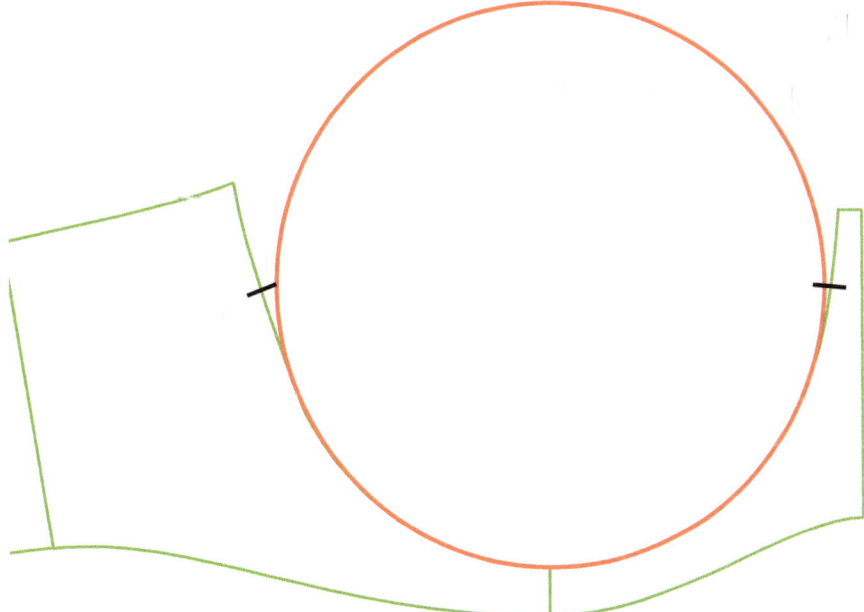

19. Place both the top and bottom cup together at the seam and the circle from the band draft. Adjust both the top and bottom cup to line up to the wire line. The new cup shape will include the small area between the circle and the wire line of the band.

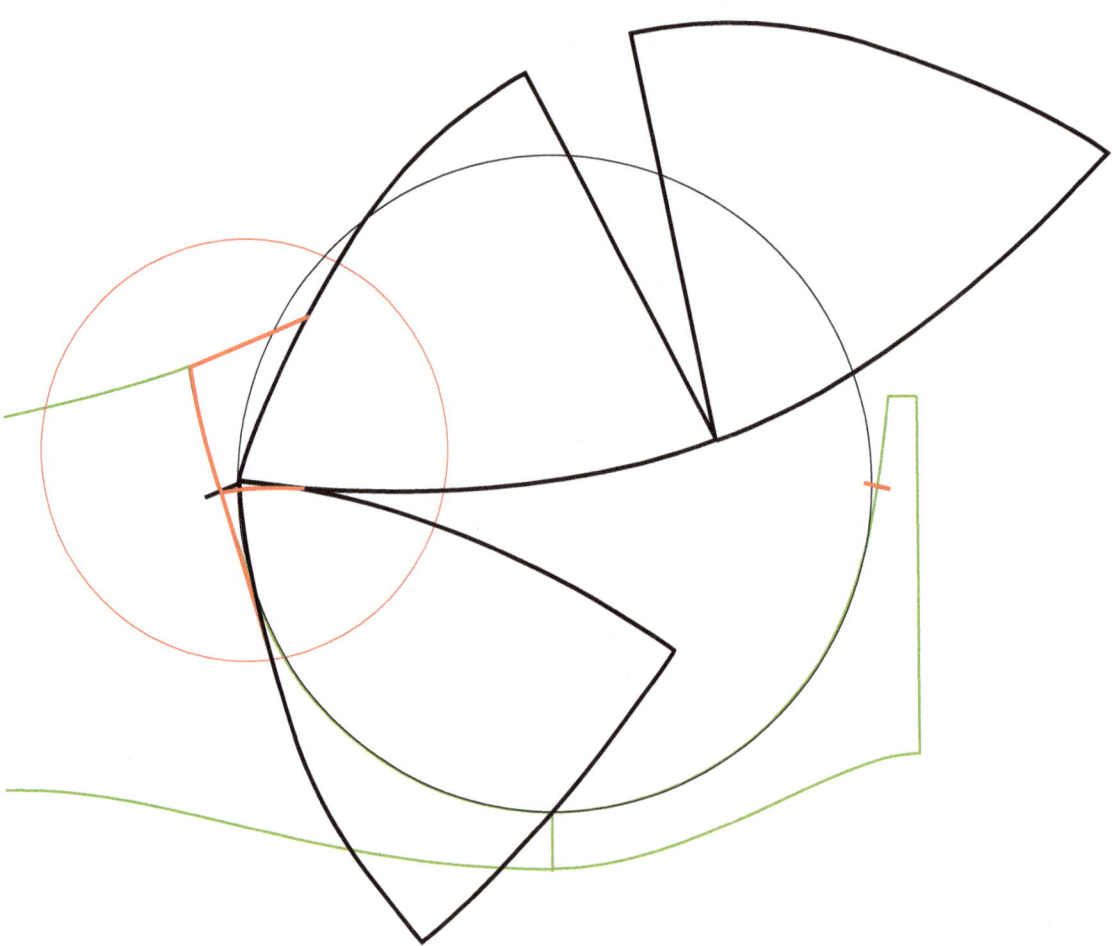

20. The center of the cup is adjusted in the same manner. Alter both cup pattern pieces.

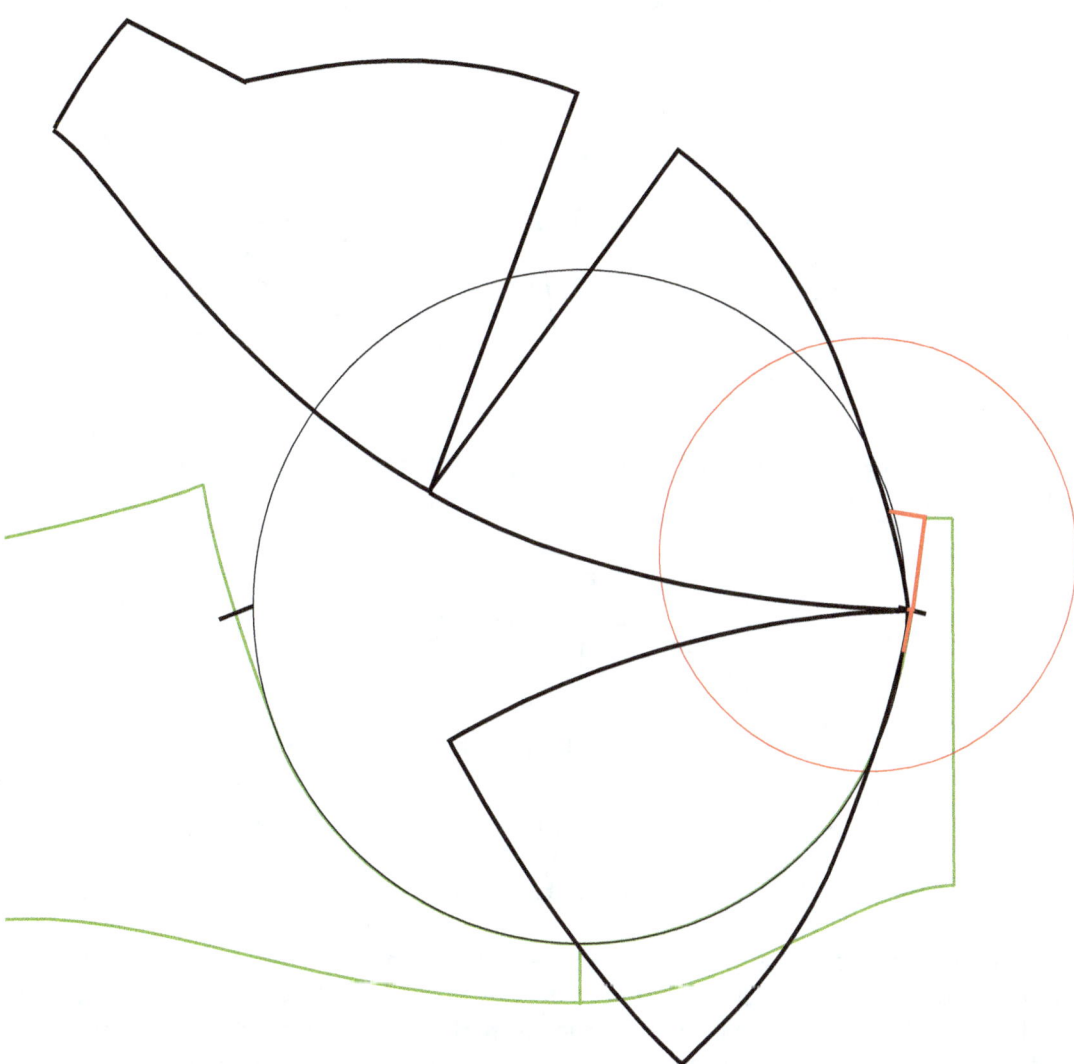

STRAP PLACEMENT

21. On the upper cup, determine the center of the cup. Draw a line from tip to tip of the wire line, then divide it in half by folding the paper in half.

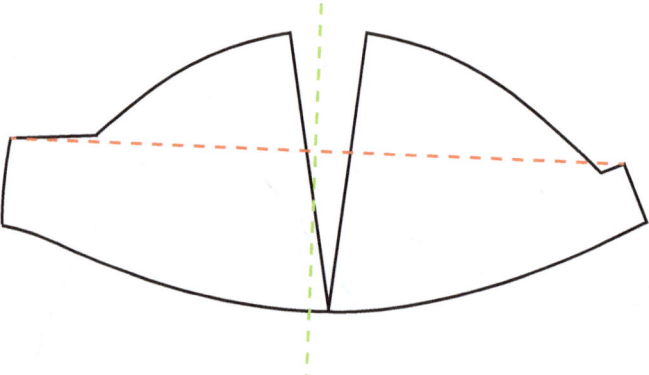

22. The strap placement is determined based on the calculation in Chapter 14. Measure to the left of the center line, the amount calculated for the strap position.

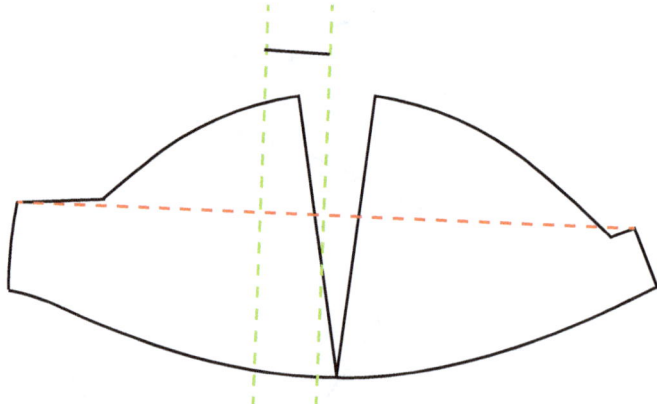

23. Use the height of the cup as the strap height. Depending on the strap attachment, you can alter the strap point for preference. In this step, the strap point is 1/2" or 12.5mm wide, but small cups could use as little as 1/4" or 6mm and large cups as much as 1" or 25mm. Likewise, the strap position can be a different shape entirely, such as the pattern provided in this book.

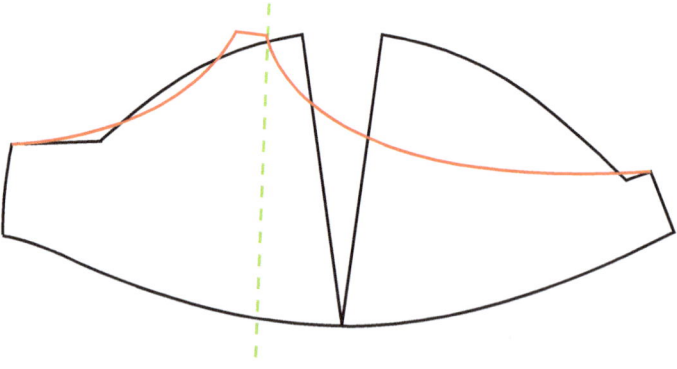

DRAFTING BY ILLUSTRATION SOFTWARE

The Porcelynne Pattern Drafting Method can be replicated in Illustrator.

1. a. Using the *Ellipse Tool,* create an ellipse using the horizontal diameter as the width and the vertical diameter as the height.

   b. Use the *Scissors Tool,* cut the ellipse in quarters and separate to work on one quarter of the ellipse.

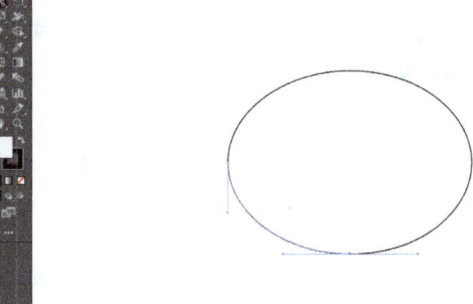

2. With the section separated, determine the length of the curve or path of the one quarter section. Navigate to **Window -> Document Info -> Object**. Select the curve and in the window, it will show the path length. Record this amount.

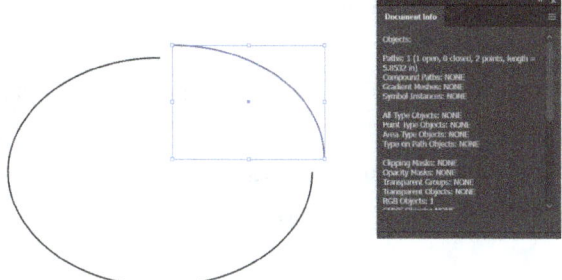

3. Use the *Pen Tool* to draw in the full quarter pie. Hold the shift key down to keep the lines straight and aligned.

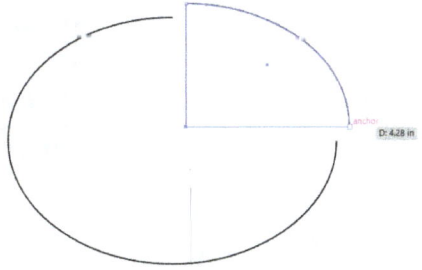

4. The next portion involves a little math. The line needs to be changed to a length determined by step 6 from hand drafting.

   a. Take the quarter wire circumference measurement and divide it by the path length shown in the previous step. This creates the angle of the path.

	Left	Right
Quarter circumference		
	/	/
Path Length		
Angle of Path		

   b. Multiply the angle of the path by 90 degrees. This results in the angle in which to divide the curve.

	Left	Right
Angle of Path		
	× 90	× 90
Angle to Divide Curve		

   c. Subtract the result from 90 degrees.

	Left	Right
	90 -	90 -
Angle to Divide Curve		
Line Segment Angle		

5. Use the **Line Segment Tool** starting at the pie corner. Create a line segment slightly longer than the apex height to extend past the curve of the ellipse. Use the angle determined in the previous step. Delete the remainder of the oval.

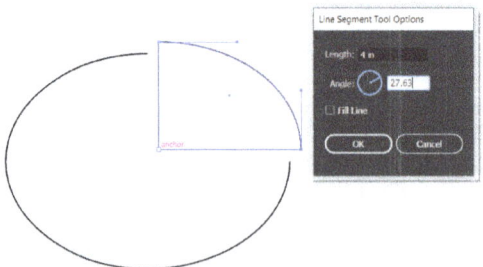

6. Use the *Scissors Tool* and cut the curve where the line intersects.

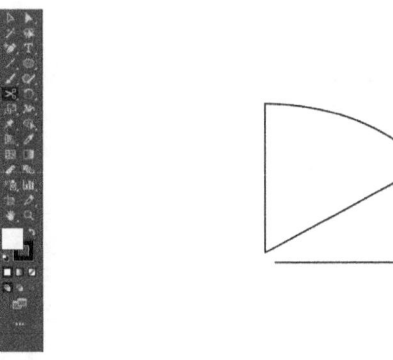

7. Delete the small lower portion of the pie shape. Copy the remaining portion and flip it horizontally for the bottom cup.

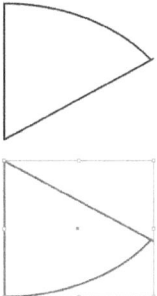

8. a. Take the amount from Step 10.b of the hand draft and divide the amount by two.

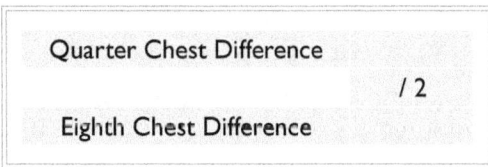

b. Use the *Line Segment Tool* and draw a line to the left of the top piece the amount from the previous step. Use the *Pen Tool* to connect that point back to the tip of the pie shape.

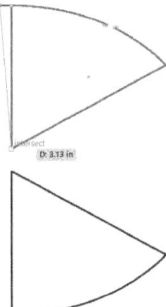

c. Make the grid visible. This grid is based on the imperial system and is displayed in eighths of an inch. For metric, the grid is in tenths of a centimeter.

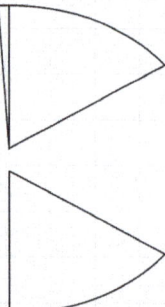

9. Rotate the top piece cup to sit against a vertical grid line. If the bust height needs to be adjusted, do so at this point. Lower or raise the bottom cup at the top of the cup. To make the top cup stay balanced, adjust the top of the top cup to raise or lower the cup height.

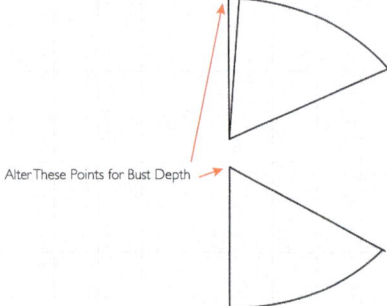

10. a. Following the curve guide recommendations from Step 14 of hand drafting, mark the division of the line accordingly, on the diagonal straight line of the top, draw a short guide with the **Line Segment Tool** at a 90 degree angle in the amount from step 14.

  b. Lock all line segments and use the **Pen Tool**. Draw a new curve to the apex passing through the mark.

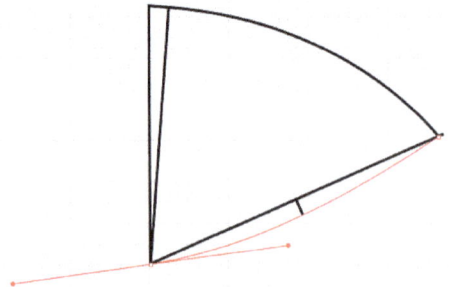

11. Unlock all segments, select the pattern, copy and flip vertically. Group all pieces and name as the top cup.

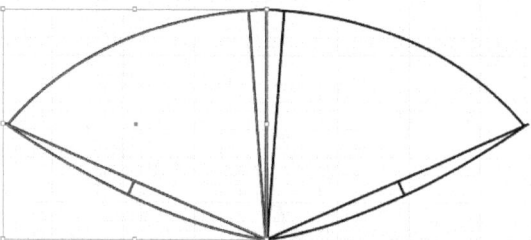

12. On the lower cup, add the markings based on Step 14 from the previous section. Draw a short guide with the **Line Segment Tool** at a 90 degree angle in the amounts from Step 14. Draw your curves and copy the bottom cup, flipping it vertically.

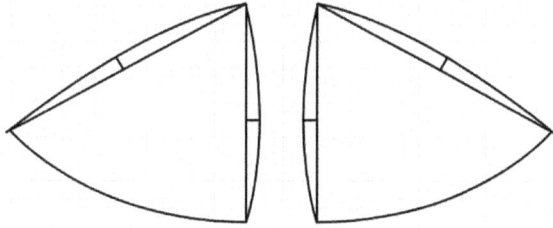

13. a. Rotate both cups so they line up on the left side by about 1/4" or 6mm. Using the same measurements from the band hand drafting for the wire, use the **Line Segment Tool** to draw lines from the intersection of the cup pieces.

   b. Draw in a smooth line from that point down to the lower cup.

   c. Draw in a horizontal line meeting that line to the center where the cups meet.

   d. Split the new lines using the **Scissors Tool**.

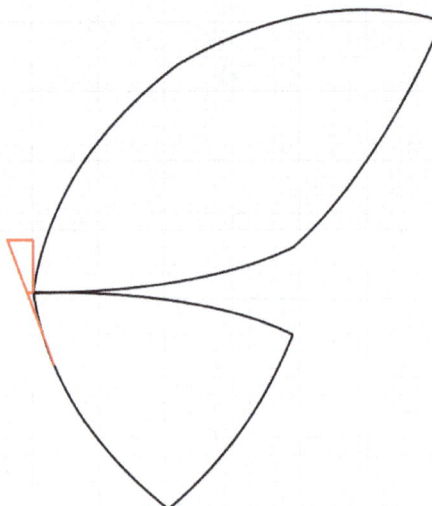

14. Group the new pattern piece extensions with the top and bottom cups. Repeat on the right side using the band drafting specifications for the wire.

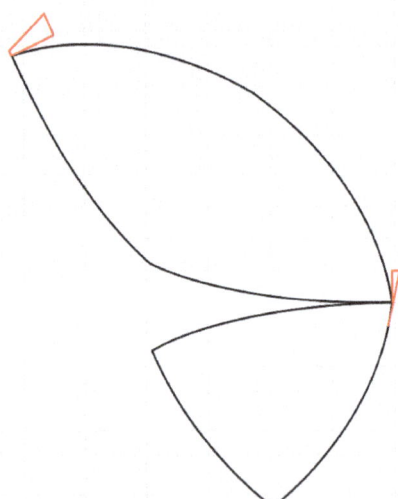

15. To determine the strap placement, draw a line from tip to tip on the top cup, navigate to ***Object -> Path -> Add Anchor Point***. This will add an anchor point in the center of the line.

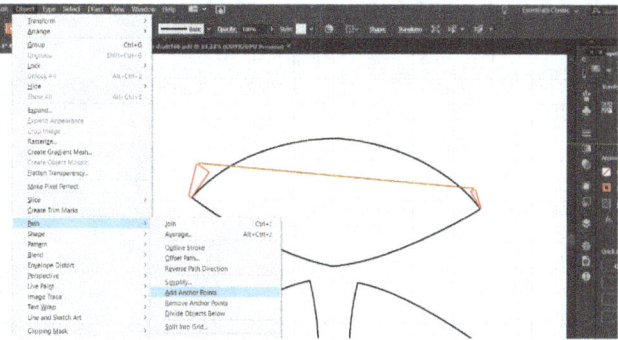

16. Mark the strap position based on the strap calculation, from the center point of the cup. Draw a perpendicular line to align to the height of the top of the cup.

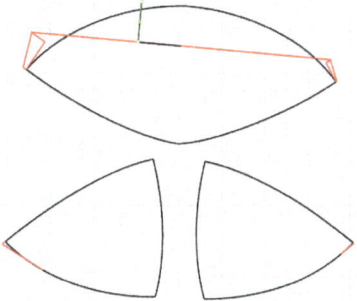

17. Lock the top cup under layers and use the pen tool to draw in the underarm and neckline curves. Line up all intersecting points on the pattern to ensure that each seam lines up. If the top cup at the apex is too pointed, remove up to 1/2" or 12.5mm at the tip, but whatever is removed, add it back to the top of the cup to balance the cup volume.

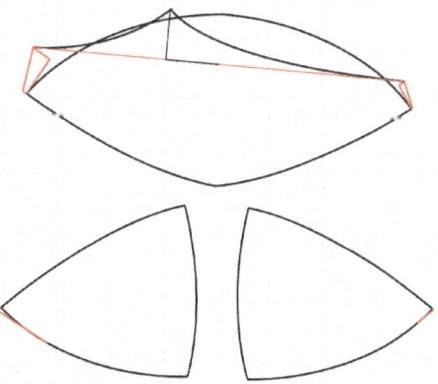

CHAPTER 17
PATTERN DIRECTIONS

This chapter prepares the drafted patterns for sewing. Directions are included for both hand drafting and Adobe® Illustrator®.

SEAM ALLOWANCE BY HAND

BRA BAND
When creating the pattern for a bra, consider how the elastics and edges are finished. These decisions can affect the seam lines and allowances.

1. Separate the front and back pattern pieces.

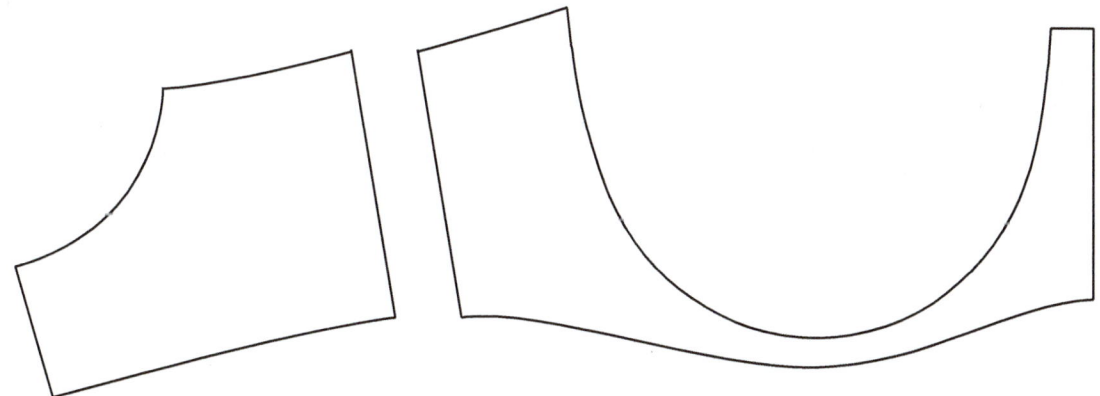

2. Add 1/4" or 6mm seam allowance around the wire curve, joining band seam(s) and any location in which a picot elastic is applied.

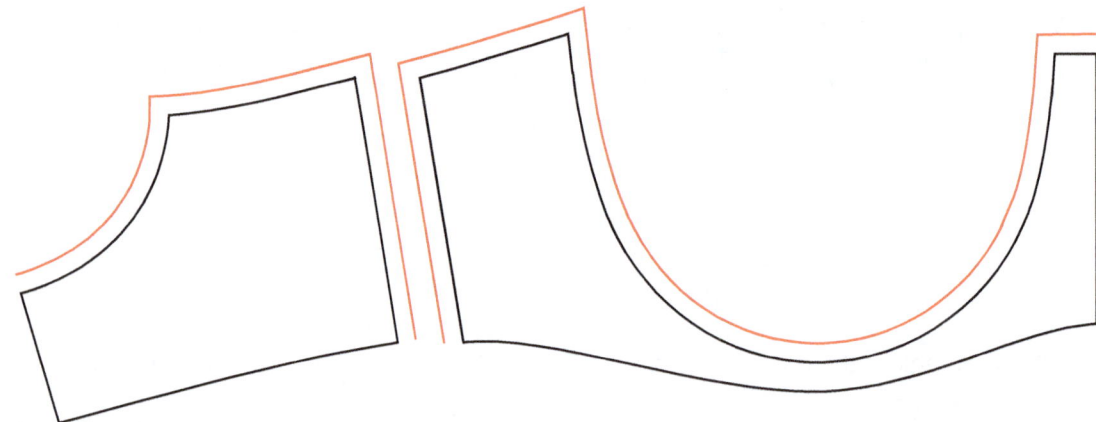

3. On the center front, the pattern is placed on the fold. On the center back, the hook and eye is stitched over the end by about 1/2" or 12.5mm. If the hook & eye overlap is smaller, adjust this amount to equal that amount.

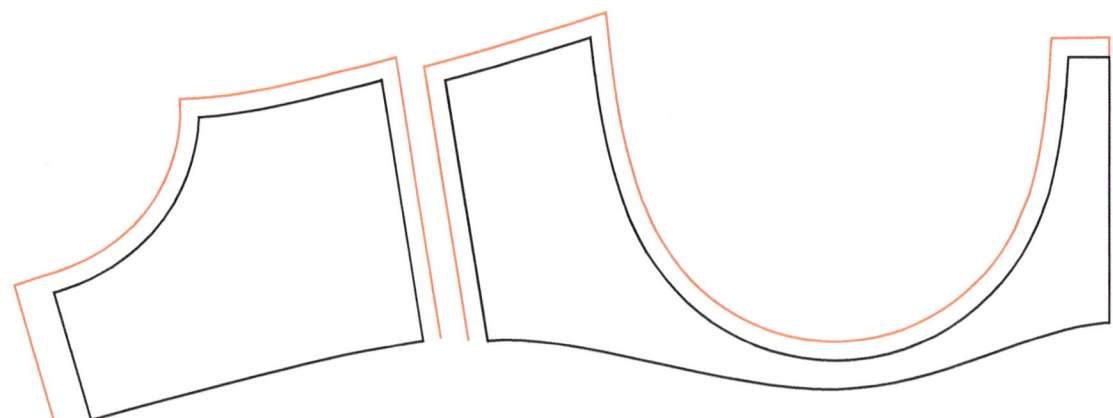

Advanced / Pattern Directions | 191

4. The waistline attachment is the final step. For a wider elastic finish, the elastic can be finished by overlapping the elastic on the edge by 1/4" or 6mm. In this case, the seam allowance is 1/4" or 6mm. If the elastic is stitched and folded under to only have the edge of the elastic shown, then the seam allowance required equals the width of the elastic.

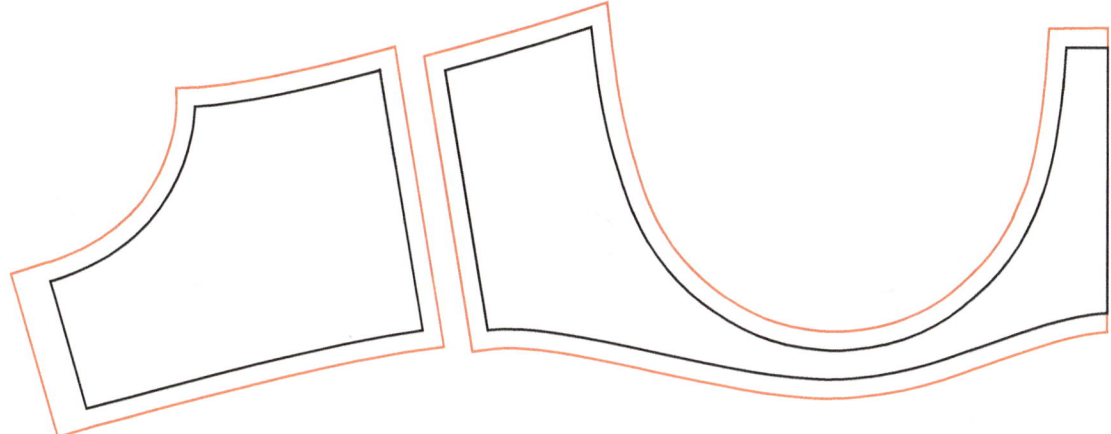

BRA CUP

4. Separate and lay out the basic cup patterns.

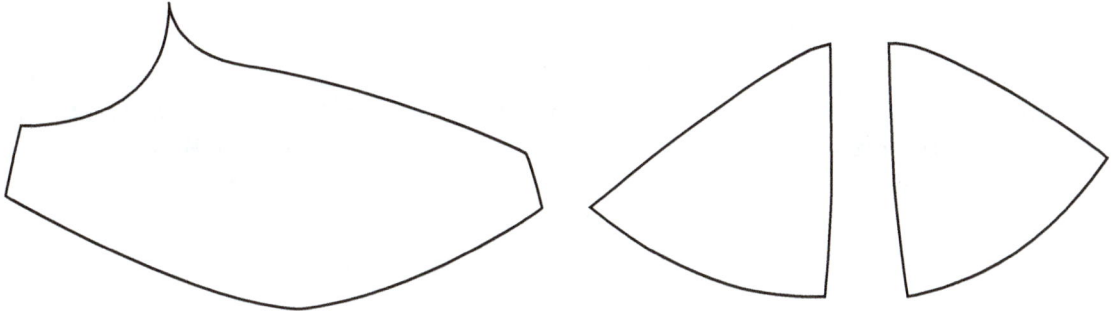

5. Around the wire line and where picot elastic is attached, the seam allowance is 1/4" or 6mm.

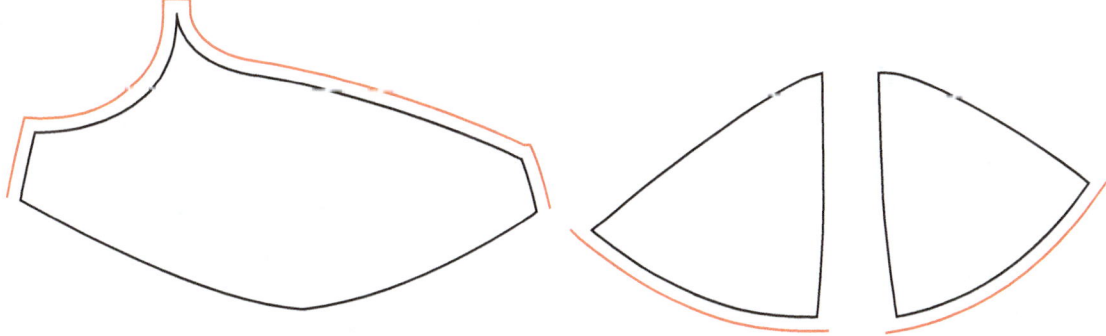

6. Interior seam lines can have a seam allowance of 1/8" or 1/4" (3mm or 6mm). In manufacturing, the interior seam allowance will often be 1/8" or 3mm. For most custom clothiers, a seam allowance of 1/4" or 6mm is more practical.

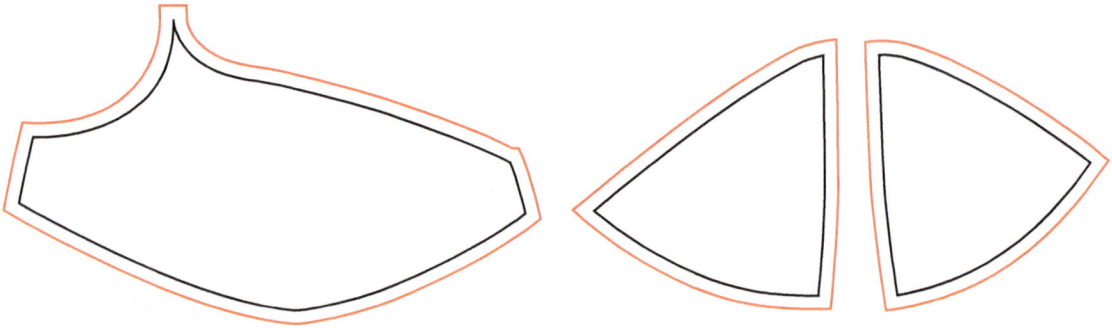

SEAM ALLOWANCE BY ILLUSTRATION SOFTWARE

In Adobe® Illustrator®, all lines need to be joined in order to have a single path for the pattern piece. If the paths are not joined, this process will not be very smooth.

1. Select the pattern piece to add seam allowance to. Choose a seam allowance that most of the seams use for that pattern piece. Add a uniform seam allowance by selecting the **Offset Path Tool** under the **Object Menu**. Indicate the amount of the seam allowance and select **Miter**.

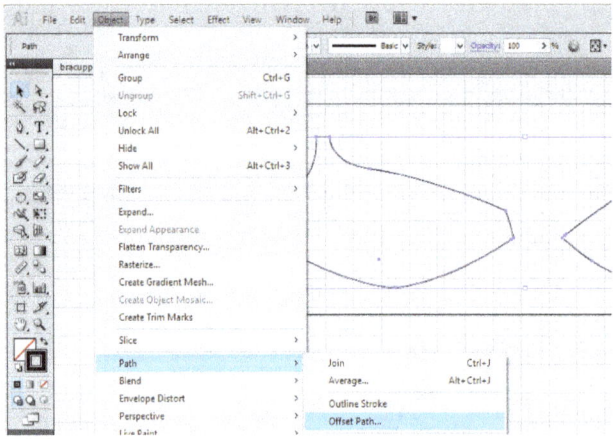

2. If the pattern looks like the illustration below, after the offset, the path was not completely joined. At this point, delete the additional lines that were created and correct the shape. If adding an unequal amount for seam allowances, manually adjust the seam allowances that are different from the uniform offset. This is relatively easy to do when using the software with grid view visible.

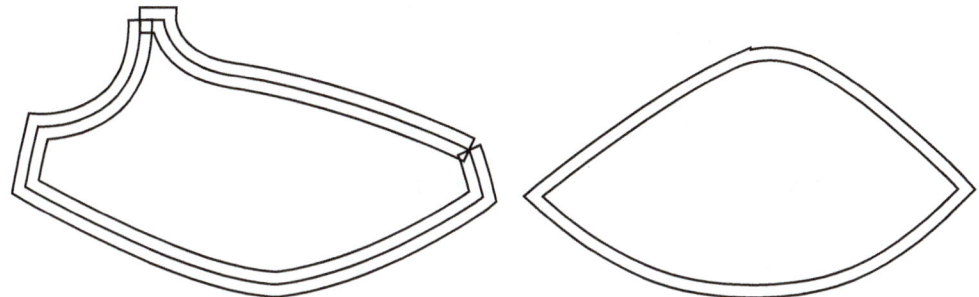

GRAINLINES

The last step in creating patterns is to add grainlines and pertinent pattern information. Pattern information should include the style name and/or number, piece name, size and cutting instructions.

GRAINLINES VS. DIRECTION OF GREATEST STRETCH

In traditional pattern drafting, the grainline indicates the measurement of least stretch, which is generally the grain parallel to the selvage of fabric. All pattern professionals, including factories, sample makers and pattern makers use the traditional definition of grainlines.

In the home sewing & indie pattern making realm of the bra-making industry, it has become common for pattern makers to mark the direction of greatest stretch (DOGS) instead of grainlines. Please make note on the patterns what is being used, write "Grainline" or "DOGS" on the indicator line. These directions refer to the grainline or the direction of least stretch.

1. On the back band, line up the grainline parallel to the center back.

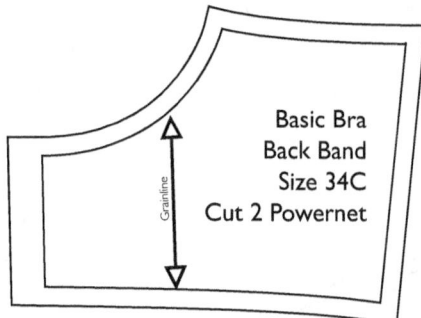

2. On the front band, line up the grainline to the center front.

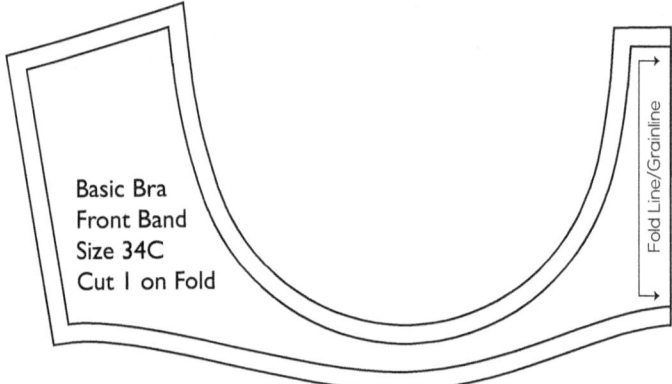

3. On the cup pieces, the grainline can vary based on the style lines. In order for seams to refrain from puckering when sewn, the grainline should be at an angle that does not place the most stable portion of the fabric on a seam line. Envision a pie. When cutting a pie piece, the point of most stability in the piece is in the center, as the sides of the pie piece flow out. The exact center of the pie piece is the grainline, or the most stable part of the pie piece.

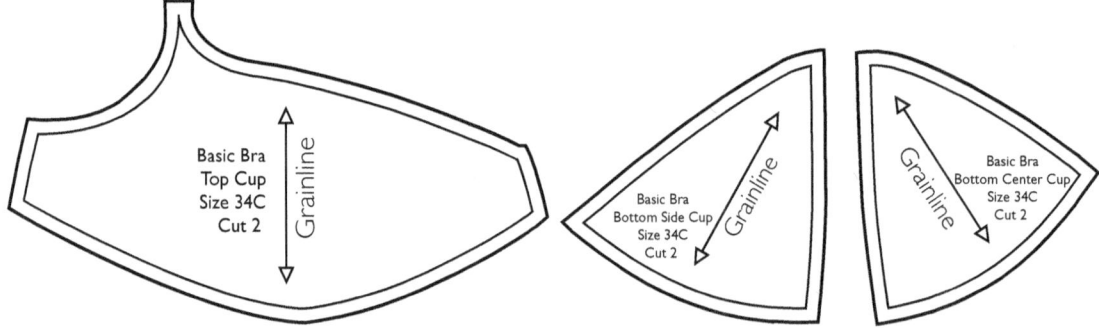

CHAPTER 18
CREATE A SLOPER: PORCELYNNE PATTERN MANIPULATION METHOD

Separate slopers are created for the cup, front and back bands. The cup sloper is created using the Porcelynne Pattern Drafting and Manipulation Method. These slopers are used to create the drafts in the following three chapters.

CUP SLOPER

1. On the custom draft from Chapter 16, draw in straight lines from each point on the outer edge of the cup to the apex of the cup. If the apex was raised for seam curving, use the original apex point for this step.

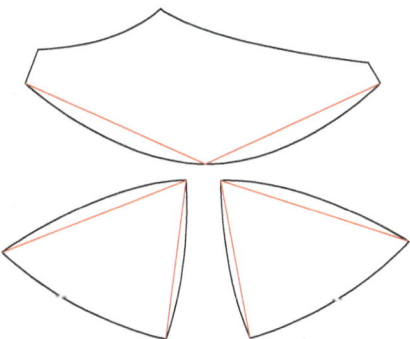

2. Cut on the straight lines and tape the bottom pieces to the top piece on the center horizontal seam. Be sure to line up the apex of each cup.

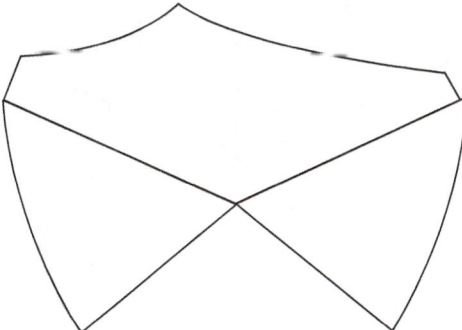

3. Smooth the joining seams on the side and front of the cup to remove the points and smooth the curve.

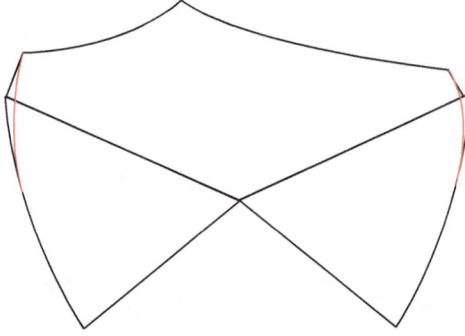

GUIDELINES

The guidelines for the sloper will help determine the amount of volume that is added for any particular design. Follow the charts under the next heading to determine the curved amounts for each area.

4. The original seamlines will indicate both the horizontal and vertical guidelines. Mark the horizontal as H and Vertical as V. Take a straight line up from the apex to the top of the cup for the vertical position on the top cup. This does not have to be precise, as it is only a guideline.

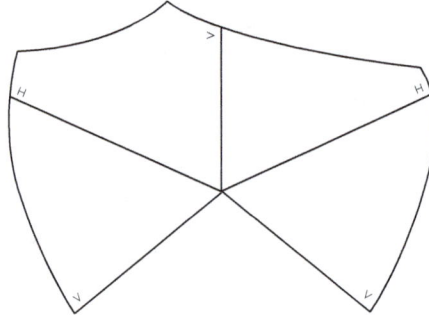

5. Draw diagonal lines, dividing each section in half. Mark these diagonal lines as D. This does not have to be precise, as it is only a guideline.

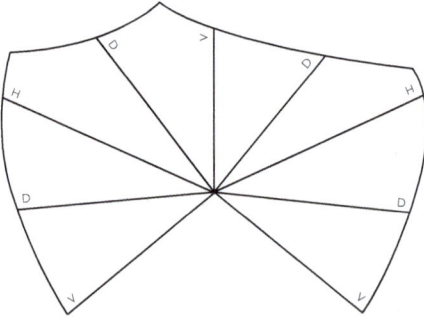

Advanced / Create a Sloper: Porcelynne Pattern Manipulation Method | 197

6. For all seams that do not go through the apex of the cup, the amount of cup curve does not need to be as extreme as its further away from the apex. These lines appear in a star like pattern because we are dividing each part of the cup in half. Mark the halfway points of each horizontal and vertical line and create new lines. Label the new horizontal lines as H/2 and the vertical lines as V/2.

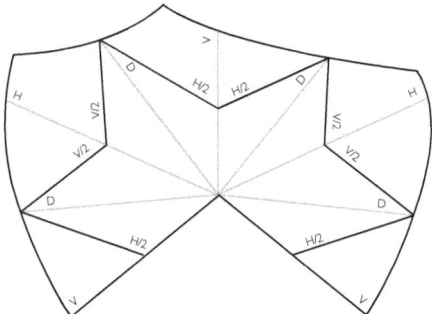

7. Add half way diagonal guide lines, dividing the remaining areas in two, mark these lines as D/2.

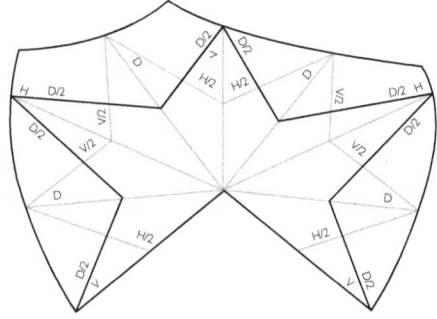

CUP CURVES

When drafting from the sloper, there is variation to the volume added for each draft. This amount varies based on two factors. The first is based on how many seams are in the cup and the second is where the seam lines are located.

8. Each interior line of the cup, indicates a position for adding volume. Based on the cup size on the original draft, indicate the horizontal and vertical measurements.

| Horizontal Measurement |
| Vertical Measurement |

9. For the curves on the cup, there is a direct correlation to the diameter of the cup, vertically, horizontally and diagonally. To get the diagonal amount, add the horizontal to the vertical amounts and divide by 2.

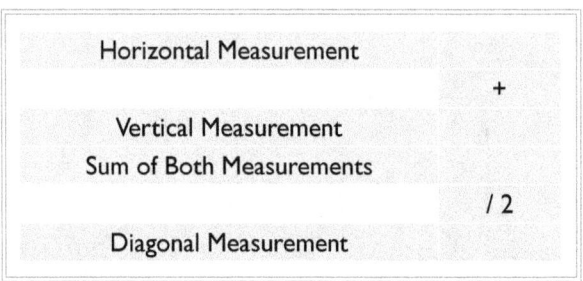

10. Every design varies in style lines. The volume needs to be based on its individual design. Refer to these charts to create a custom chart for the sloper. This chart indicates the amount of cup curve based on the vertical, horizontal or diagonal measurements and the quantity of pattern pieces in the cup. Using these charts, multiply the percentage by the measurement to get a custom chart.

Regular Wire Curve Chart	1 Piece Cup	2 Piece Cup	3 Piece Cup	4 Piece Cup	5 Piece Cup	6 Piece Cup
Percentage for V, H & D	7.5%	3.75%	2.5%	1.875%	1.5%	1.25%
Percentage for V/2, H/2, D/2	3.75%	1.875%	1.25%	0.9375%	0.75%	0.625%

Vertical Wire Curve Chart	1 Piece Cup	2 Piece Cup	3 Piece Cup	4 Piece Cup	5 Piece Cup	6 Piece Cup
Percentage for V, H & D	15%	7.5%	5%	3.75%	3%	2.5%
Percentage for V/2, H/2, D/2	7.5%	3.75%	2.5%	1.875%	1.5%	1.25%

Example Chart	1 Piece Cup	2 Piece Cup	3 Piece Cup	4 Piece Cup	5 Piece Cup	6 Piece Cup
V	0.47	0.23	0.16	0.12	0.09	0.08
V/2	0.23	0.12	0.08	0.06	0.05	0.04
H	0.64	0.32	0.21	0.16	0.13	0.11
H/2	0.32	0.16	0.11	0.08	0.06	0.05
D	0.55	0.28	0.18	0.14	0.11	0.09
D/2	0.28	0.14	0.09	0.07	0.06	0.05

Custom Chart	1 Piece Cup	2 Piece Cup	3 Piece Cup	4 Piece Cup	5 Piece Cup	6 Piece Cup
V						
V/2						
H						
H/2						
D						
D/2						

FRONT BAND SLOPER

1. Create a straight line down from the center bridge. Draw a straight line across at the bottom of the band, perpendicular to the center front.

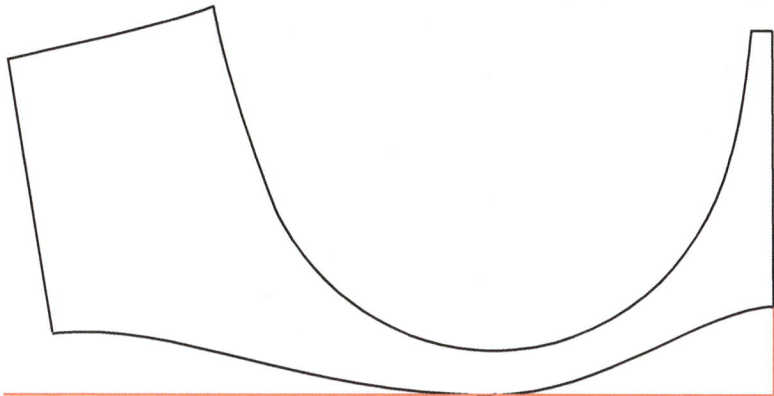

2. Continue the side seam down to the straight line.

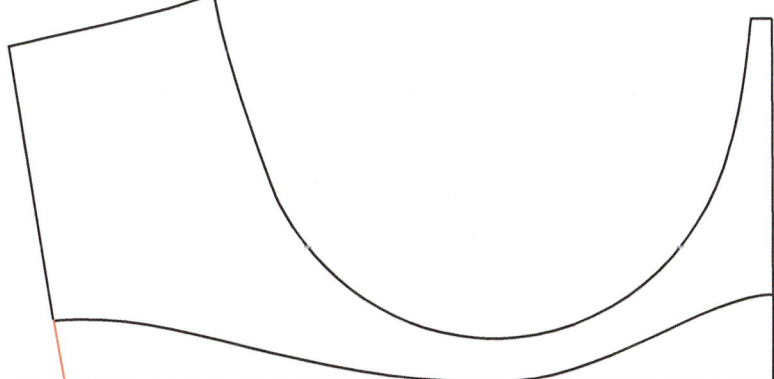

3. To finalize the front sloper, place a notch or marking where the original curved points were on the center front and side seam. Indicate the center of the cup. It is recommended to indicate the width of the band elastic that the original draft was created for.

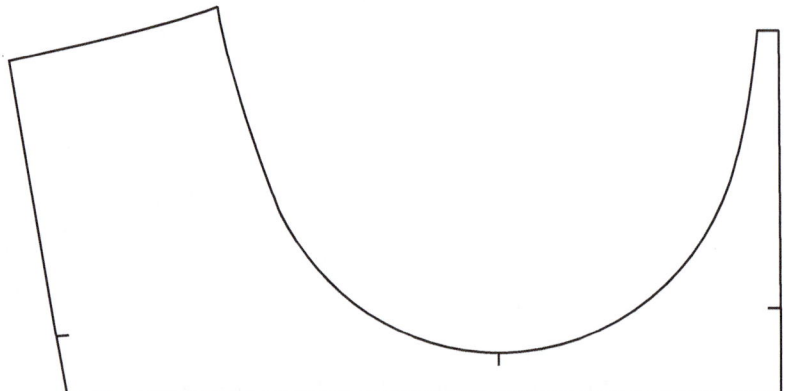

BACK BAND SLOPER

1. Line up the back band to the front band sloper.

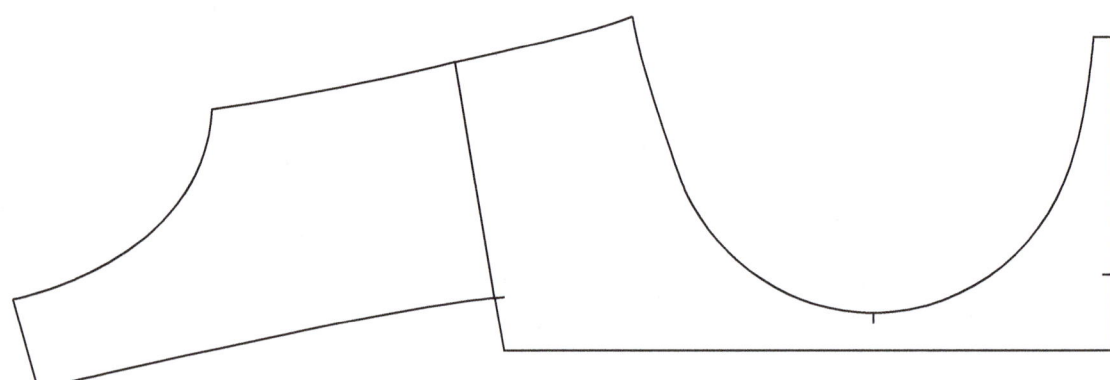

2. Draw a straight line down the side seam to extend it to match the front band. From the bottom of the side seam, draw a straight line to the bottom of the center back.

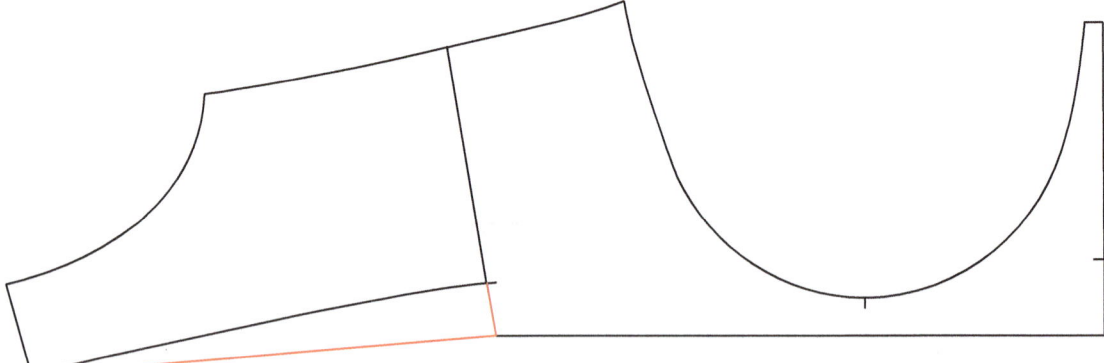

3. To finalize the back sloper, place a notch or marking at the original side seam. Notate the stretch of the fabric that the back band was drafted for. Separate slopers should be created for stretch variations.

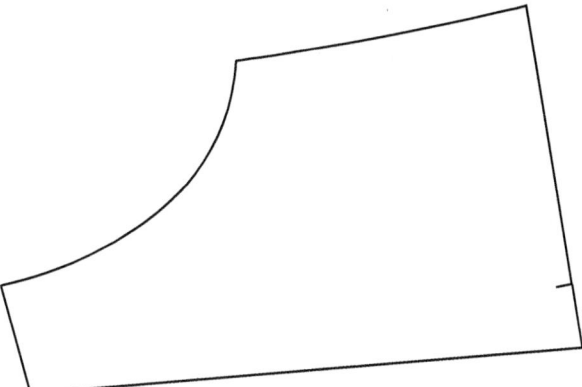

CHAPTER 19
PORCELYNNE PATTERN MANIPULATION METHOD

1. Sketch the design and trace the bra sloper to a secondary piece of paper.

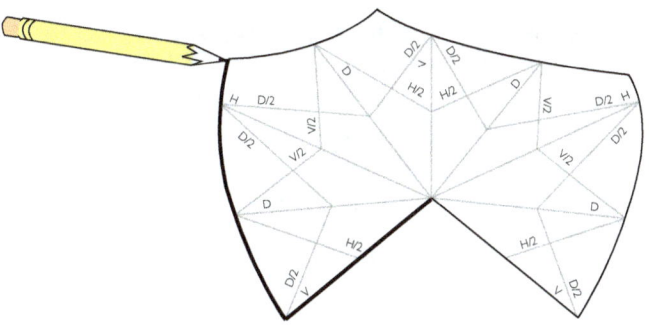
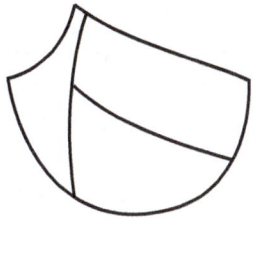

2. Determine where the style lines converge according to the sloper. Use straight lines and think of the sloper in relationship to the position of the bust. All seams will appear curved on a sphere, despite whether they are straight or not.

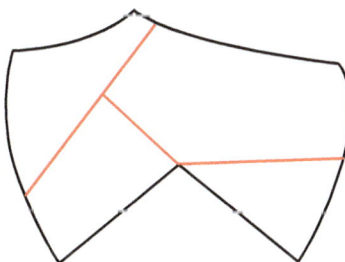
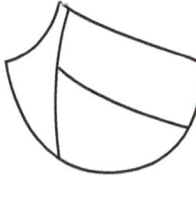

3. On the draft, refer to the sloper and indicate on each interior line how much of a curve is needed referring to the chart created in the previous chapter. Be sure to mark each portion of the line since the draft will be cut apart. Draw in a temporary line extending the diagonal line through the side of the cup. Additional volume will be added to the side of the cup based on the curve of the diagonal line on the top and bottom cups.

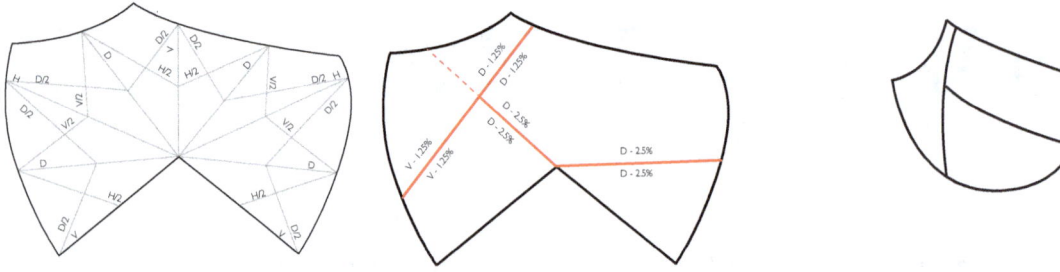

4. Prior to cutting the pattern apart, mark either the half way or the third way points on each line, based on the original draft preference. On lines that do not intersect the apex in any form, the center of the line is used. It is then divided in two sections, for above and below the center horizontal position.

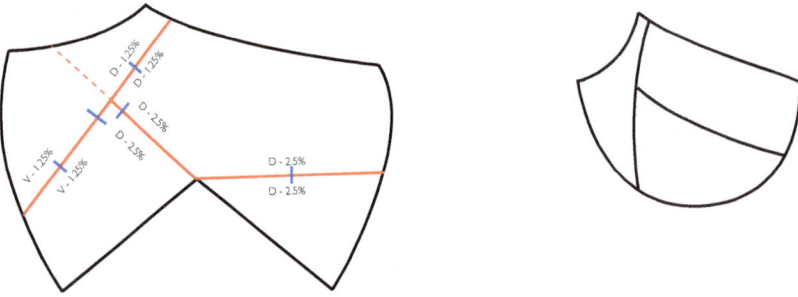

5. Cut along each of the style lines and tape the bottom cup together.

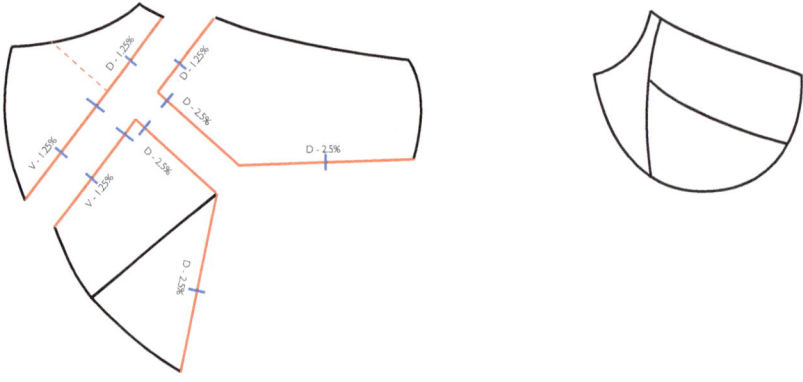

Advanced / Porcelynne Pattern Manipulation Method | 205

6. Add the curves to each of the right side vertical lines, measuring the amount required for volume on the top and bottom cup.

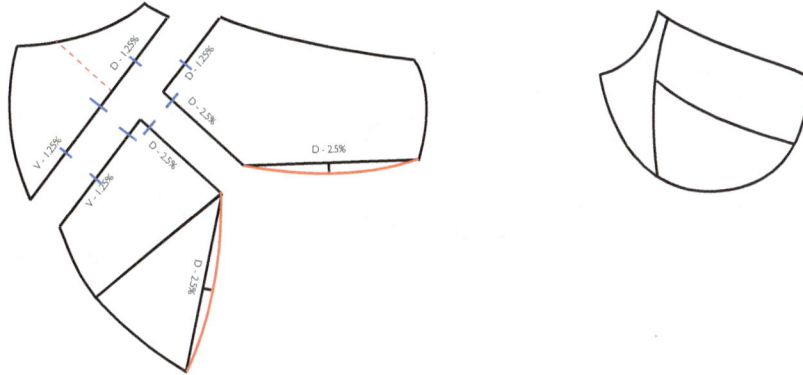

7. For the diagonal seam on the side of the cup, add the volume to the curve as if it were to extend through to the armhole.

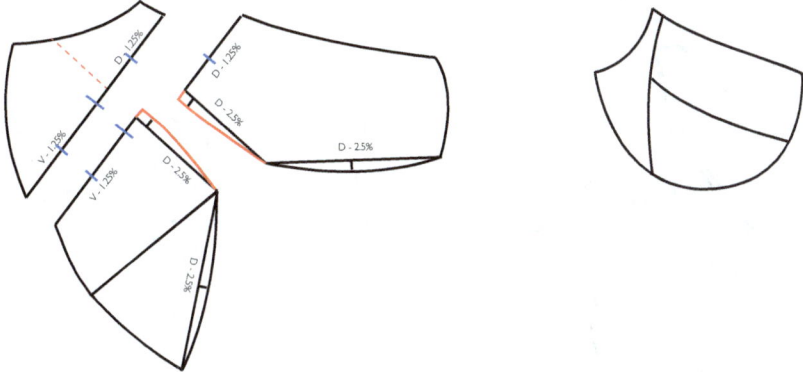

8. The amount of volume added to the side of the diagonal seam needs to be added to the side of the adjacent pattern piece. Cut from the interior seam to the armhole, but do not separate the pattern in two. Open the pattern piece by the combined total added to the matching seams.

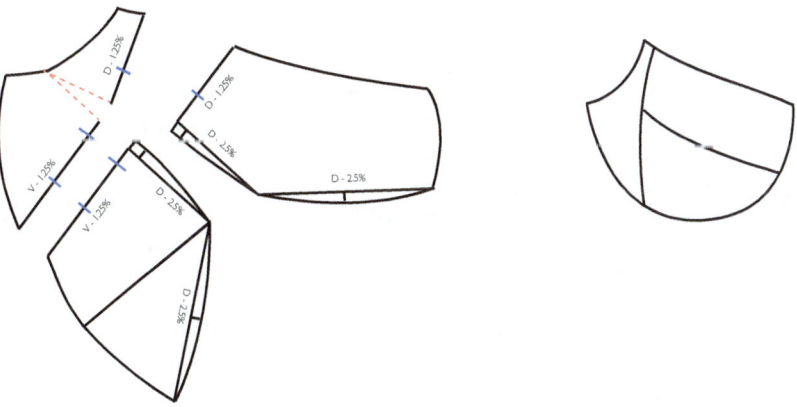

9. Create a curve for the side cup taking into consideration the amount of curve to add to the top and bottom. Try to keep the center point of the seam touching or close to the original pattern. Reshape the armhole curve of the cup.

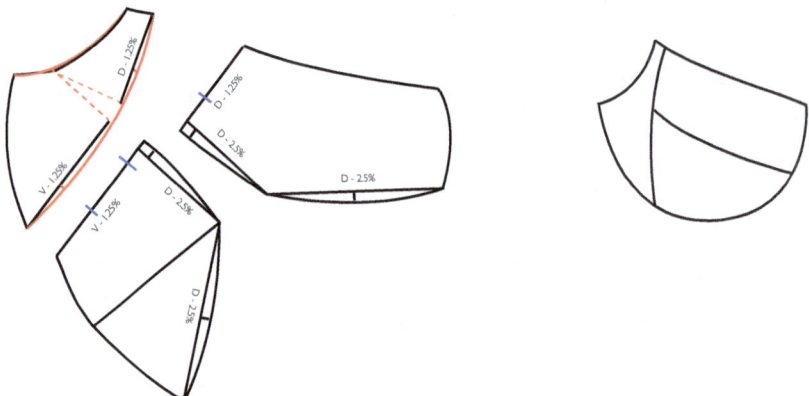

10. On the joining seams of the top and bottom cup to the side cup, add the cup curve.

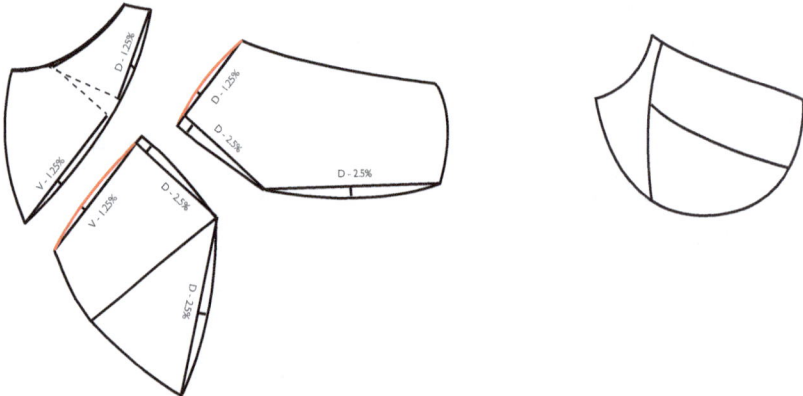

11. Line up the joining pattern pieces and be sure the seam edges are smooth. The front of the cup needs to be blended to create a smooth curve.

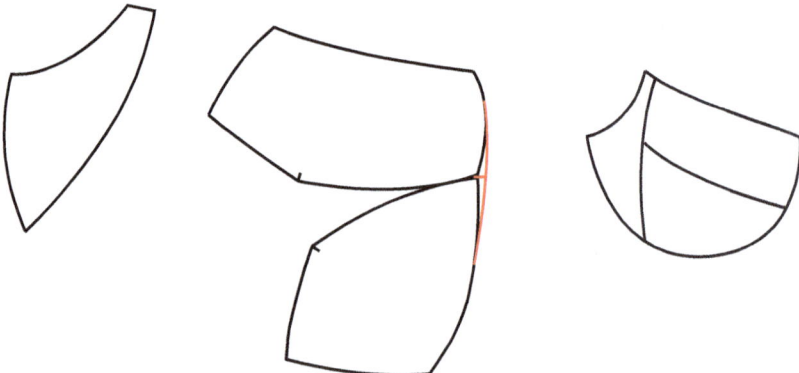

12. Align the side cup up to the bottom cup and align the top and bottom cups at the joining seam. Correct all joining seam edges.

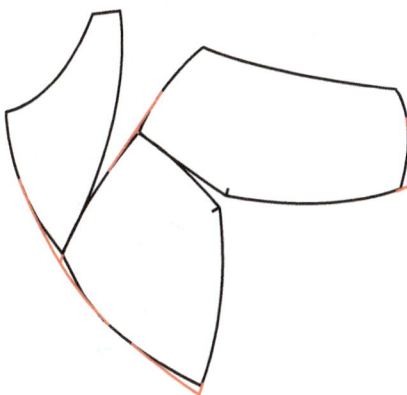 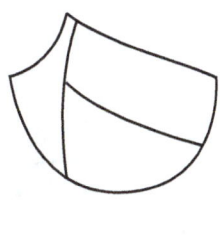

13. The last piece to align is the top of the cup with the side cup.

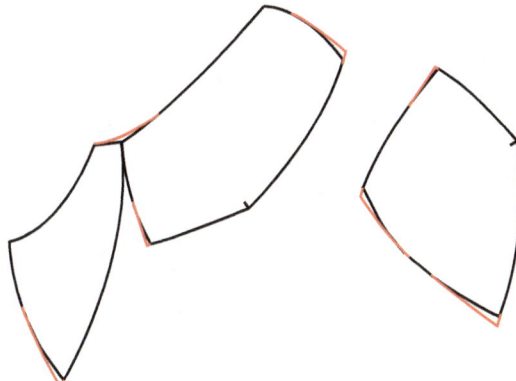 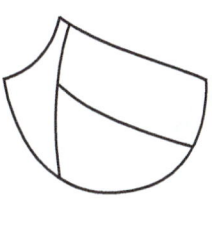

14. Blend the point out of the apex and double check joining seam lines to make sure the matching seams align in length.

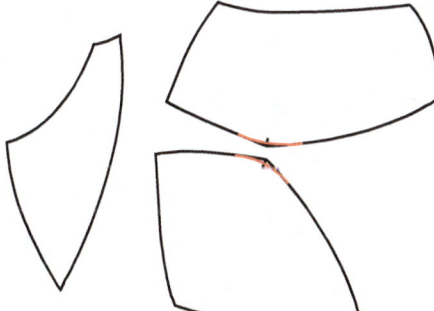 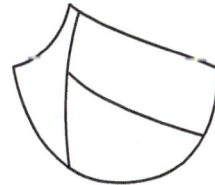

15. Place grainlines on the patterns based on the original sloper. The cup grain was adjusted slightly to keep the neckline and seamlines off grain. Restricting the stretch on the neckline can cause tightness on the neckline.

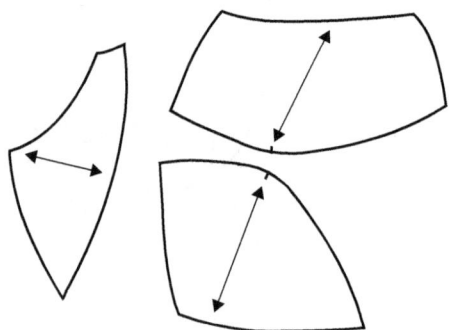 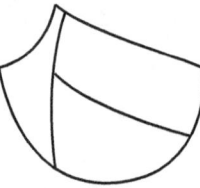

CHAPTER 20
PATTERN MANIPULATION: BRALETTE

A bralette is a bra without the support of an underwire. It is often worn by individuals with a smaller cup size, including being worn as a sleep bra or training bra. The syle drafted in this exercise has a single darted cup, an encased elastic waistband and a simple strap that ties behind the neck.

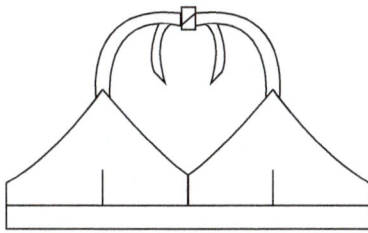

1. The band is a simple straight band encased with elastic around the body. At the bottom of the front band wire curve, draw a line across the band.

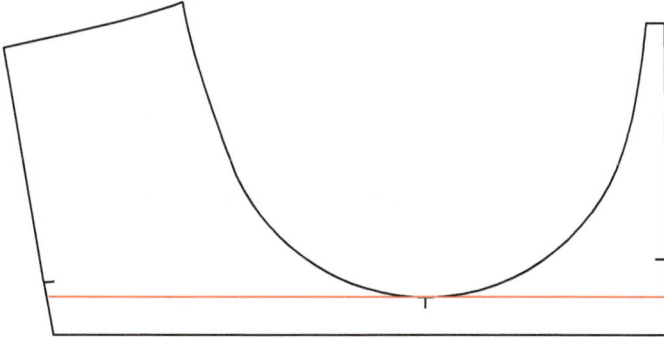

2. The back band is altered by marking the same amount that is marked on the front.

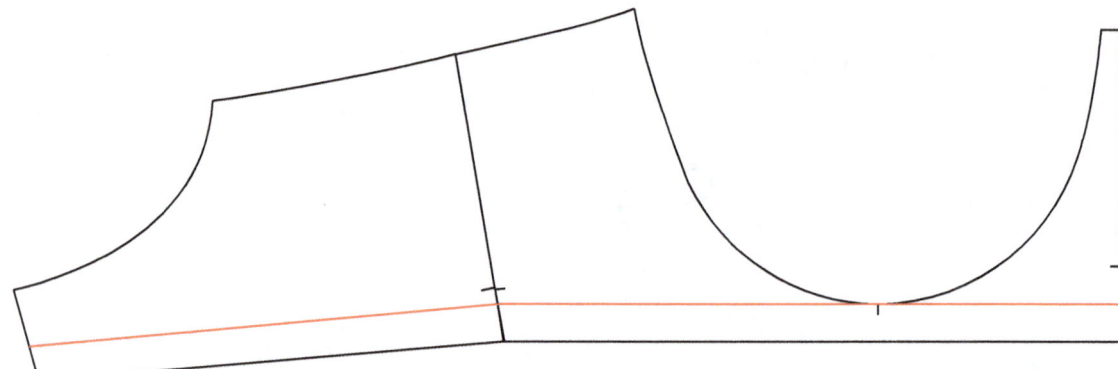

3. This bralette utilizes the sloper lower vertical seam as a dart. Line up the front of the cup sloper to the front part of the band by matching both the top and bottom points together. The center of the curves may overlap, but this is ignored since there is no wire in a bralette.

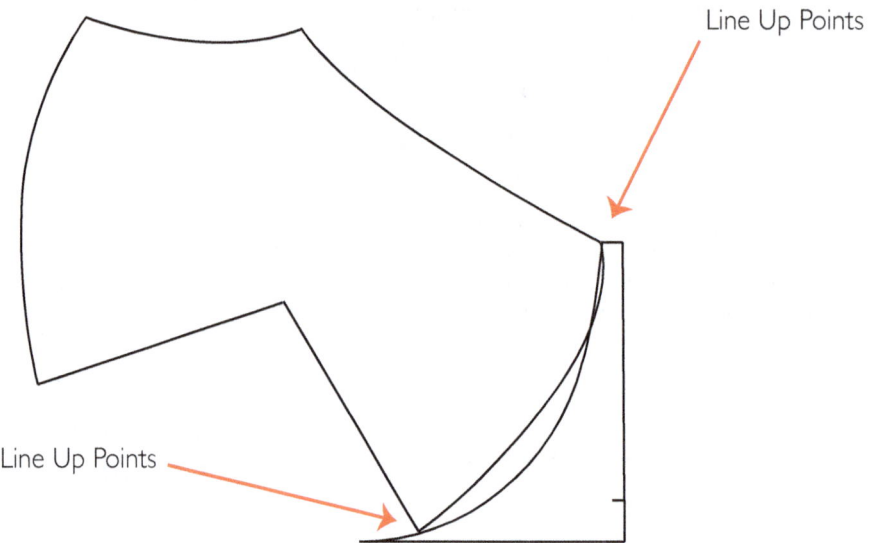

Line Up Points

Line Up Points

4. Line up the side of the cup in the same manner as the front.

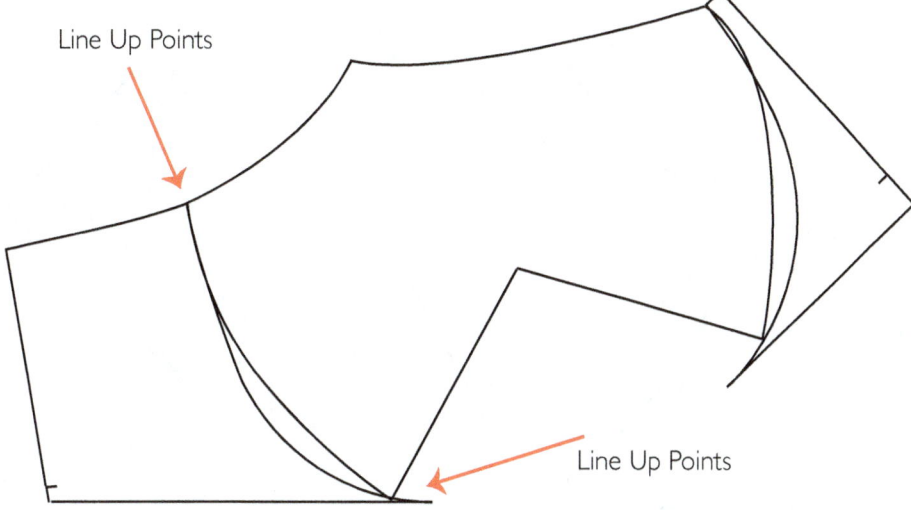

5. Alter the neckline of the front, including the attached band.

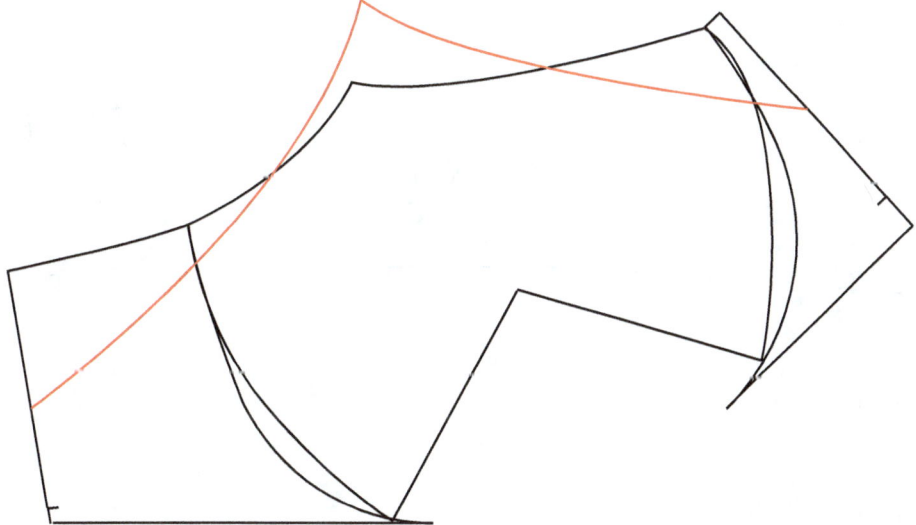

6. Add curves for a one-piece cup.

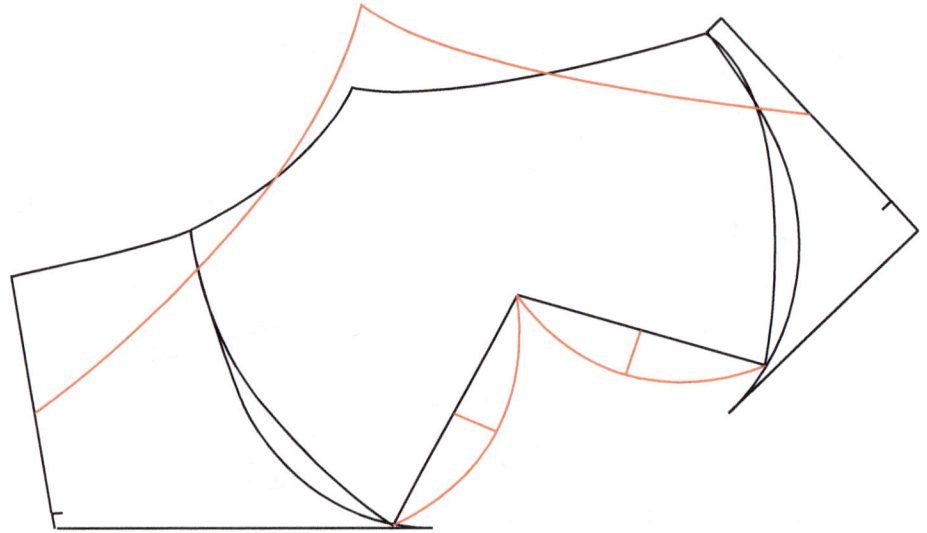

7. Line up the top portion of the back back to the front and reshape the back.

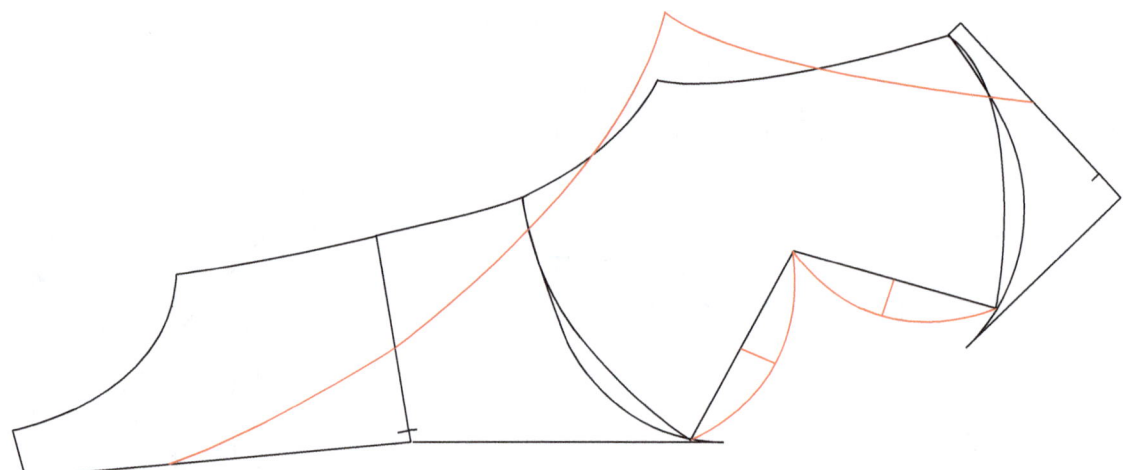

8. The body of the bralette is in one combined pattern piece for both the right and left sides of the pattern. The grainline is best placed at the center front to keep that area from stretching out of shape.

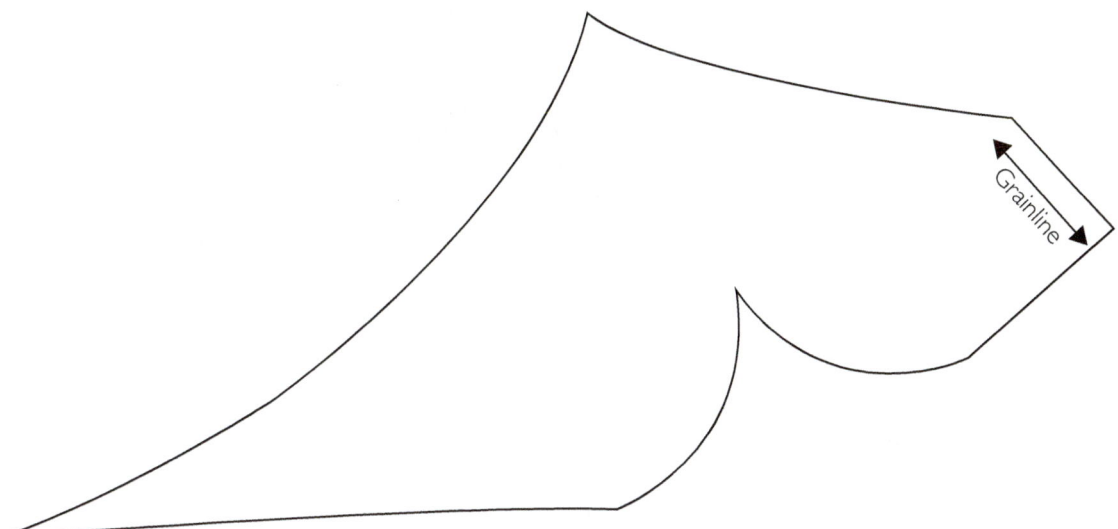

9. The band width needs to match the chosen hook & eye attachment. The back waistband is straightened to keep the fabric from twisting when elastic is inserted.

10. To make an encased elastic waistband, the band needs to be twice the height of the elastic. The waistband can be combined to be a continuous band from front to back. In this exercise, the front is cut on the fold and the back is a separate pattern.

11. Add seam allowances to the bra as previously demonstrated. The bottom of the dart seam allowance is squared down from the dart to ease the construction process of attaching the cup to the band. The elastic at the waistband is encased in fabric. A wider seam allowance of 1/2" or 12.5mm was chosen for the waistband. A pattern for the strap is not necessary unless it is a fabric strap.

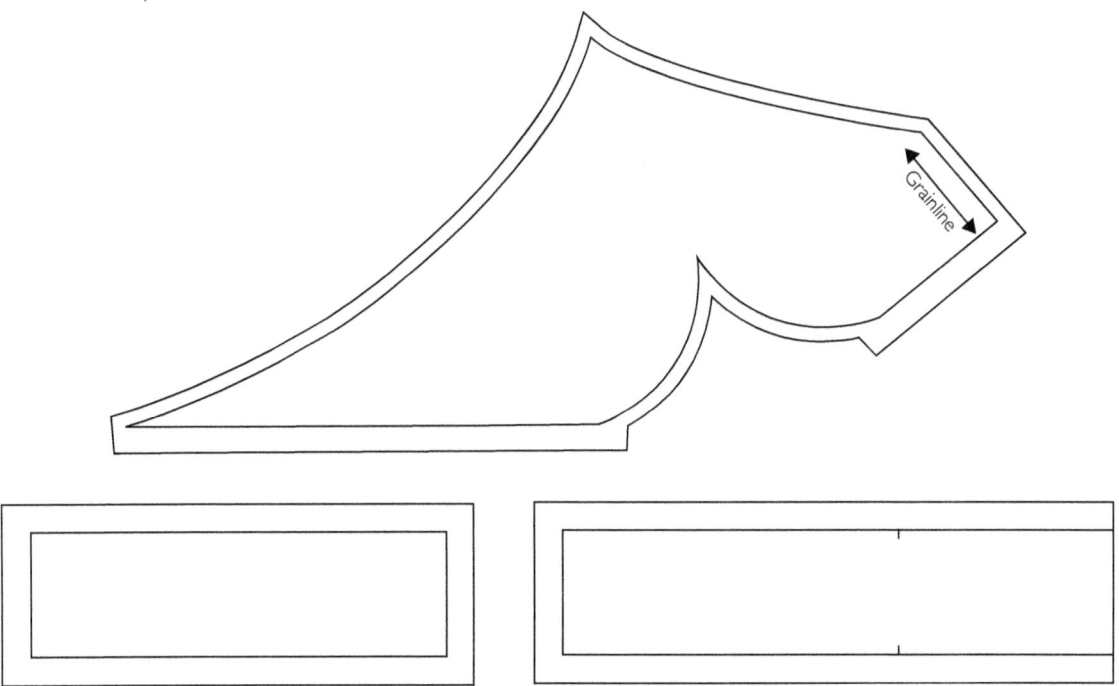

CHAPTER 21
PATTERN MANIPULATION: NON-WIRED SOFT BRA

This chapter creates a non-wired soft bra from the slopers created in Chapter 18. The style demonstrated in this exercise is pictured below.

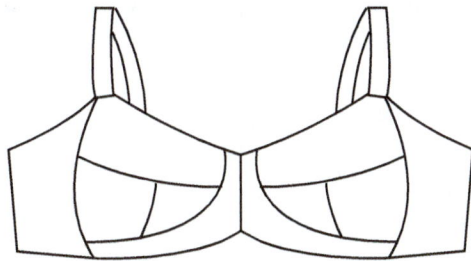

1. In this exercise, the side of the cup is combined with the band up to the strap point. Line up the side of the cup sloper to the wire curve of the band, matching the underarm point and the point in which the new seam line will fall.

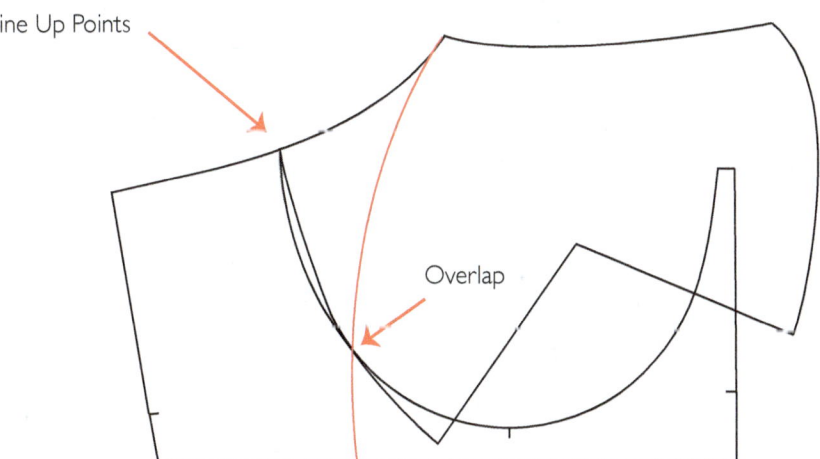

2. Draw the additional styling of the band. The center front and side seam are raised. The center front ends at a point to create a "Gothic arch."

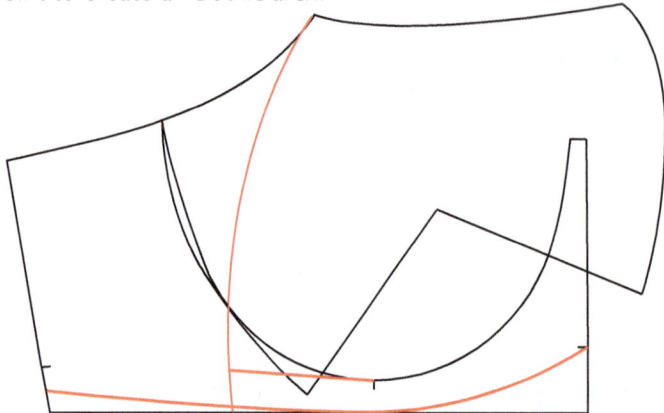

3. Separate the side cup/band from the cup and band sloper. Add the small portion of the band to the bottom of the cup on the left side. Smooth the shape between the cup and band joining point.

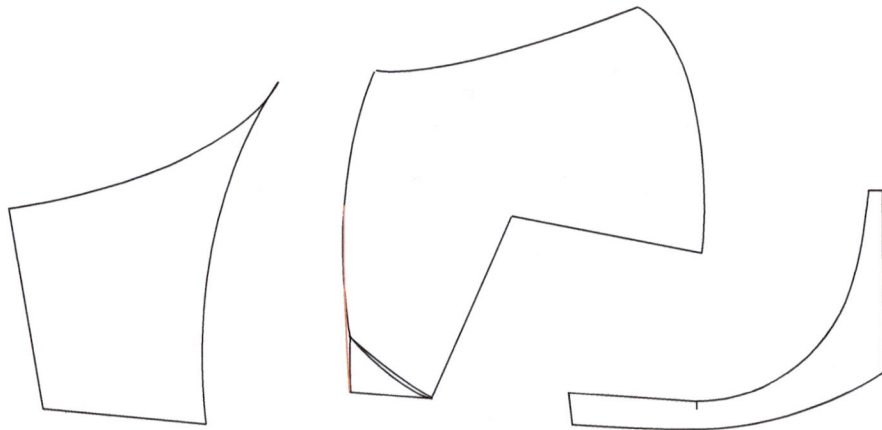

4. Draw in the seam lines for the cup. Indicate which line on the sloper this falls closest to, in order to determine the cup curves. Mark the side cup/band with a mark to line up the seam of the cup.

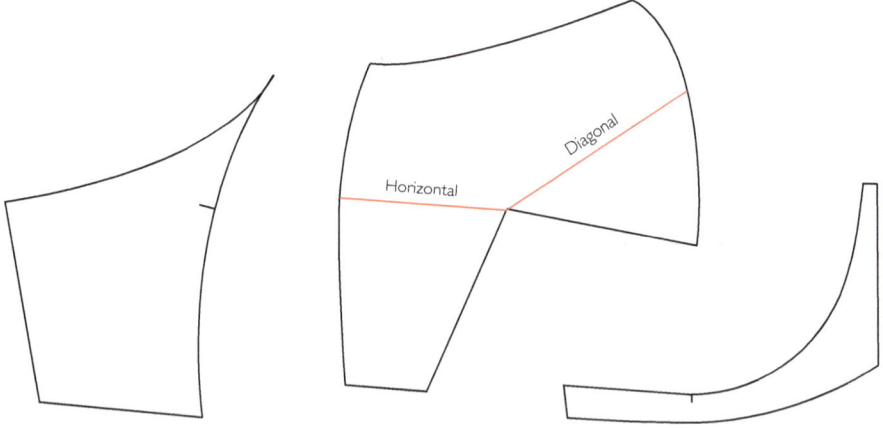

5. Separate the cup and add the corresponding volume at the seams. Since this cup does not have an underwire, the side of the cup does not need to have the same added volume. Consider this cup as a three piece cup for calculation purposes. Draw a line across the side cup from the marking placed on the side cup/band.

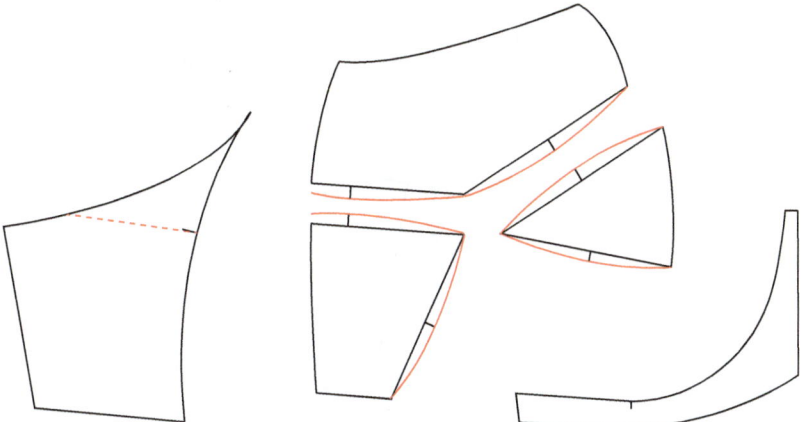

6. Slash and spread the side cup on the line to open it the same volume that was added to the horizontal seam. Create a new smooth curve for the side cup.

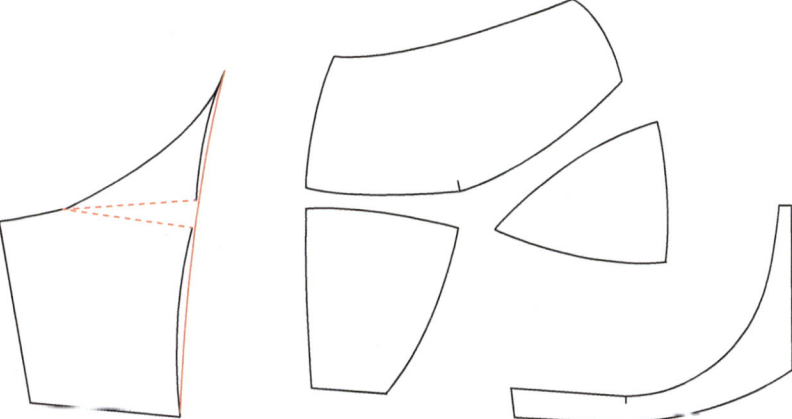

7. The back band needs to be adjusted to the side band/cup. The back band can also be combined with the side band to create one pattern piece. Despite stretch not being calculated in the front portion of the band, the band can be combined with little, if not any, adjustments for stretch on the front band.

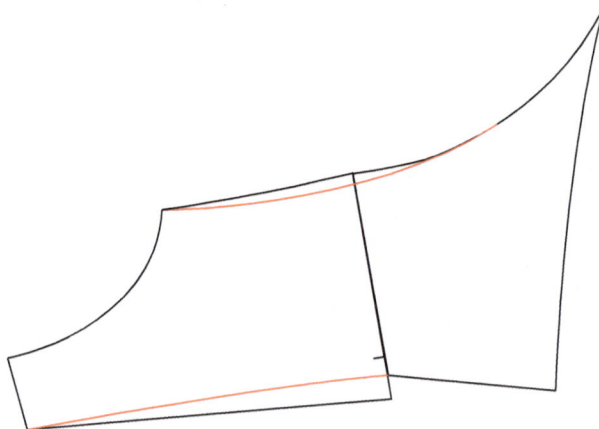

8. Add seam allowances to the pattern as previously demonstrated. The grain on the back can be placed in a number of locations, but this exercise places it in the center of the band.

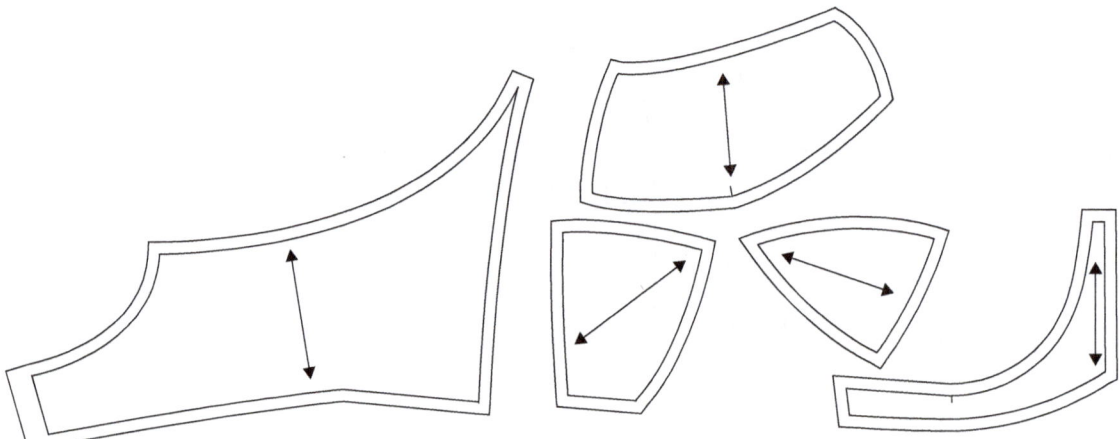

CHAPTER 22
BRA BAND GRADING

The bra band is graded in two manners. The first is for the wire size and the second is for the band size. Instructions are provided for both hand grading and grading with Adobe® Illustrator®.

GRADE RULES

Determining the grade rules for the band is the first step. In Chapter 14, the grade of the bra band was discussed briefly. The total grade amount needs to be broken down into "rules" to accommodate all points that are being graded.

The grade for a wire size on the front of the band is based on wire growth. Wire widths grade by 5/16" or 8mm. Wire lengths can grade in length by 1/2" to 5/8" (12.5mm to 15mm). The following chart is based on a regular wire with a growth of 1/2" of 12.5mm which corresponds to the general grade amount created by using the scaling method for the cup.

The wire height amounts also vary depending on whether it is a long wire, short wire or regular wire. The side seam height grade is a variable amount based on preference. This exercise uses the front wire height grade for the side seam height grade. This grade keeps the bra in a balanced position on the body.

The back grade for wires are generally only graded at the side seam to match the side seam height grade on the front. The following table represents a general wire grade. This may differ by wire manufacturer. Use the custom column to add your own.

WIRE GRADE RULES

	Imperial	Metric	Custom
Full Cup Wire Width Grade	5/16"	8mm	
Half Cup Wire Width Grade	5/32"	4mm	
Front Wire Height Grade	3/16"	5mm	
Side Wire Height Grade	7/32"	6mm	
Side Seam Height Grade	3/16"	5mm	

The grade for band size is slightly different and can be done in two different manners. Each starting band size has a corresponding cup size. For example, a 34C graded to a 36 band would be a 36B. The 34C graded to a 32 band would be a 32D. All three of these sizes use the same wire. This is called sister sizing.

The easiest method for grading a band is to create sister sized front bands, meaning the front band is stationary and does not change based on band size. This method moves the entire band grade to the back band. This method is a way to save money on cutting and additional pattern work. This is the method I covered in the first and second editions of this book.

The second method grades both the front and back for the band size. For further grading information, both methods are covered in this book. Both methods are correct and both are based on preference. The sister size method is preferred by indie pattern makers.

FRONT BAND GRADE RULES

	Imperial	Metric	Custom
Sister Size - Side Seam Width Grade	0	0	
Traditional - Side Seam Width Grade	1/2"	12.5mm	

The back grade is slightly different than the front. The back grade needs to be modified for the stretch of the fabric. Refer to the stretch reduction chart in Chapter 14 to determine the fabric stretch. In this example, a medium-heavy weight power mesh is used. The measurements for the quarter of the body is multiplied by the stretch reduction of 0.75 for a fabric with a 50% stretch.

Using the method in which the band grade is split between the front and back, this total grade is split between the front and back. The stretch reduction is then multiplied by the grade designated for the back.

Using the method in which the full band grade is taken in the back, the amount multiplied will be the total grade for the front and back. That total amount is then multiplied by the stretch reduction for the back grade.

The strap placement on the back is also graded based on the draft. If the back strap point was drafted as indicated in this book, the back strap point would be 1/3 of the total back grade. Customize your back grade to correspond to the fabric you are using.

BACK BAND GRADE RULES			
	Imperial	Metric	Custom
Stretch Multiplier	.75	.75	
Sister Size - Back Grade	3/4"	20mm	
Sister Size - Strap Grade	1/4"	6mm	
Traditional - Back Grade	3/8"	10mm	
Traditional - Strap Grade	1/8"	3mm	

GRADING BY HAND FOR WIRE SIZES

BAND FRONT

1. Begin with the front band draft.

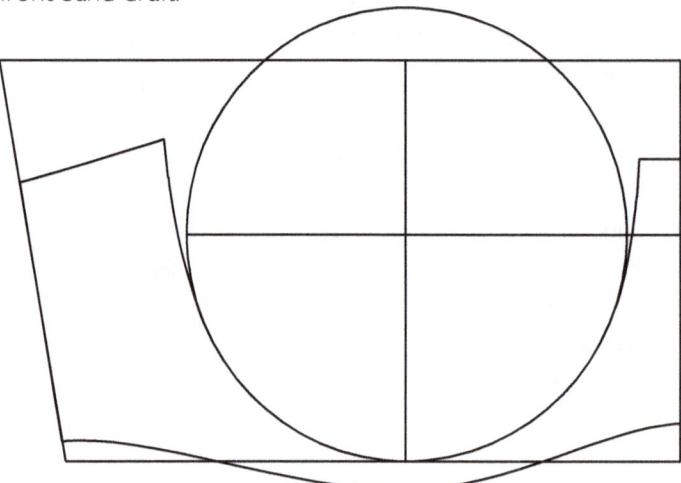

2. Vertical Grade Guides - To visually see where the grade hits the band, add the following vertical grade guides.

    a. Right side of the wire curve. This indicates the zero grade.

    b. Center line of the cup. This indicates the half wire grade.

    c. Left side of the wire curve. This indicates the full grade.

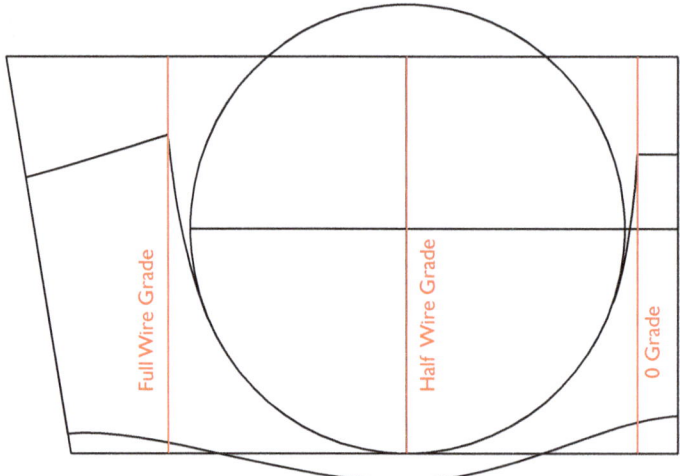

3. **Horizontal Grade Guides** - To visually see where the grade hits the band, add the following horizontal grade guides.

   a. Bottom of the circle. This indicates the zero grade.

   b. Center of the circle. This indicates the half grade

   c. Top of the circle. This will represent a full cup grade.

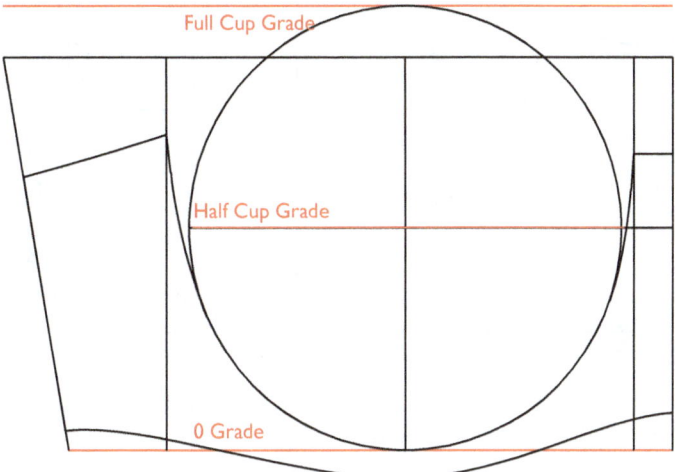

4. **Wire Grade Guide**

   a. Imperial Grade - Divide the area between the half and full cup into five equal amounts. Each division is a 1/32" grade. Add this increment to the half grade of each of the division lines. The first mark above the half cup is 6/32" or 3/16".

   b. Metric Grade - Divide the area between the half and full cup into four equal amounts. Each division is a 1mm grade. Add this increment to the half grade of each of the division lines. The first mark above the half cup is 5mm.

   c. Find the closest division for the top of the wire grade. For the center front of the wire grade, one can alternate between a 6/32" (3/16") and 7/32" (or 5mm to 6mm), but the side of the wire grade will be a constant 7/32" or 6mm grade.

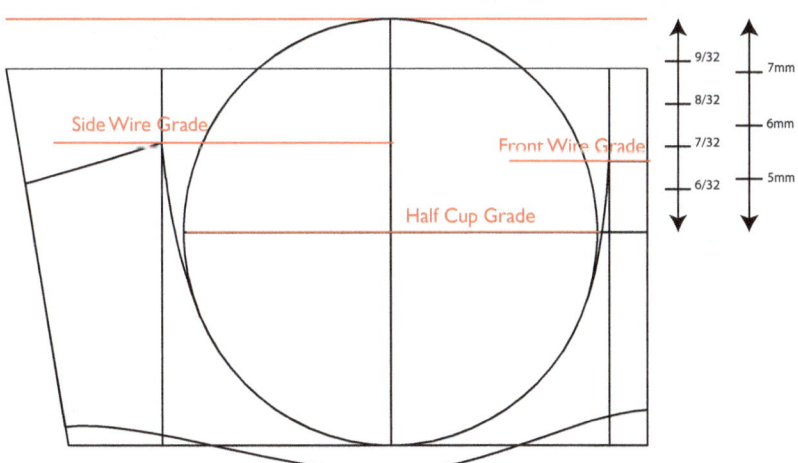

5. a. At the top of the wire at the center front, draw in the new wire height.

  b. On the left side of the wire, draw in your new wire height.

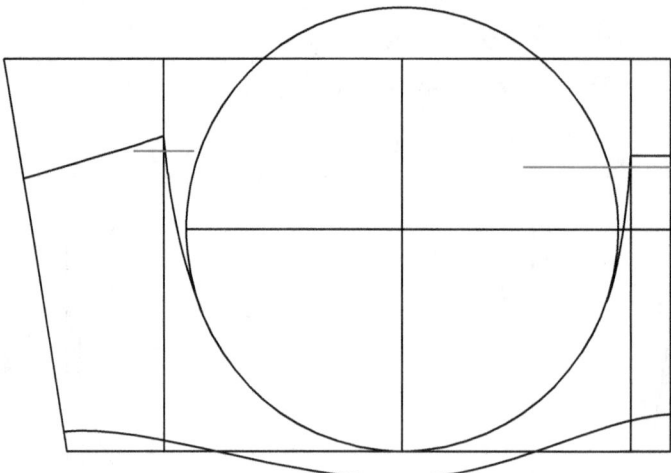

6. The height of the side seam grades at the same amount as the center front of the band alternating between 3/16" and 7/32" (5mm and 6mm) or utilize a custom amount based on preference.

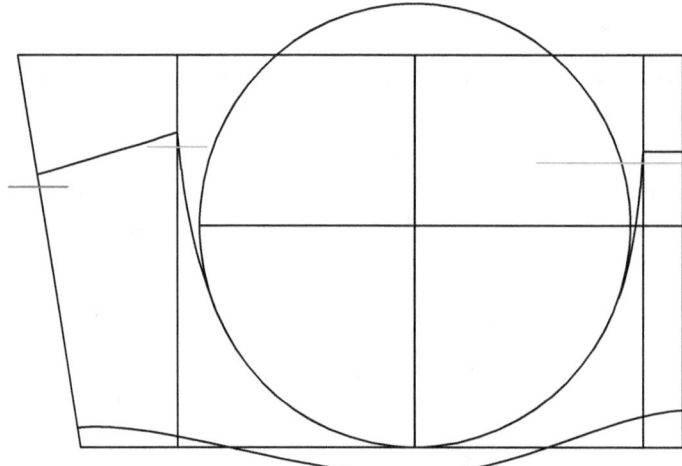

7. Create the center of the wire grade by drawing in the center cup half grade change of one size both horizontally and vertically.

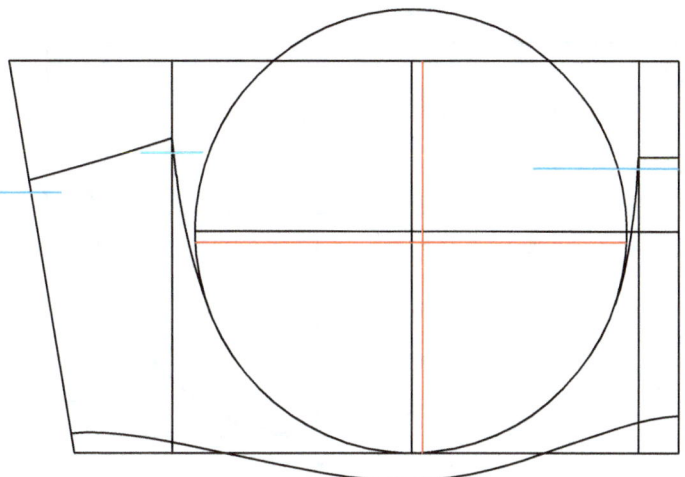

8. Take the compass and draw in a circle using the new center point at the tip of the compass.

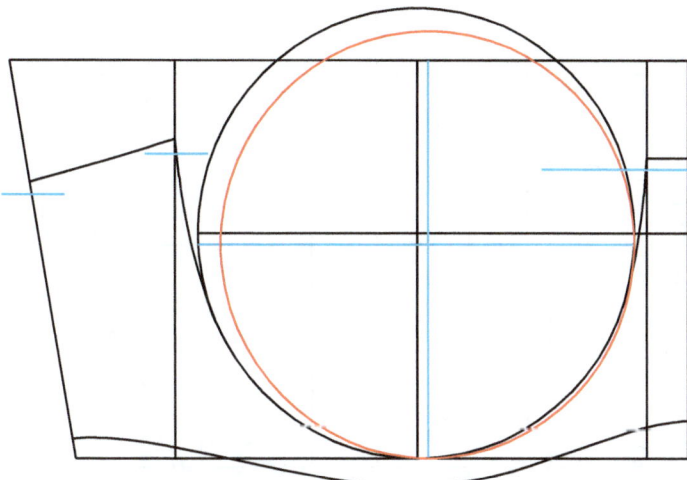

9. The left side of the wire curve changes in width by the full grade.

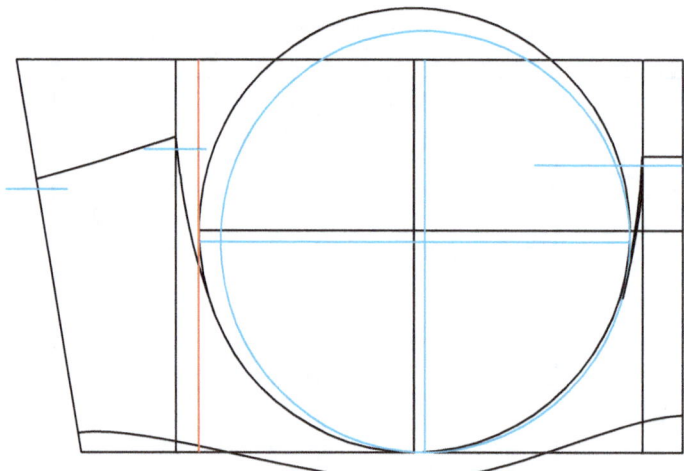

10. a. Blend a curve from the lower half of the circle up to the top of the new wire line.

    b. Draw in the new underarm curve from the side seam to the side of the wire curve.

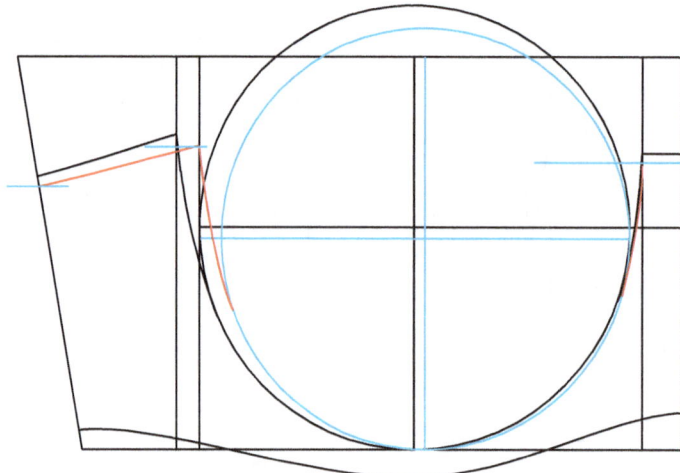

BACK BAND

11. Horizontal Grade Guides - Align the center back of the back band vertically on the paper. Line the back up to the front and duplicate the horizontal guides from the front to the back at a perpendicular angle from the side seam. There are no vertical changes for the back band for the cup grade.

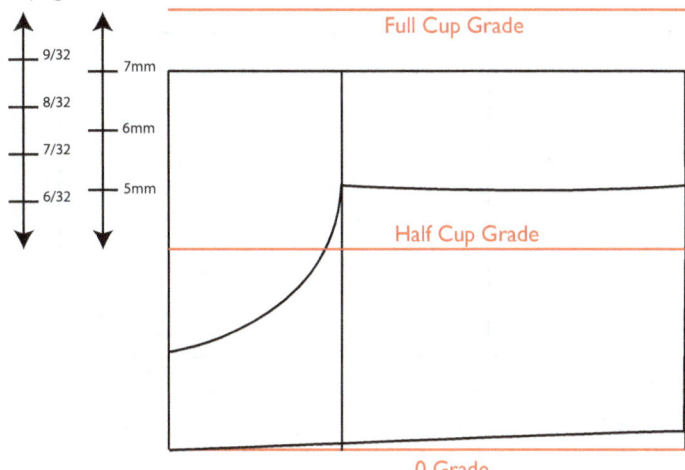

12. The center back increases or decreases in size based on the size of the hook & eye attachment. For this example, the center back is decreased by 1/2" or 12.5mm for a hook & eye with one less row of hooks & eyes.

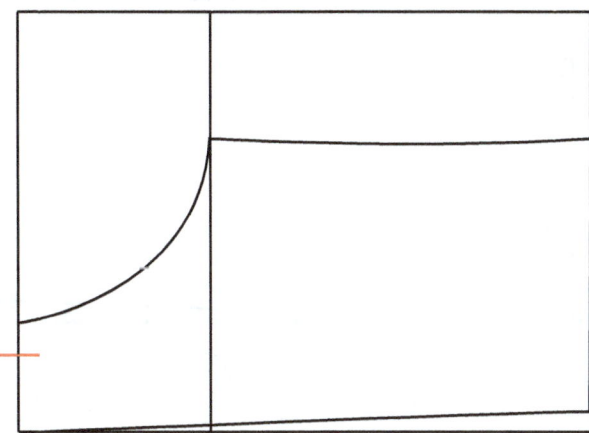

13. The side seam height and strap point height have the same grade as the front.

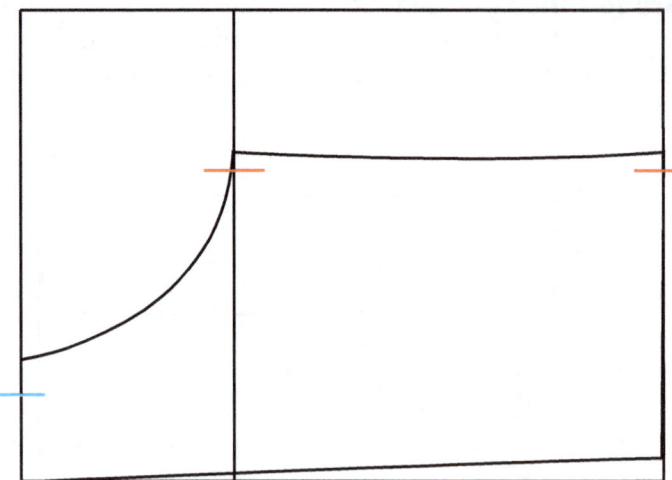

14. Draw in the new neckline curve from the center back, through the strap point and to the side seam. Match this curve up to the front to be sure the transition from front to back is a smooth shape.

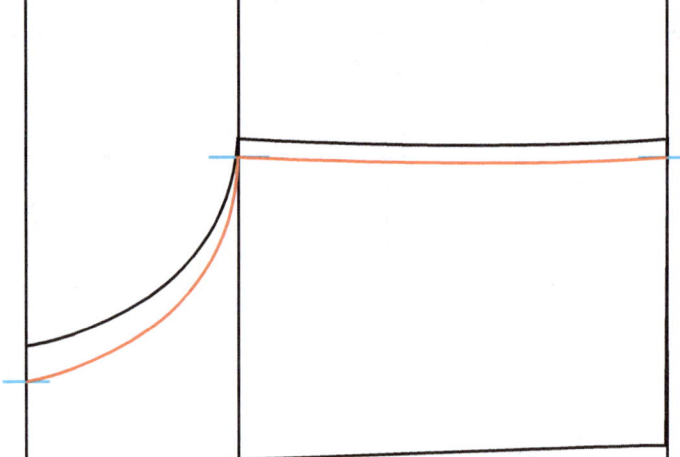

GRADING BY HAND FOR BAND SIZES

FRONT BAND

1. Vertical Grade Guides - The front band grade only applies to the traditional grading method in which the grade is split between the front and back grade. Indicate the full grade amount at the side seam. There are no horizontal grade points for the band grade.

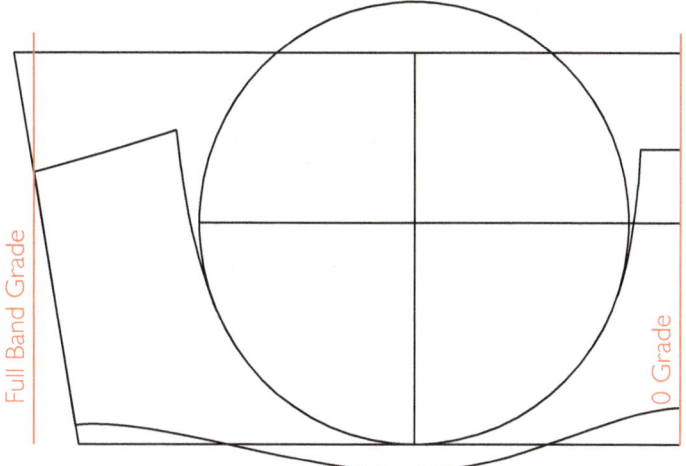

2. Increase the width of the side seam by the grade amount of 1/2" or 12.5mm, keeping the horizontal point stationary.

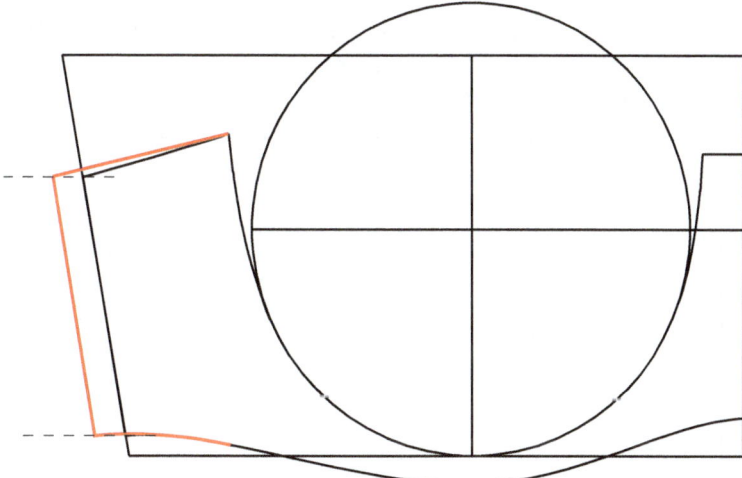

BACK BAND

3. Vertical Grade Guides - The back grade method is similar for both grading techniques discussed. The only difference is the amount of the grade. Align the center back of the back band vertically on the paper and add the following vertical grade guides. There are no horizontal grades for the band size grade.

    a. The strap point. This indicates the third grade.

    b. Center of the back band. This indicates the half grade.

    c. The side seam. This indicates the full grade.

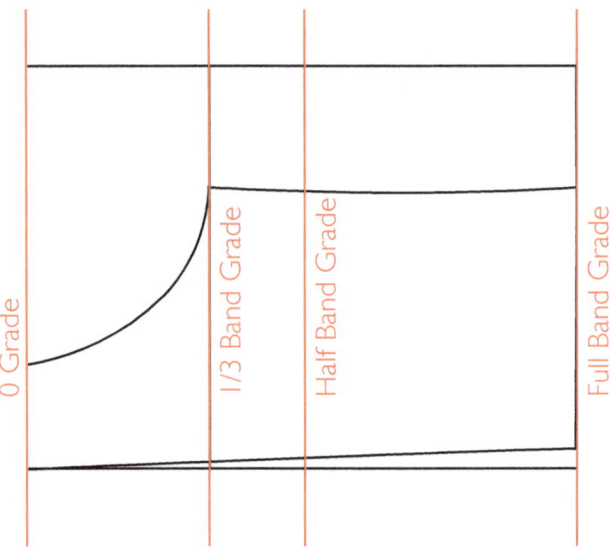

4. Following the predetermined grade rules, there are only two places for adjustments: the side seam and the back strap position. Indicate the grade point amounts from the side seam and strap point parallel to the original points.

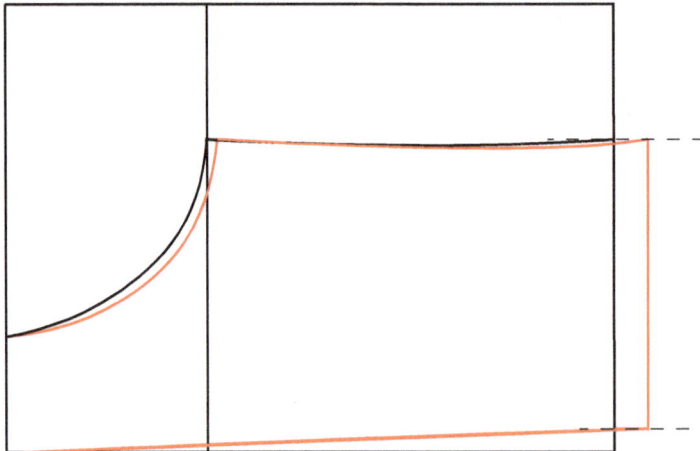

WIRE LINE ADJUSTMENTS

After creating the band grade, compile a list of measurements from the band wire lines. Use the following chart to compare the total wire line length of the graded pattern to the lengths of the wires used for reach size. There should be at least 1/2" or 12.5mm of wire play on the wire line to allow for sewing and wire movement.

Pattern Size	Pattern Wire Line	Wire Size	Wire Length	Adjustments

GRADING IN ILLUSTRATION SOFTWARE

The first step is to prepare the pattern to grade in the software. If the pattern was not drafted in Adobe® Illustrator®, the pattern needs to be imported into the software. The simplest way to transfer a pattern from paper to computer, is with the use of a flatbed scanner at 100%. If unsure that the scan is at 100%, draw a measurement square on the pattern. A 1" by 1" or a 1cm by 1cm square is ideal.

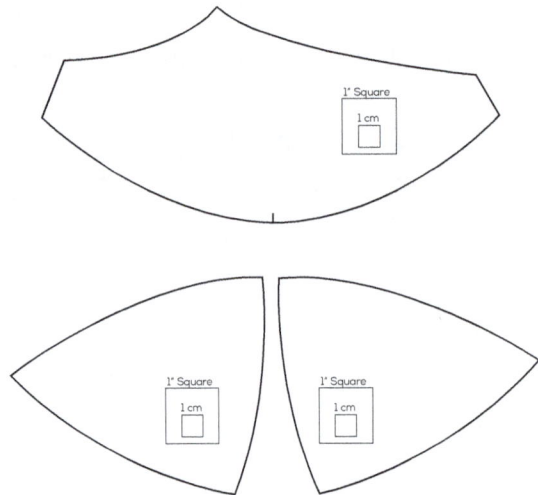

If the pattern has been imported through a scanner, use the basic vector drawing tools to recreate the pattern pieces. Be sure to add all necessary notches.

GRADING BY SOFTWARE FOR WIRE SIZES

FRONT BAND

1. For grading the band with Adobe® Illustrator®, join all lines to create one path. One option is to keep the front band as a single pattern piece, but in these steps, it is divided for a variation to hand grading. Below is a more in depth grade segmentation of the front band. This can also be used for grading by hand, but it will prove more useful for computer grading.

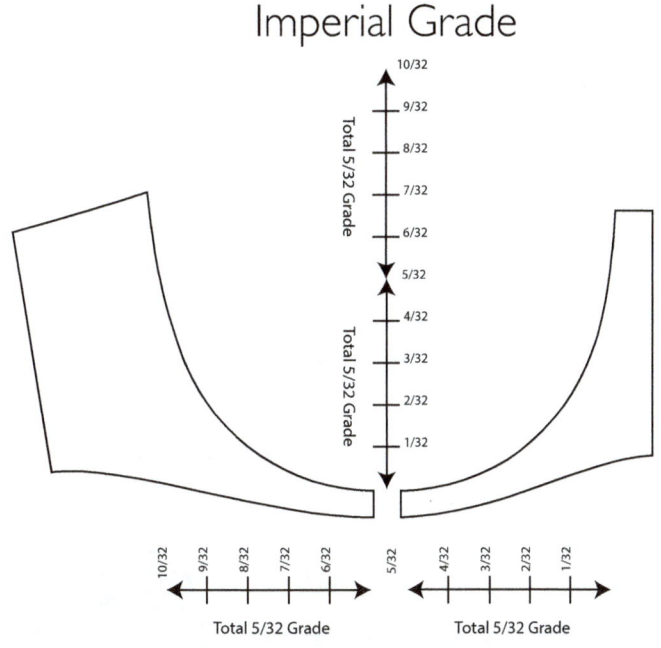

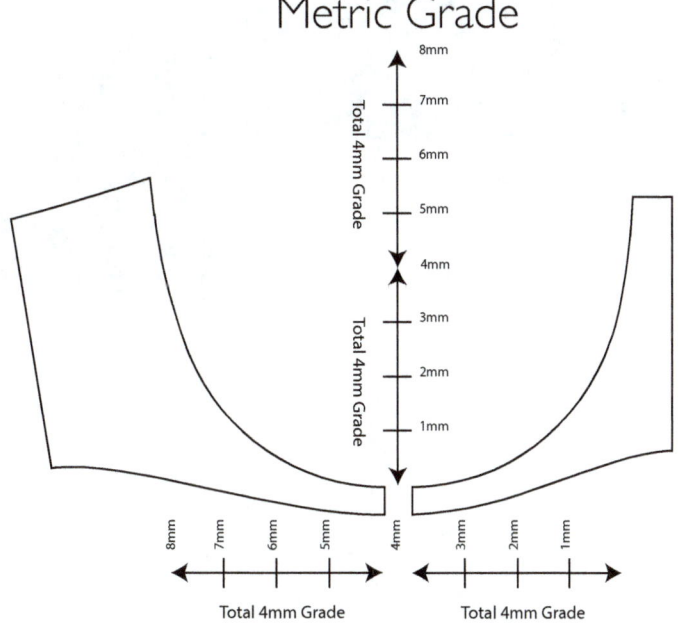

2. When beginning the grade, it may be helpful to indicate the exact amounts on the screen using the *Text Tool*. When grading in Adobe® Illustrator®, horizontal and vertical amounts are graded at the same time. Horizontal amounts are on the X axis, moving from left to right and vertical amounts are on the Y axis, moving up and down. Program settings indicate the direction negative amounts move. Note that these settings are not universal settings.

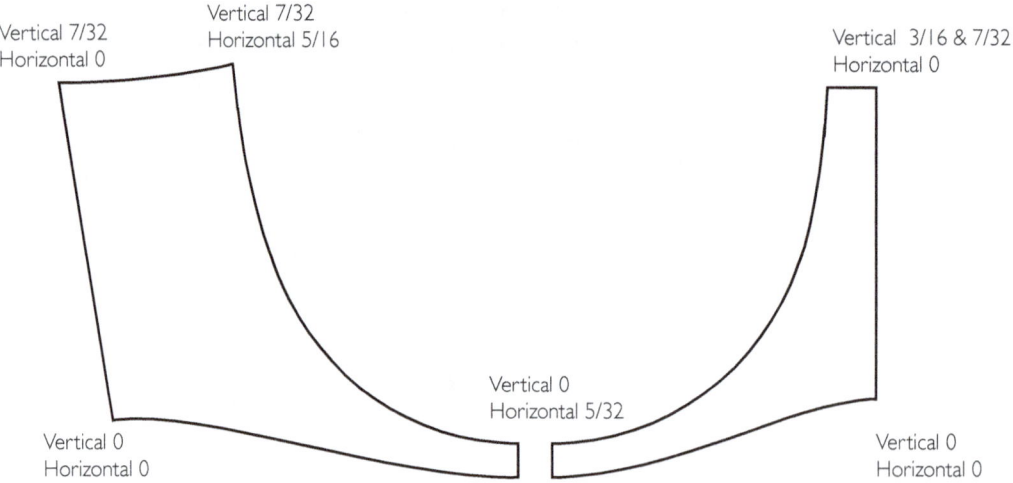

3. Copy the pattern and place directly in front of the previous pattern. Name both the new and original pattern pieces and lock the original in the *Layers Window*.

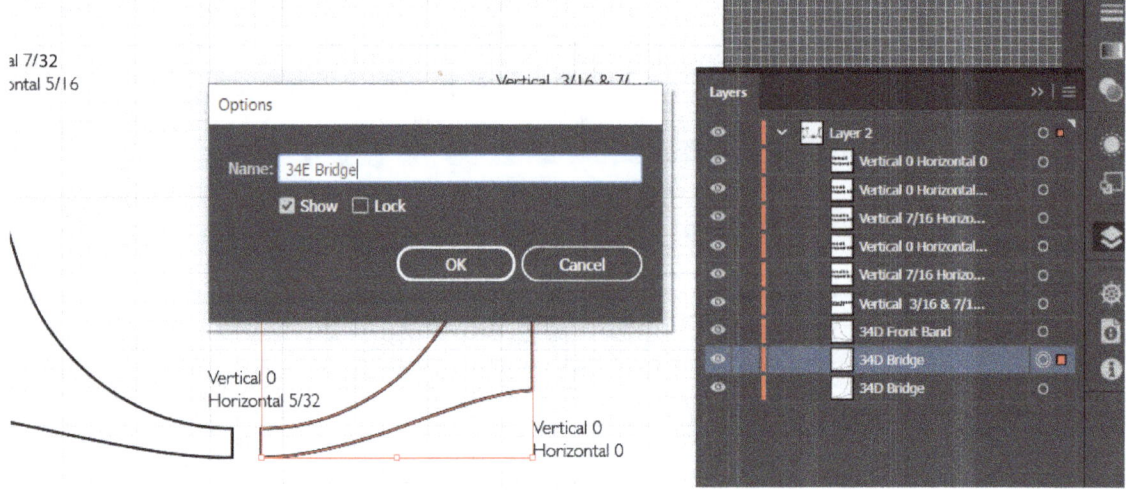

Advanced / Bra Band Grading | 235

4. Select the grade point with the *Direct Selection Tool* and hit the *Enter Key*. Enter the *Horizontal* and *Vertical* grade amounts for each point and each new size.

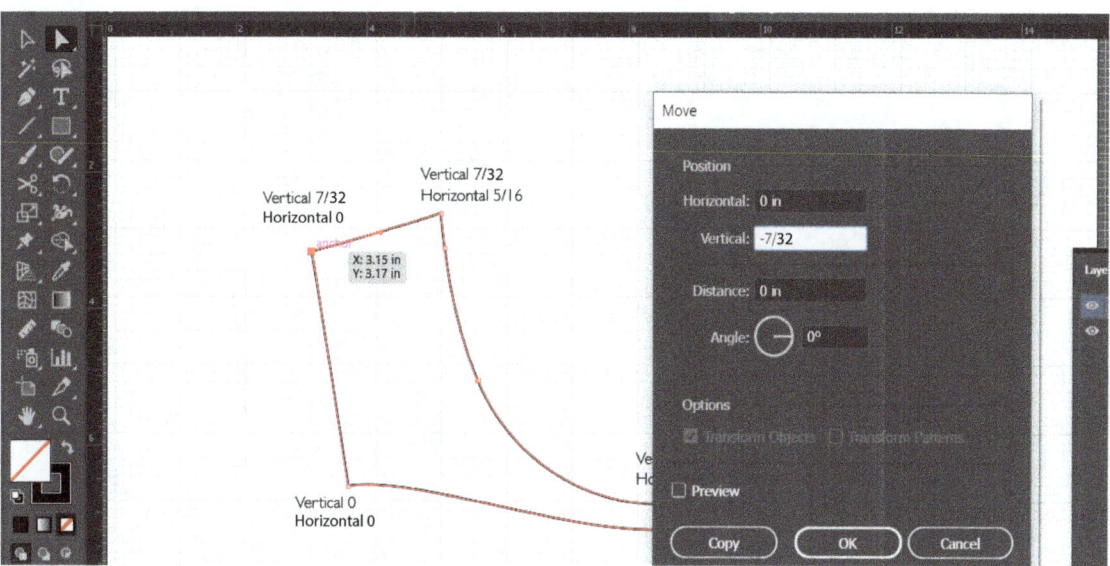

5. For points around the curve, manually move the point with arrow keys to smooth the curve or create grade amounts for each point based on the grade rules on the previous pages. Shown here is an additional grade rule for a point on the curve on the side of the wire curve.

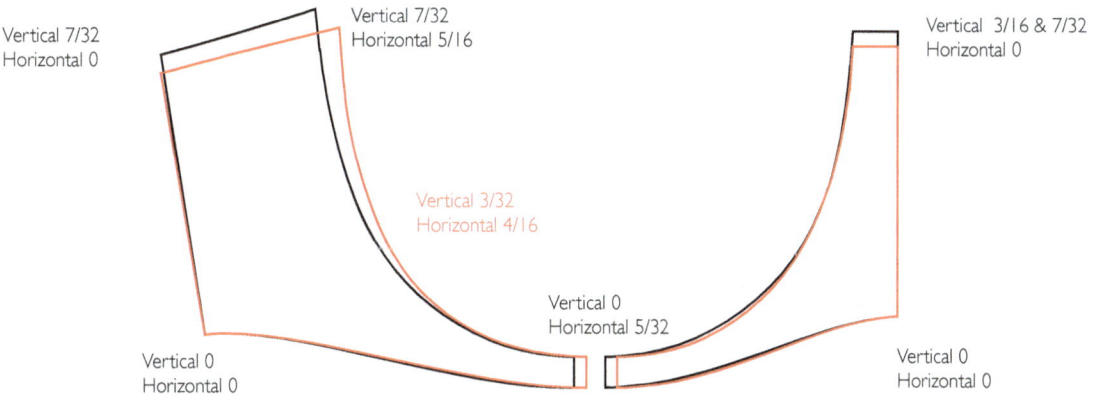

BACK BAND

6. Align the center back vertically on the screen. Label the grade amounts for each point on the back band.

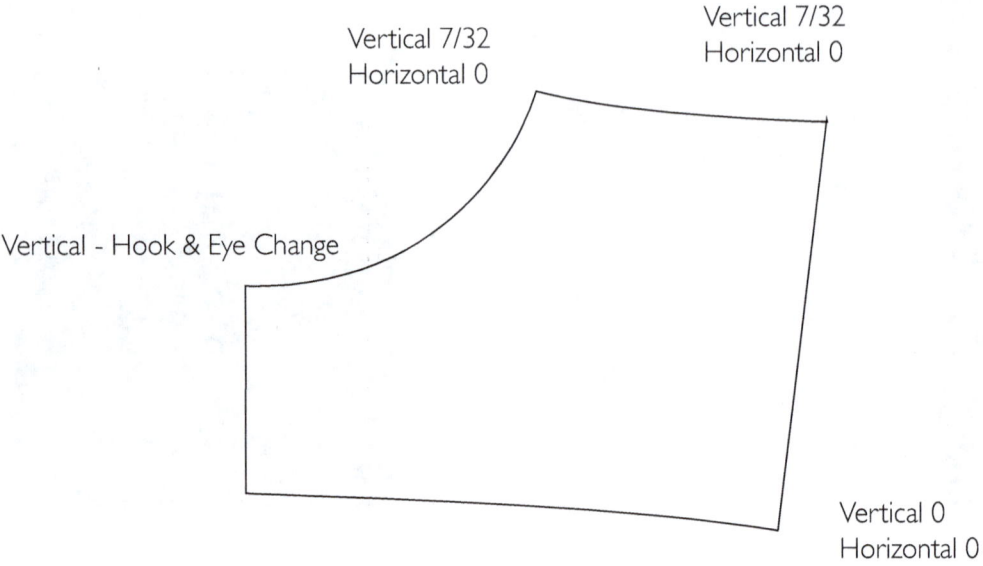

7. Follow the steps previously demonstrated. Grade the new size for the back.

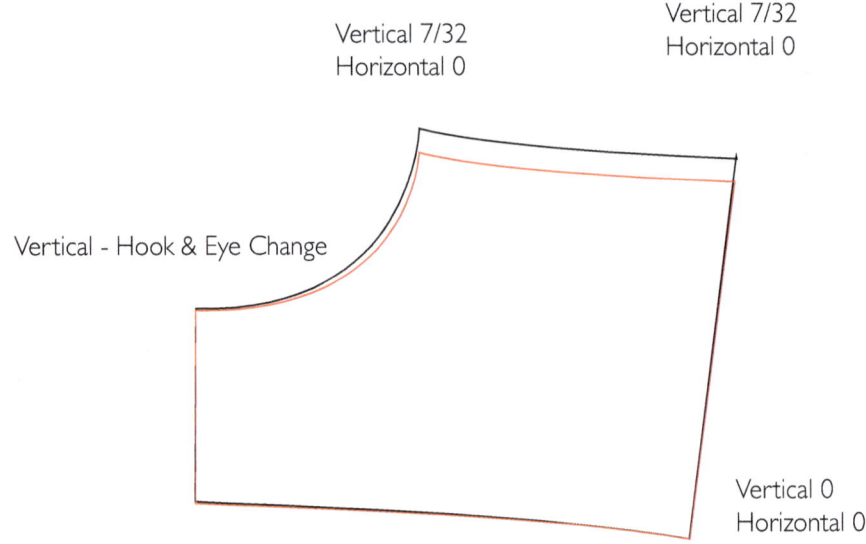

CHAPTER 23
BRA CUP GRADING

Grading a cup is unlike any other grading. The 0 grade falls at the apex of the cup and the grade radiates from the apex, meaning that the largest graded amount on a cup is technically a half grade. For grading a cup, create a grade rule for the cup size grade.

The cup changes by 1/2" or 12.5mm in diameter for the US, UK and all European countries. Australia utilizes a different cup grade entirely. The following chart breaks down the grade into rules for half and quarter cup grades. All the following directions will refer to this chart. These directions describe grading down one size. The same method applies to grading up a size.

	US/UK	Europe	Australia
Full Diameter	1/2"	12.5mm	10mm
Half Cup Grade	1/4"	6mm	5mm
1/4 Cup Grade	1/8"	3mm	2.5mm

SISTER SIZING A CUP GRADE

It is common place in this industry to grade cups using "sister sizing." Sister sizing refers to stepping up or stepping down a cup and band size. For example, a 36D cup is the same as a 34E (DD), 32F (DDD), 38C and 40B. The volume for the bust remains the same and so does the wire, but the band changes the position in which the bust volume is distributed on the body.

It is possible to create any cup size from an existing cup. If a grade start size is a 36E and there is a need to grade the range of 30A through 40F, grade the cup range of 36AAAA to 36G. Even though the AAAA does not ever exist in reality, keeping the grade as a "36" allows you to grade your range visually without confusion. A 36AAAA is the same as a 30A cup.

The grading of a cup can be done in three methods, radial grading, grid grading and scaling. Directions are provided for hand grading of the radial and grid grading methods. For computer grading with illustration software, the scaling method is demonstrated. The scaling method can only be done by computer and is very similar to radial grading in methodology, but very different in execution.

GRADING BY HAND

RADIAL GRADING METHOD

1. Draw a line down the center and across the paper. Line up the cups at the center point. These directions can be adapted for a two piece cup by using the same grading principles.

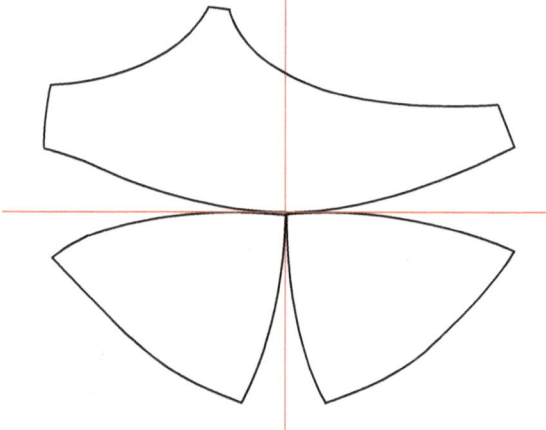

2. Circular Grade Guides - To visually see where the grade hits the band, add the following circular grade guides.

    a. The apex indicates the zero grade.

    b. Center of the cups. This indicates the quarter grade.

    c. Outer edge of the cup. This indicates the half grade.

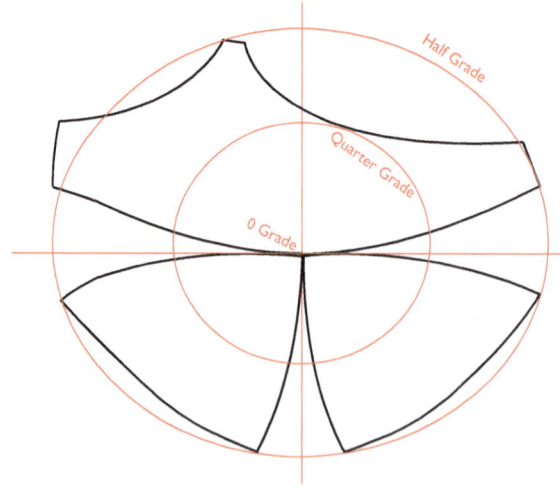

3. Diagonal Grade Guides - To visually see where the grade hits the band, add a guide line starting at the apex and passing through each grade point on the wire line.

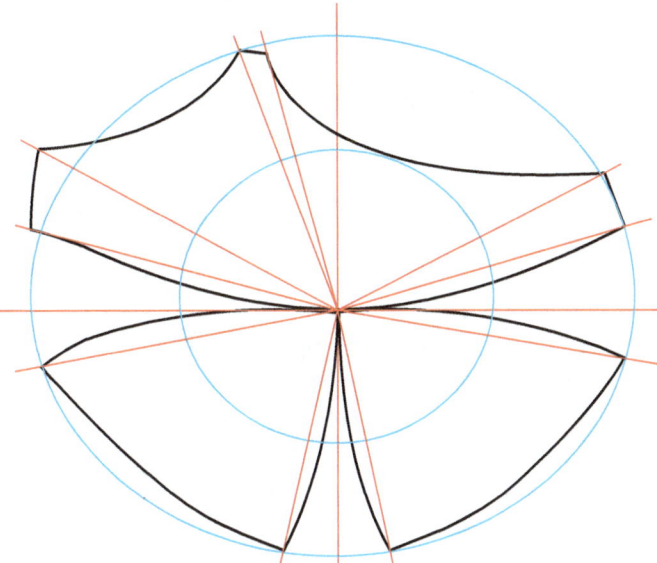

4. To decrease the outer points of the cup by one size, measure on each line, the half grade amount. Indicate with a cross mark at the end to differentiate the markings.

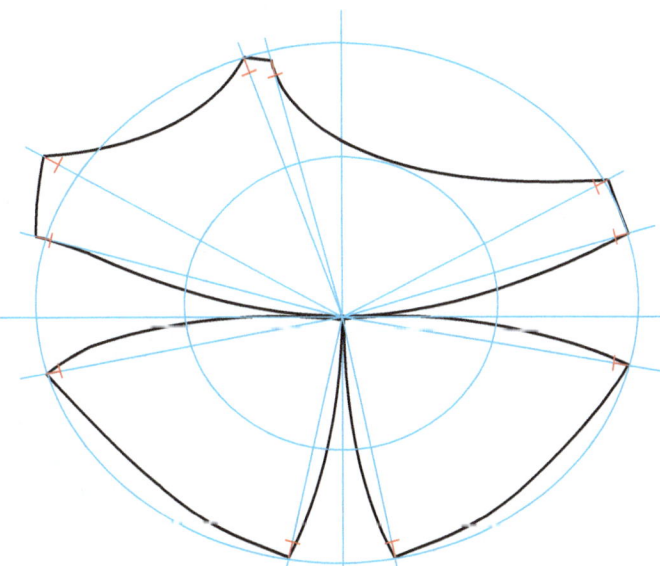

5. On the outside curves of the cup, mark the center of point with the closest grade. The neckline would use the quarter grade. The interior seam curves fall at the quarter curve. The cup seam curves were marked just off the guideline for visualization.

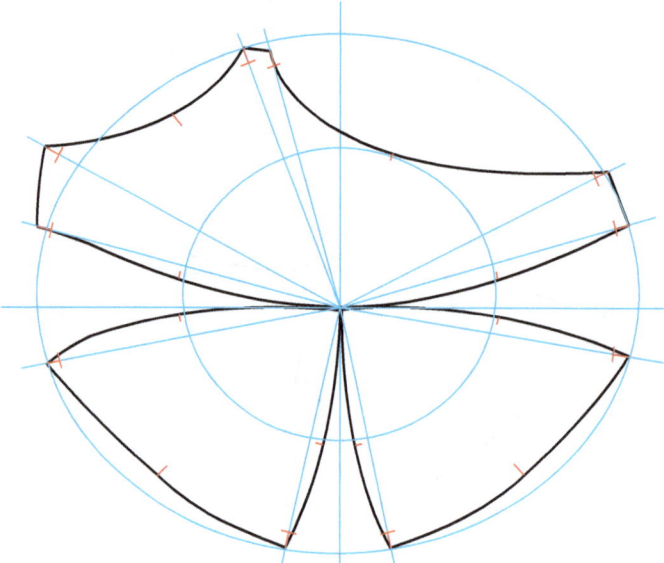

6. Draw in the new cup shapes, connecting each new grade point.

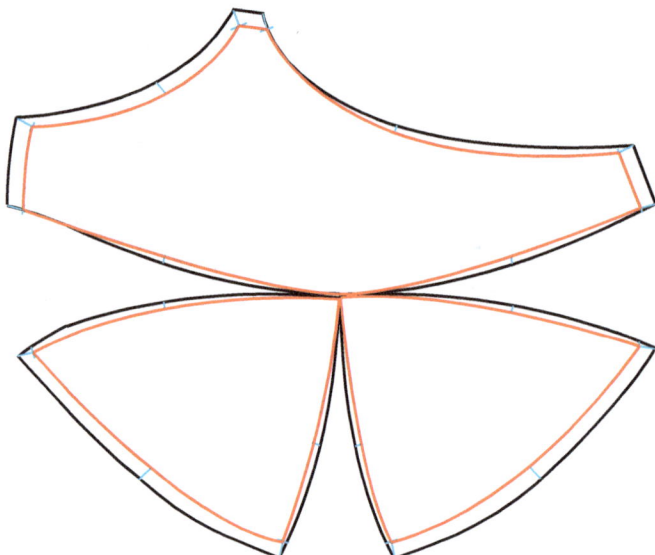

7. Once the grade is complete, use the flexible ruler to measure the new wire curve of each cup to verify that the length matches the wire line of the next wire size down on the band grade. Refer to the chart compiled in the previous chapter. Modify the top of the wire line to meet the length requirement of the band. Utilize the charts at the end of this section to compare measurements.

GRID GRADING METHOD

1. Draw a line down the center and across the paper. Line up the cups at the center point. These directions can be adapted for a two piece cup by using the same grading principles.

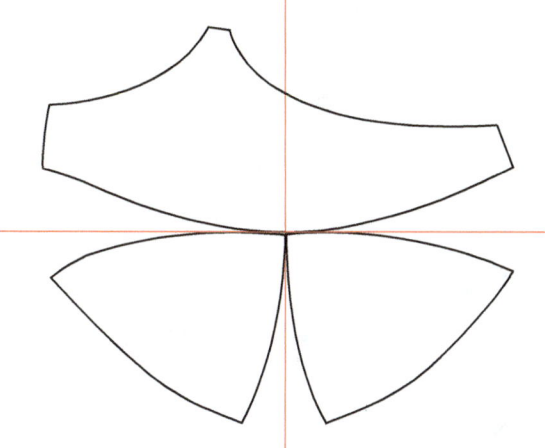

2. Horizontal Grade Guides - To visually see where the grade hits the band, add the following horizontal grade guides.

   a. The apex indicates the zero grade.

   b. Center of the cups, between the apex and outer edge of the cup. This indicates the quarter grade.

   c. Top and bottom edge of the cups. This indicates the half grade.

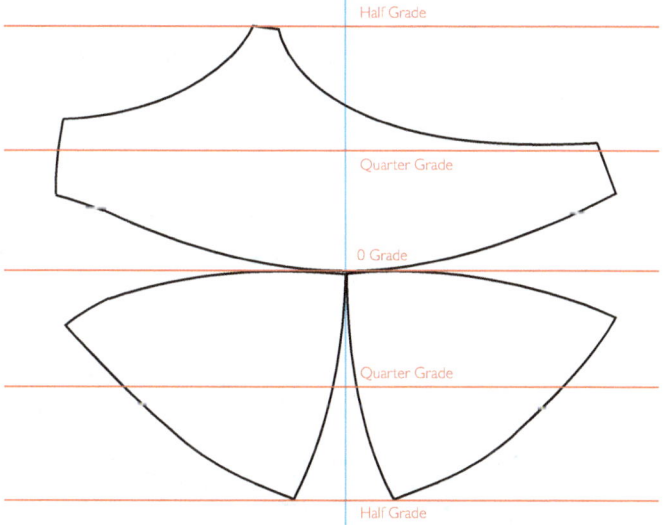

3. Vertical Grade Guides - To visually see where the grade hits the band, add the following vertical grade guides.

  a. The apex indicates the zero grade.

  b. Center of the cups between the apex and outer wire line. This indicates the quarter grade.

  c. Left and right edge of the cups. This indicates the half grade.

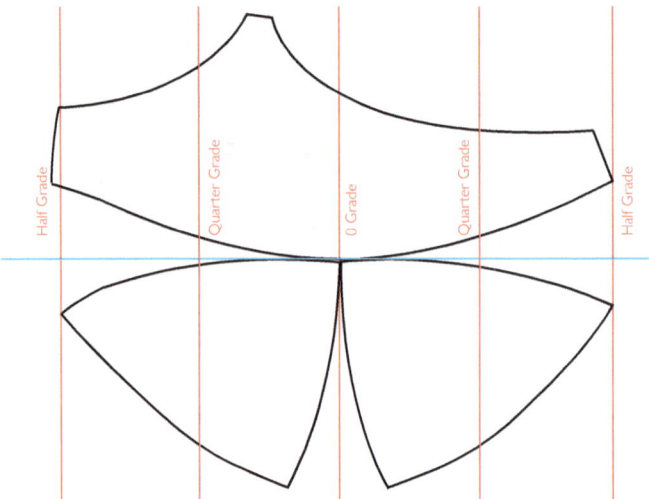

4. Begin with the vertical grade. This is the grade from the top and bottom towards the center line.

  a. Strap point, decrease the height by the full half grade amount.

  b. Top of the wire line on the cup, decrease the grade by the quarter grade amount. Indicate with a cross mark.

  c. Bottom of the top cup wire line, decrease the grade by half of the quarter grade amount. Indicate with a cross mark.

  d. Top side wire line on the bottom cups, raise the grade by half of the quarter grade amount. Indicate with a cross mark.

  e. Bottom of the cup, raise the grade by the half grade amount.

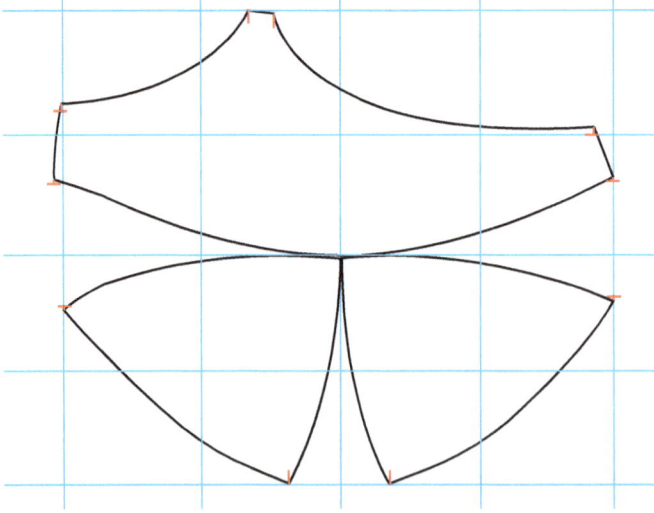

5. Continue with the horizontal grade. This is the grade from the left and right sides toward the center line.

   a. Left and right sides of the top cup and bottom cup, grade the half grade towards the center line. Indicate with a cross mark.

   b. Strap point and the bottom of the cups, grade half of the quarter grade towards the center line.

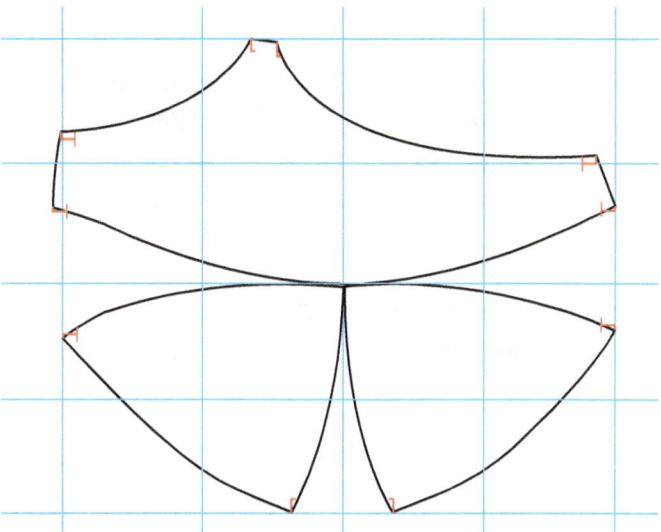

6. Create the new cup shapes.

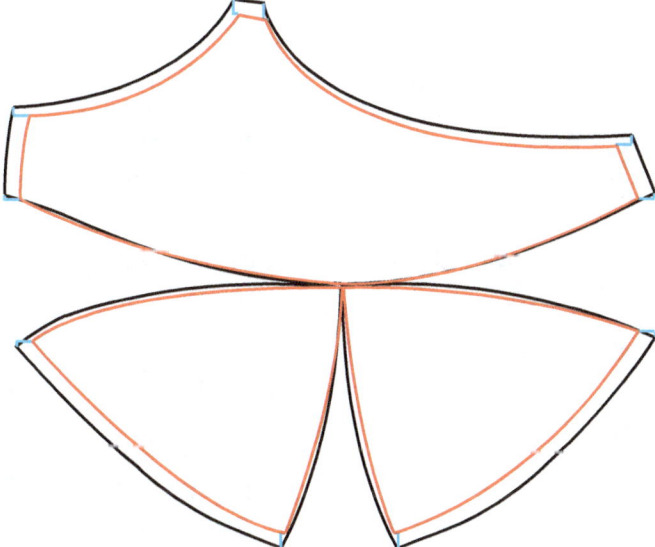

7. Once the grade is complete, use the flexible ruler to measure the new wire curve of each cup to verify that the length matches the wire line of the next wire size down on the band grade. Refer to the chart compiled in the previous chapter. Modify the top of the wire line to meet the length requirement of the band. Utilize the charts at the end of this section to compare measurements.

ADJUSTMENTS FOR CUP PATTERNS

It is important that the cup seam lines match the seams of each pattern piece, including the band. Refer to the wire line measurements from the band grades in the previous chapter and record those measurements in this chart. The cup seam lines should match within 1/32" to 1/16" (1mm to 2mm).

Cup Piece Name	Size	Wire Curve
Power Bar	36D	3 7/8
Bottom Cup	36D	5 1/4
Top Cup	36D	1 31/32
Total Cup	36D	11 3/32
Total Band	36D	11 1/16
Difference		1/32

Cup Piece Name	Size	Wire Curve
Total Cup		
Total Band		
Difference		

Cup Piece Name	Size	Wire Curve
Total Cup		
Total Band		
Difference		

Cup Piece Name	Size	Wire Curve
Total Cup		
Total Band		
Difference		

Cup Piece Name	Size	Wire Curve
Total Cup		
Total Band		
Difference		

Cup Piece Name	Size	Wire Curve		Cup Piece Name	Size	Wire Curve
Total Cup				**Total Cup**		
Total Band				**Total Band**		
Difference				**Difference**		

Cup Piece Name	Size	Wire Curve		Cup Piece Name	Size	Wire Curve
Total Cup				**Total Cup**		
Total Band				**Total Band**		
Difference				**Difference**		

Cup Piece Name	Size	Wire Curve		Cup Piece Name	Size	Wire Curve
Total Cup				**Total Cup**		
Total Band				**Total Band**		
Difference				**Difference**		

Cup Piece Name	Size	Wire Curve		Cup Piece Name	Size	Wire Curve
Total Cup				**Total Cup**		
Total Band				**Total Band**		
Difference				**Difference**		

GRADING ON THE COMPUTER

Computer grading is most accurate using the scaling method. This cannot easily be duplicated by hand, but can easily be graded on the computer. Since the cup grows proportional from the apex, it makes the most sense to grade an amount that scales the full 1/2" or 12.5mm growth of a bra cup.

Before diving into grading on the computer, whether it is on Adobe® Illustrator® or any pattern drafting and grading software, one needs to compile specific data needs to be compiled to make proportional scaling possible. This specific information stems from the cup horizontal measurement.

For a horizontal seamed cup, take the current diameter measurement of the cup being grading. This amount may be slightly over the original amount due to seam shaping. For any draft, other than a design with a horizontal seam, use the horizontal measurement from the sloper.

To determine the amount a cup is scaled, the starting cup diameter must be defined. Once the starting measurement is defined, determine the measurements for all sizes in the range. The example chart below has the 36E as the starting cup with the horizontal measurement of 10 1/4". Above and below the starting size, the cup sizes are defined including the diameters associated with each size.

The percentages in the Up and Down columns are the amounts that the previous size is scaled to achieve the desired diameter. To determine the amount to scale up, divide the new diameter by the old diameter. The same steps are taken for the down scale. Divide the new cup diameter by the old diameter. This method works for both imperial and metric amounts.

Cup Name	Diameter	Up	Down
36A	8 3/4	-	94.59 %
36B	9 1/4	-	94.87 %
36C	9 3/4	-	95.12 %
Cup Measurement - 36E	**10 1/4**	-	-
36E	10 3/4	104.88 %	-
36F	11 1/4	104.65 %	-
36G	11 3/4	104.44 %	-

Use the blank chart below to compile this data. It is recommended to make a new chart for every bra graded. I created an Excel spreadsheet that assists with all the grading steps, including this chart. The spreadsheet is available on Porcelynne.com as an option under the third edition of the book.

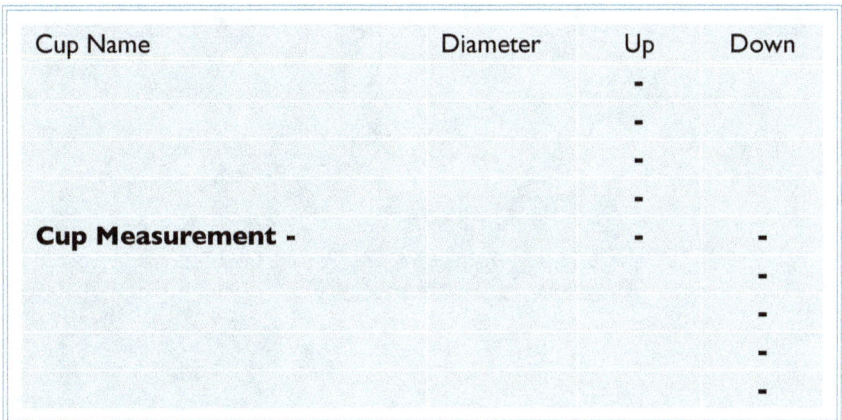

GRADING IN ILLUSTRATION SOFTWARE

1. Group and/or join all lines for each pattern piece. Rename each pattern piece with the base size and piece name.

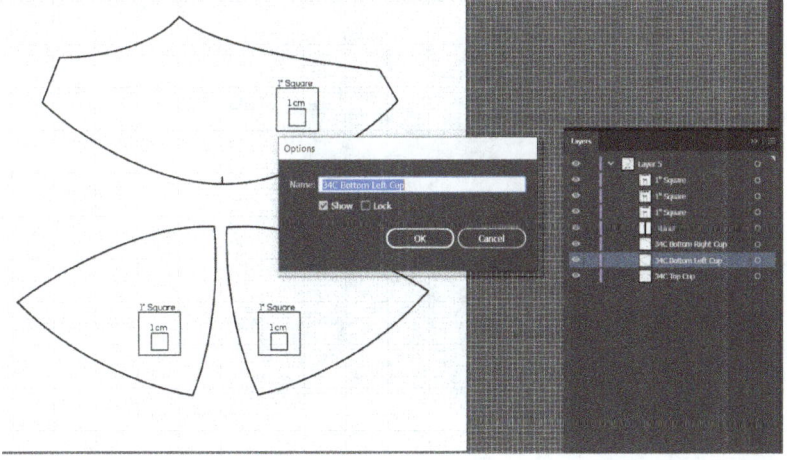

2. a. Copy the base size and rename the new cups as the next size up or down, depending on the direction of the grade.

   b. After renaming the copy, select all the cup pattern pieces of the new size, and navigate to *Object -> Transform -> Scale*.

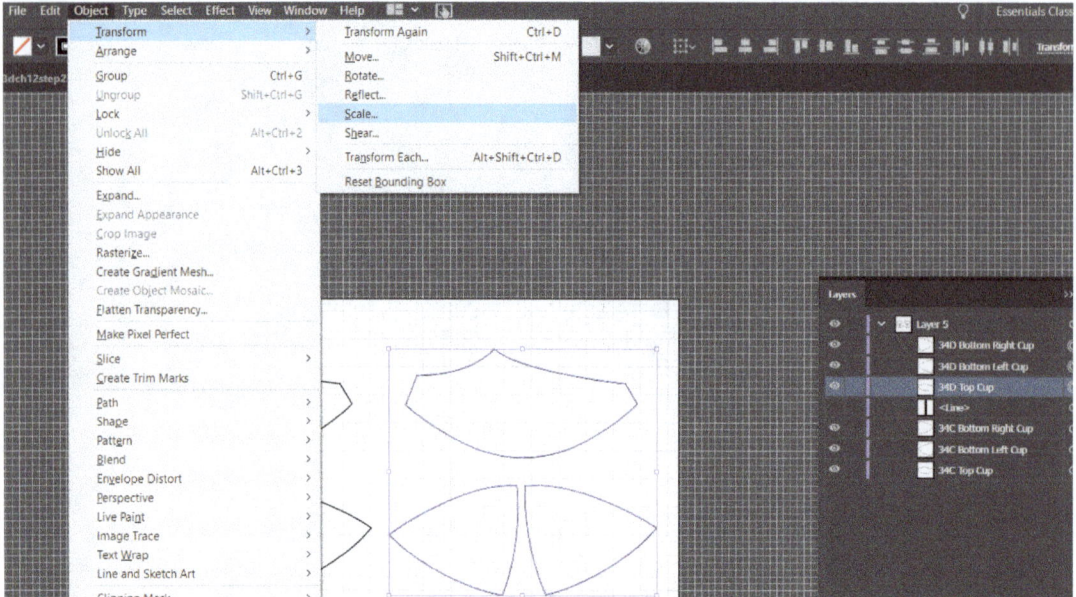

3. Select a uniform scale and use the percentages on the grade chart to grade up or down.

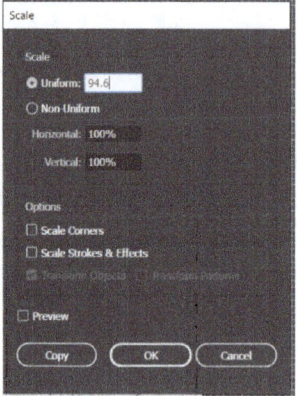

4. Repeat these steps each size in the range being graded. Copy the last size that was graded and scale to the new size. In order to avoid selecting the wrong pattern, use the **Layers Window** to lock and name each size after grading.

PATTERNS

Chapter 24: Pattern Instructions. 251

30A-30F. 253

32A-32F 257

34A-34F. 261

36A-36F. 265

38A-38F. 269

40A-40F. 273

Appendix A: PolyPattern® by Polytropon 279

CHAPTER 24
PATTERN INSTRUCTIONS

To select a size for these bra patterns, follow the charts below. Note that these correspond to all patterns by Porcelynne. These size charts are specific for these patterns and may not correlate to patterns by other designers.

These patterns were drafted for a torso shape in which the chest/overbust area is 4" or 10cm wider than the underbust measurement. See the intermediate section for adjusting the patterns for different torso shapes. The following page contains a metric measurement chart for these patterns.

US/UK BRA SIZE - IMPERIAL
Measurements in Inches

Under Bust Measurement	Full Bust Measurement							
	31	32	33	34	35	36	37	38
28-29	30A	30B	30C	30D	30E	30F		
30-31			32A	32B	32C	32D	32E	32F
32-33					34A	34B	34C	34D
34-35							36A	36B

Under Bust Measurement	Full Bust Measurement							
	39	40	41	42	43	44	45	46
32-33	34E	34F						
34-35	36C	36D	36E	36F				
36-37	38A	38B	38C	38D	38E	38F		
38-39			40A	40B	40C	40D	40E	40F

US/UK BRA SIZE - METRIC
Measurements in Centimeters

| Under Bust Measurement | \multicolumn{7}{c}{Full Bust Measurement} |

Under Bust Measurement	79-80	81-83	84-85	86-88	89-90	91-93	94-96	97-98
71-74	30A	30B	30C	30D	30E	30F		
75-79			32A	32B	32C	32D	32E	32F
80-84					34A	34B	34C	34D
85-89							36A	36B

Under Bust Measurement	99-100	101-103	104-105	106-108	109-120	121-122	123-124	125-127
80-84	34E	34F						
85-89	36C	36D	36E	36F				
90-94	38A	38B	38C	38D	38E	38F		
95-99			40A	40B	40C	40D	40E	40F

Patterns / 30A-30F | 253

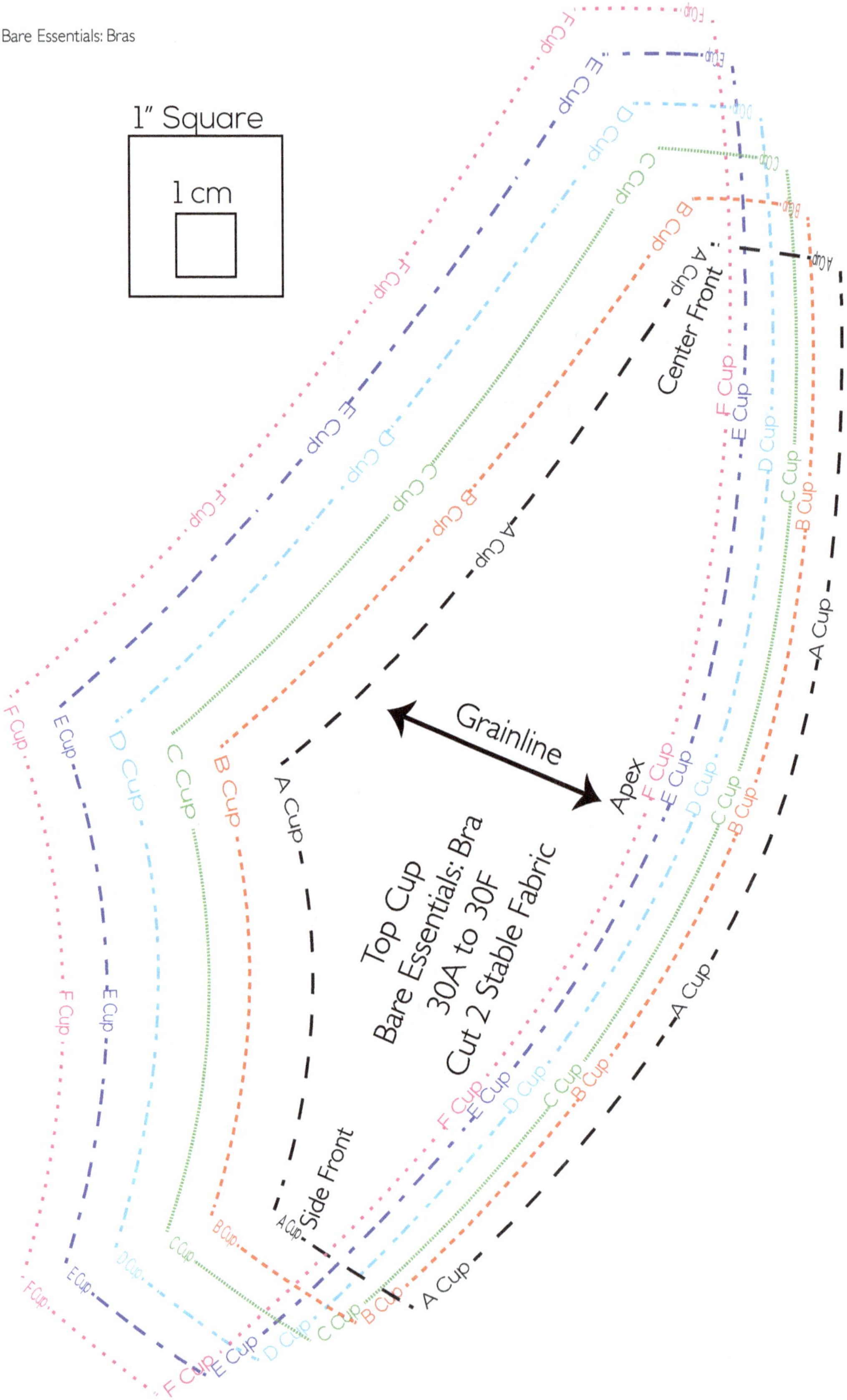
1" Square
1 cm
Top Cup
Bare Essentials: Bra
30A to 30F
Cut 2 Stable Fabric
Grainline
Apex
Center Front
Side Front
A Cup
B Cup
C Cup
D Cup
E Cup
F Cup

Patterns / 30A-30F | 255

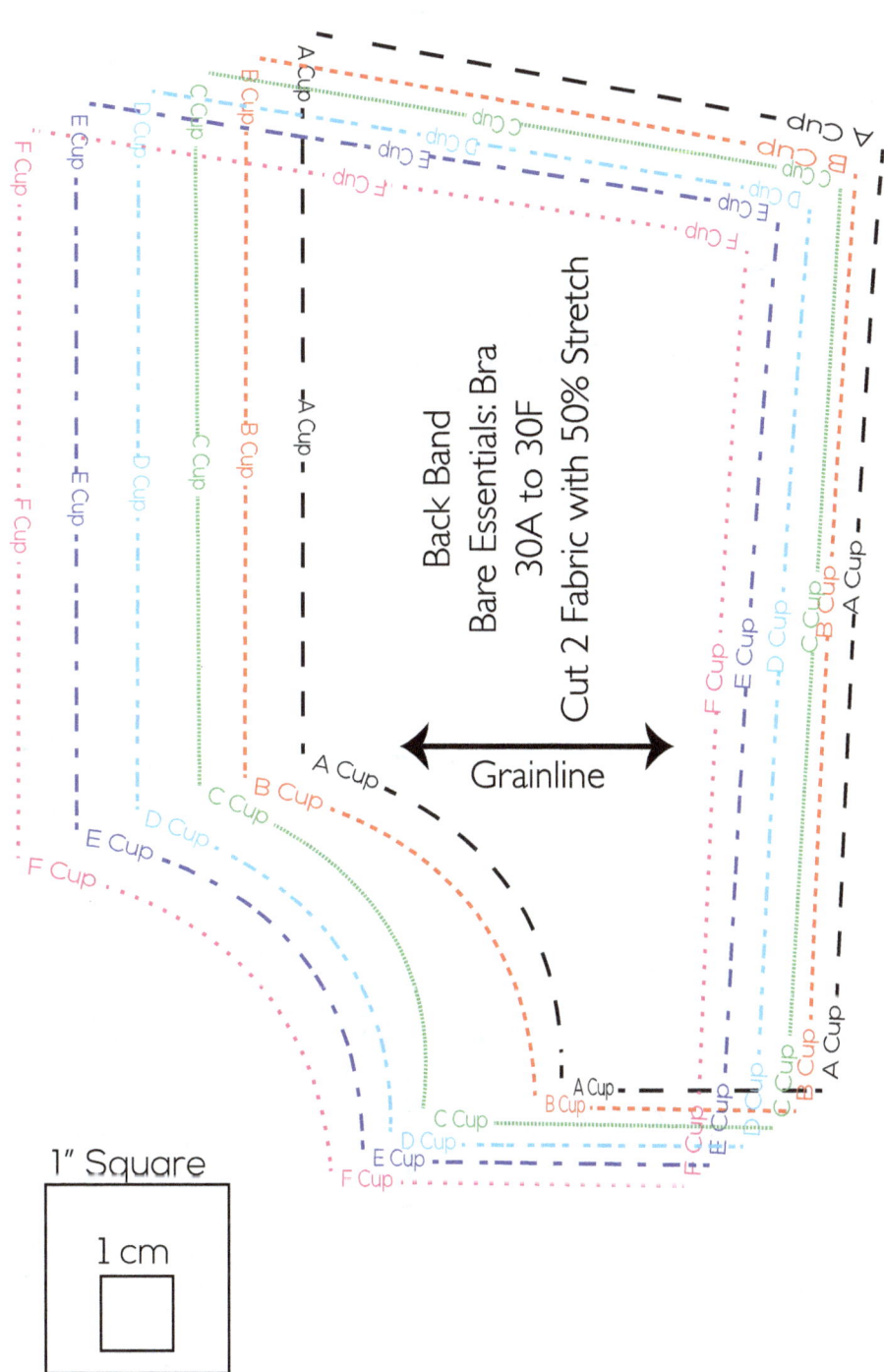

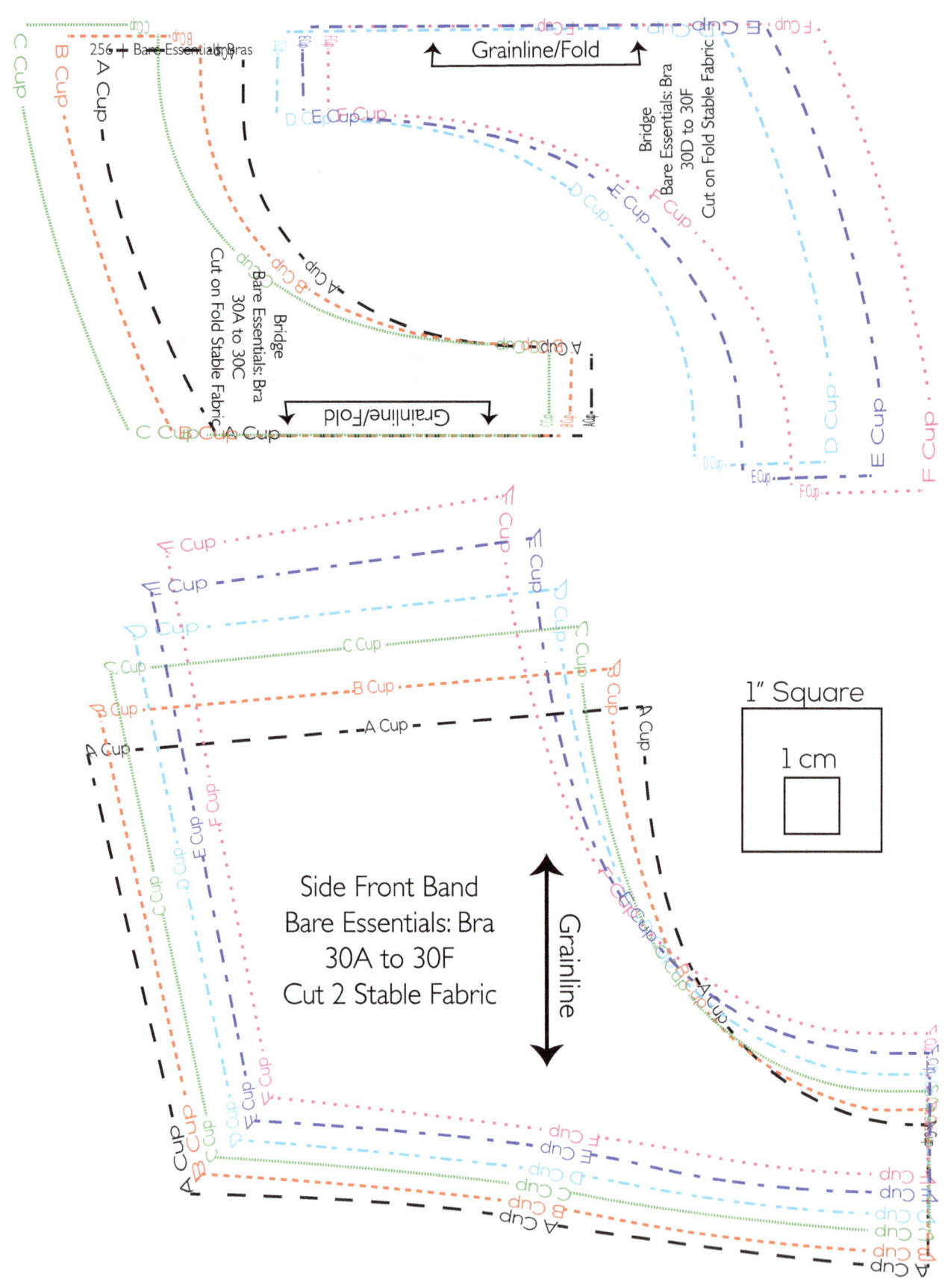

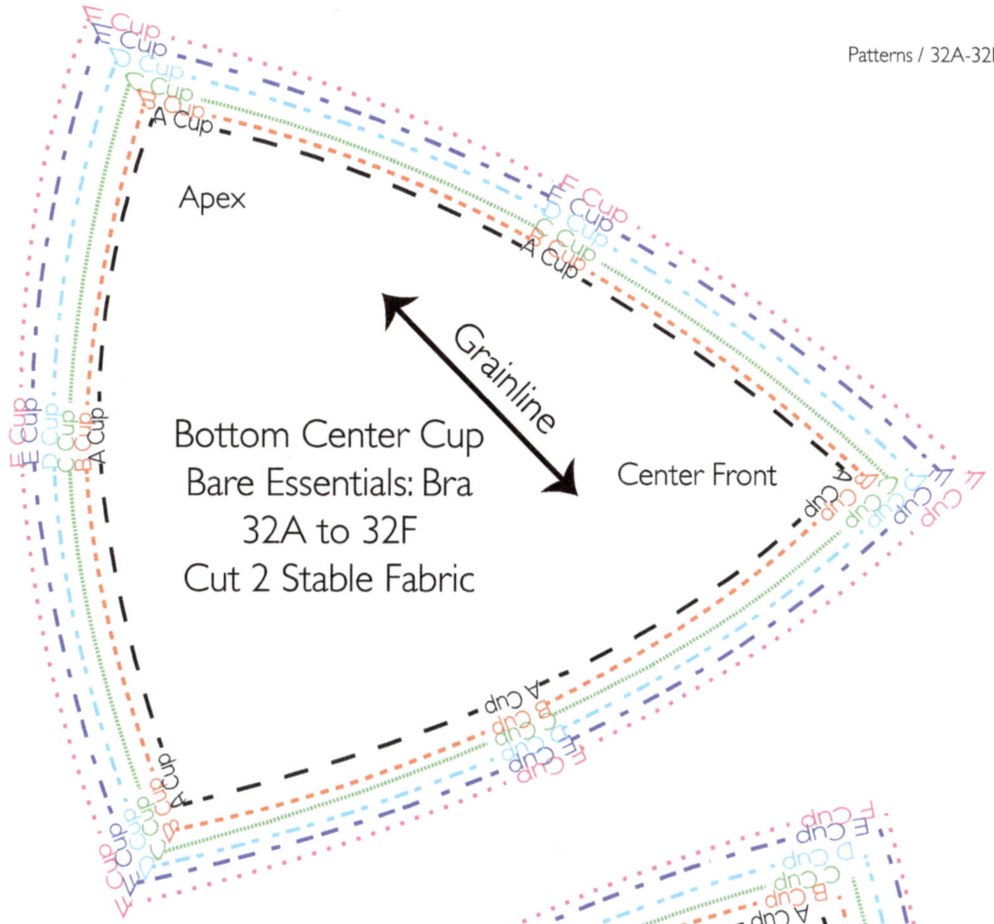

Patterns / 32A-32F | 257

Apex

Bottom Center Cup
Bare Essentials: Bra
32A to 32F
Cut 2 Stable Fabric

Grainline

Center Front

A Cup
B Cup
C Cup
D Cup
E Cup
F Cup

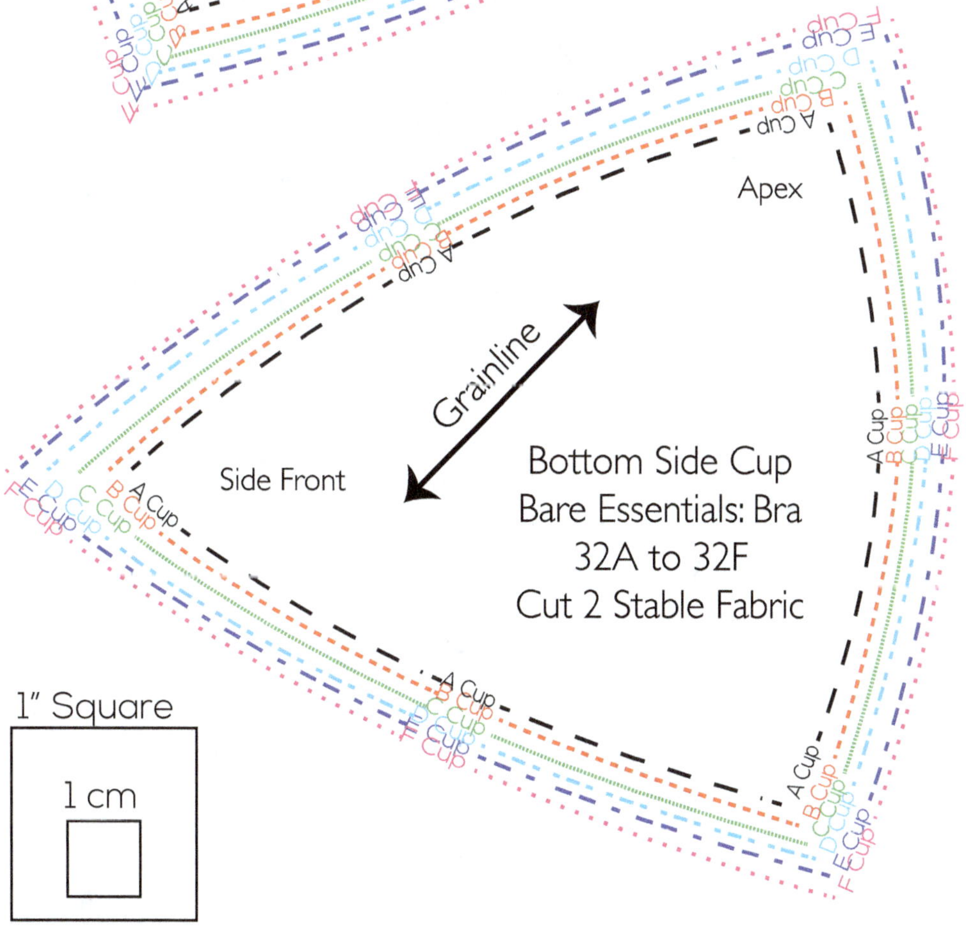

Apex

Side Front

Bottom Side Cup
Bare Essentials: Bra
32A to 32F
Cut 2 Stable Fabric

Grainline

A Cup
B Cup
C Cup
D Cup
E Cup
F Cup

1" Square

1 cm

258 | Bare Essentials: Bras

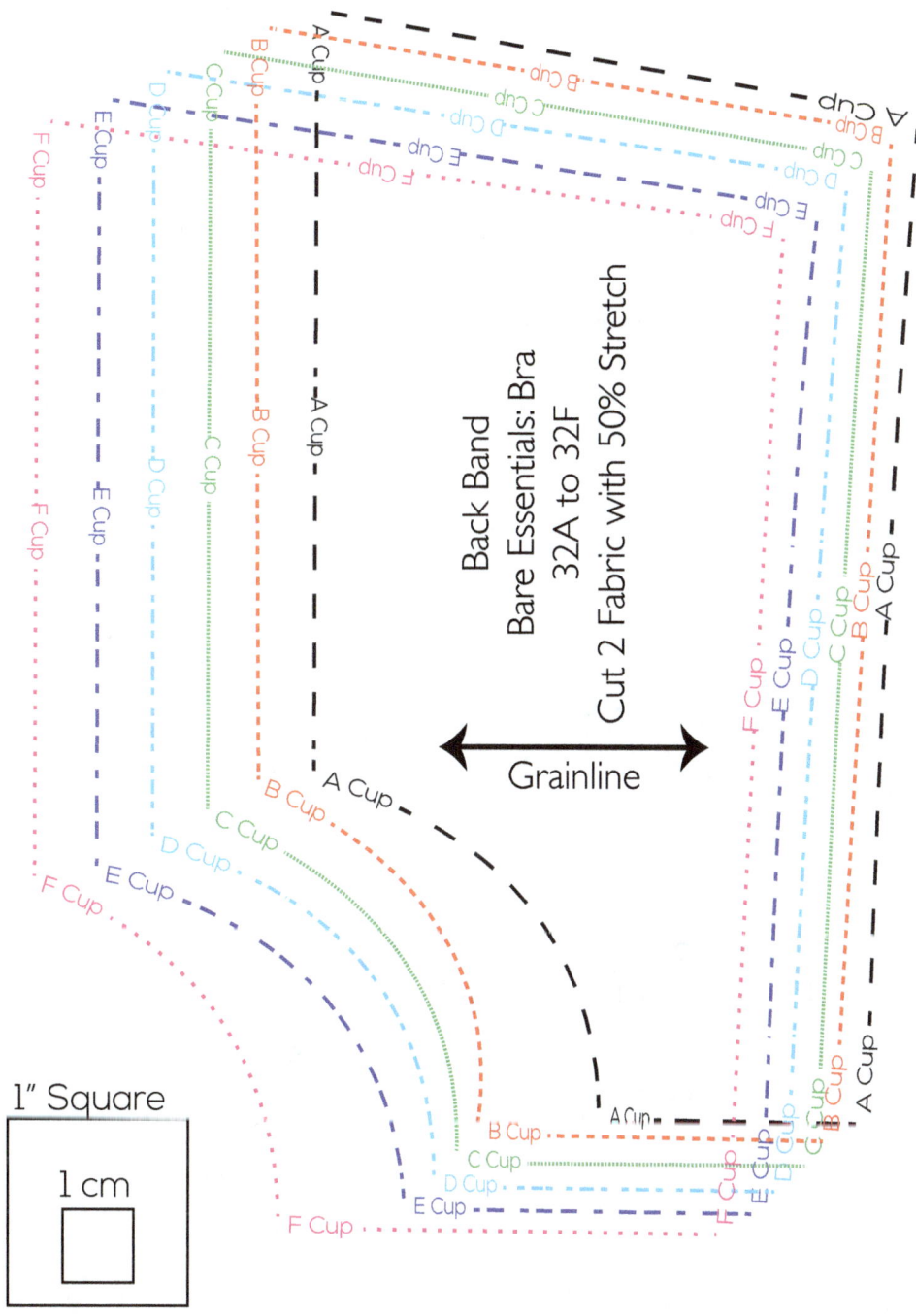

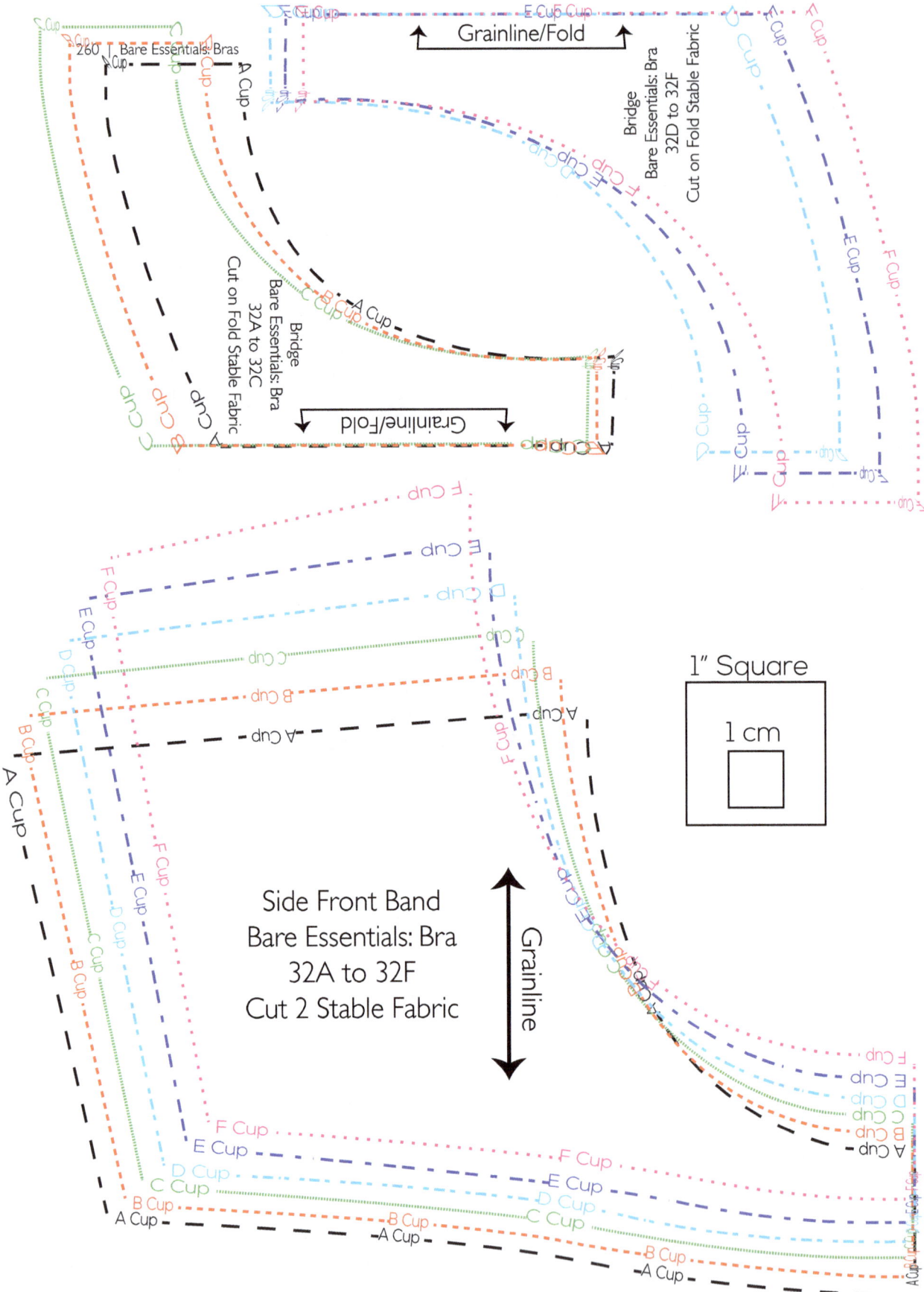

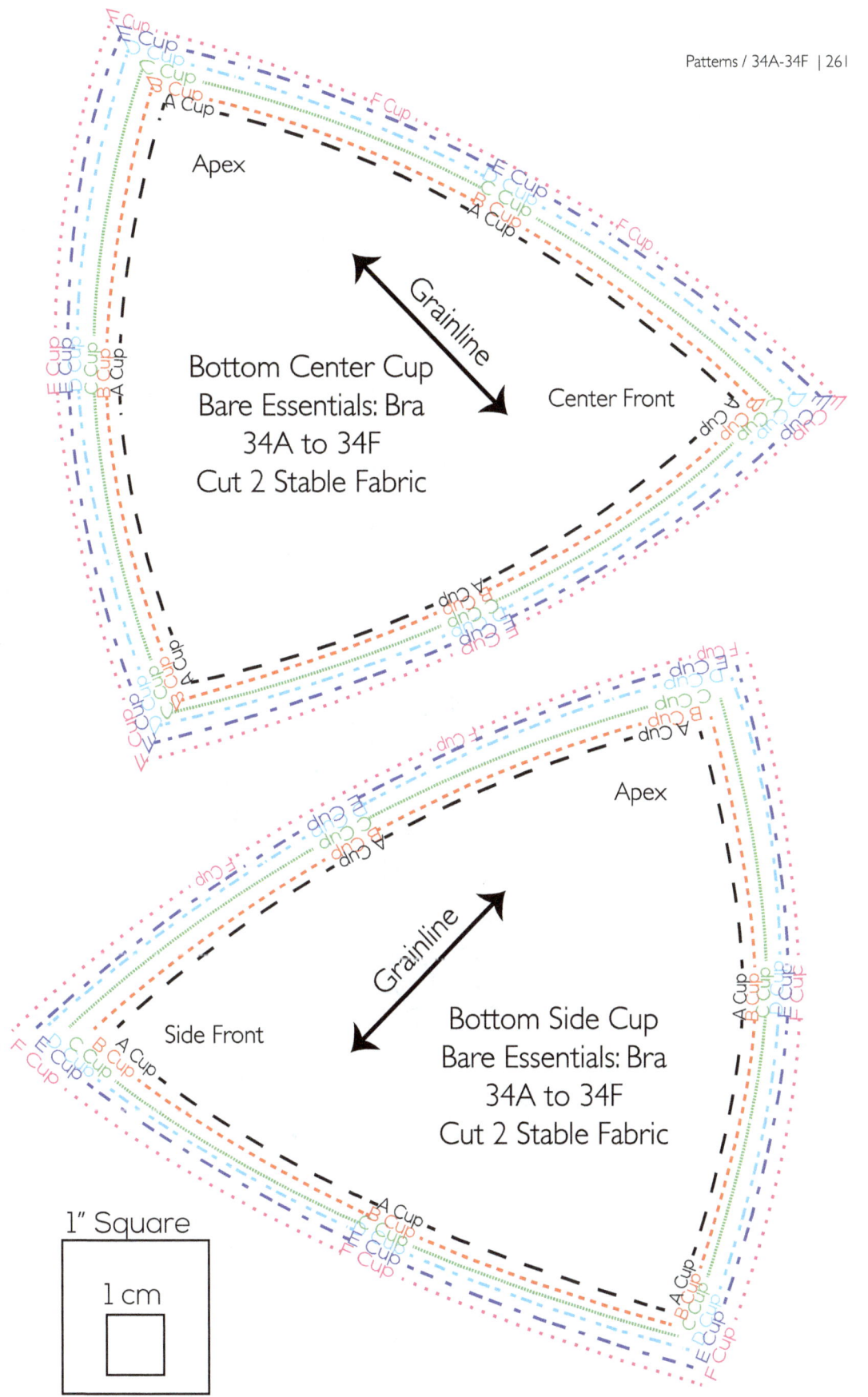

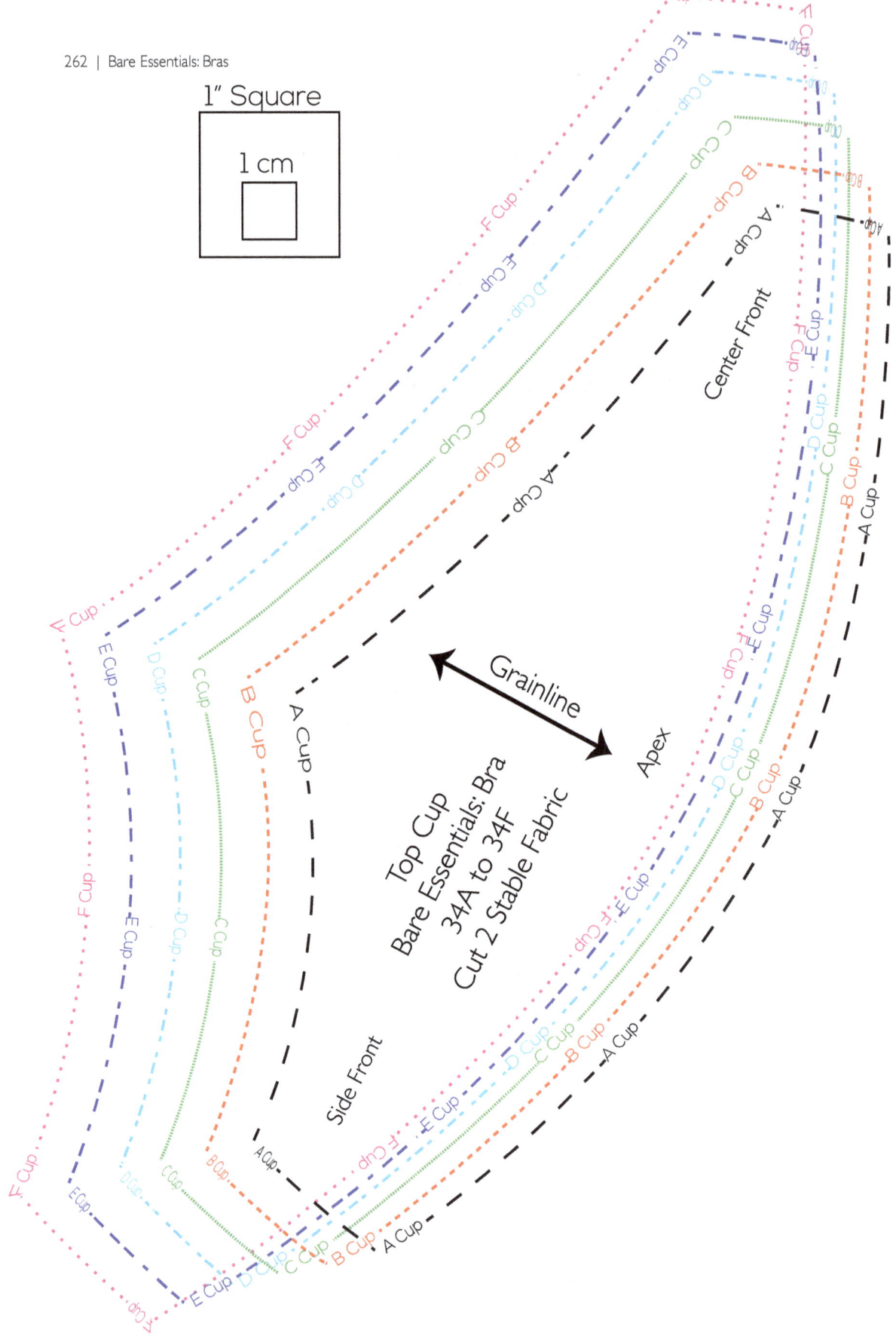

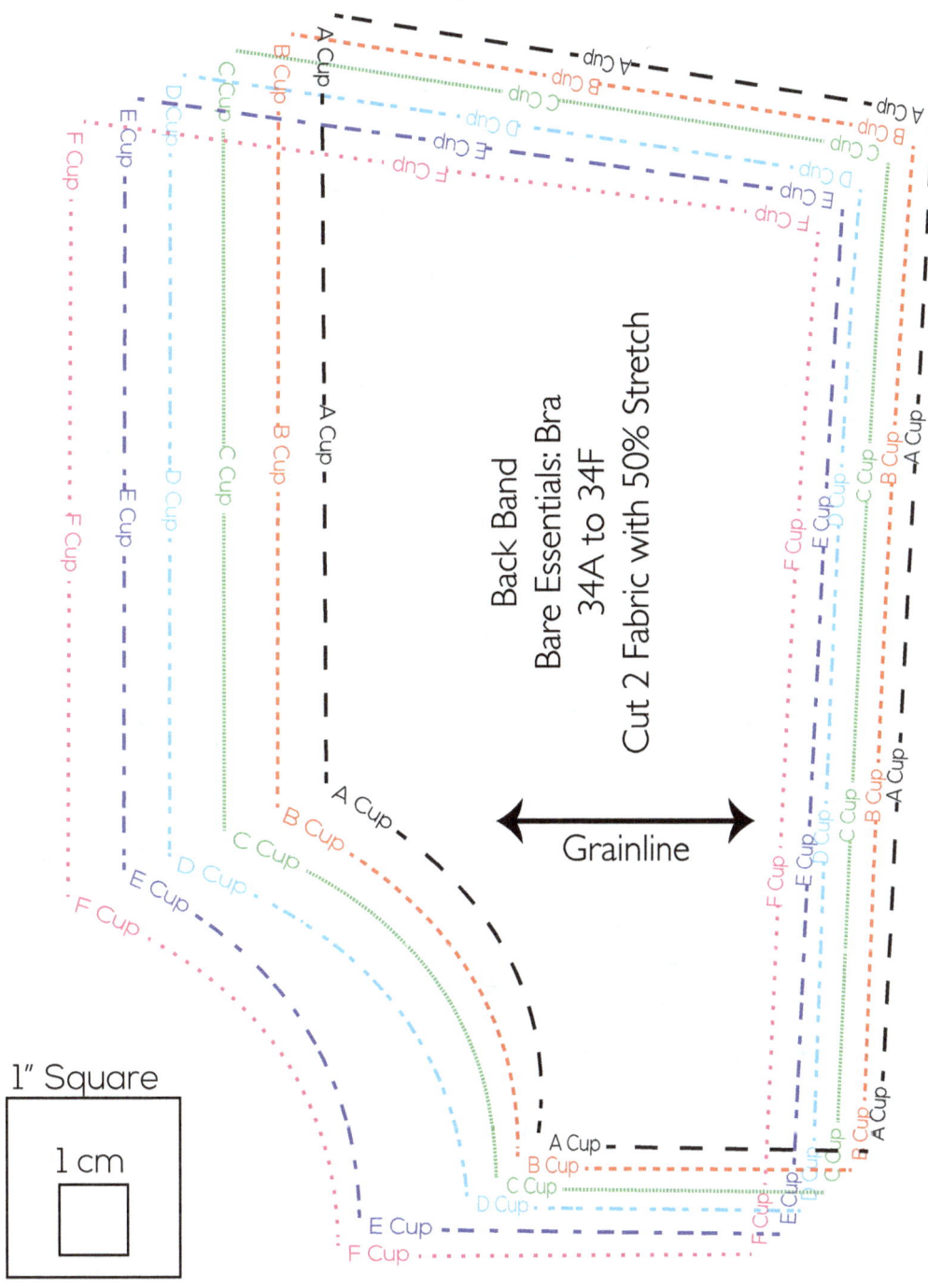

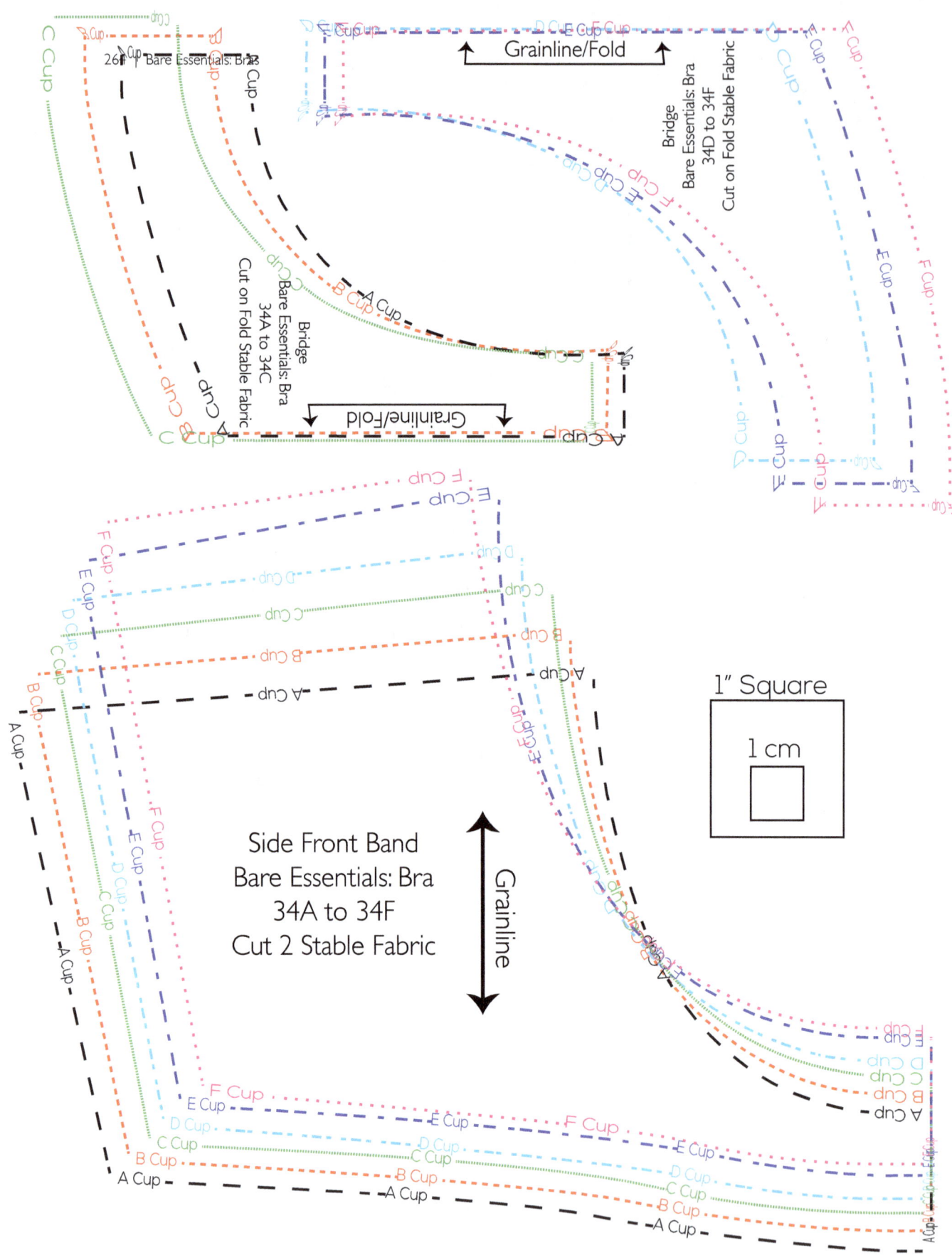

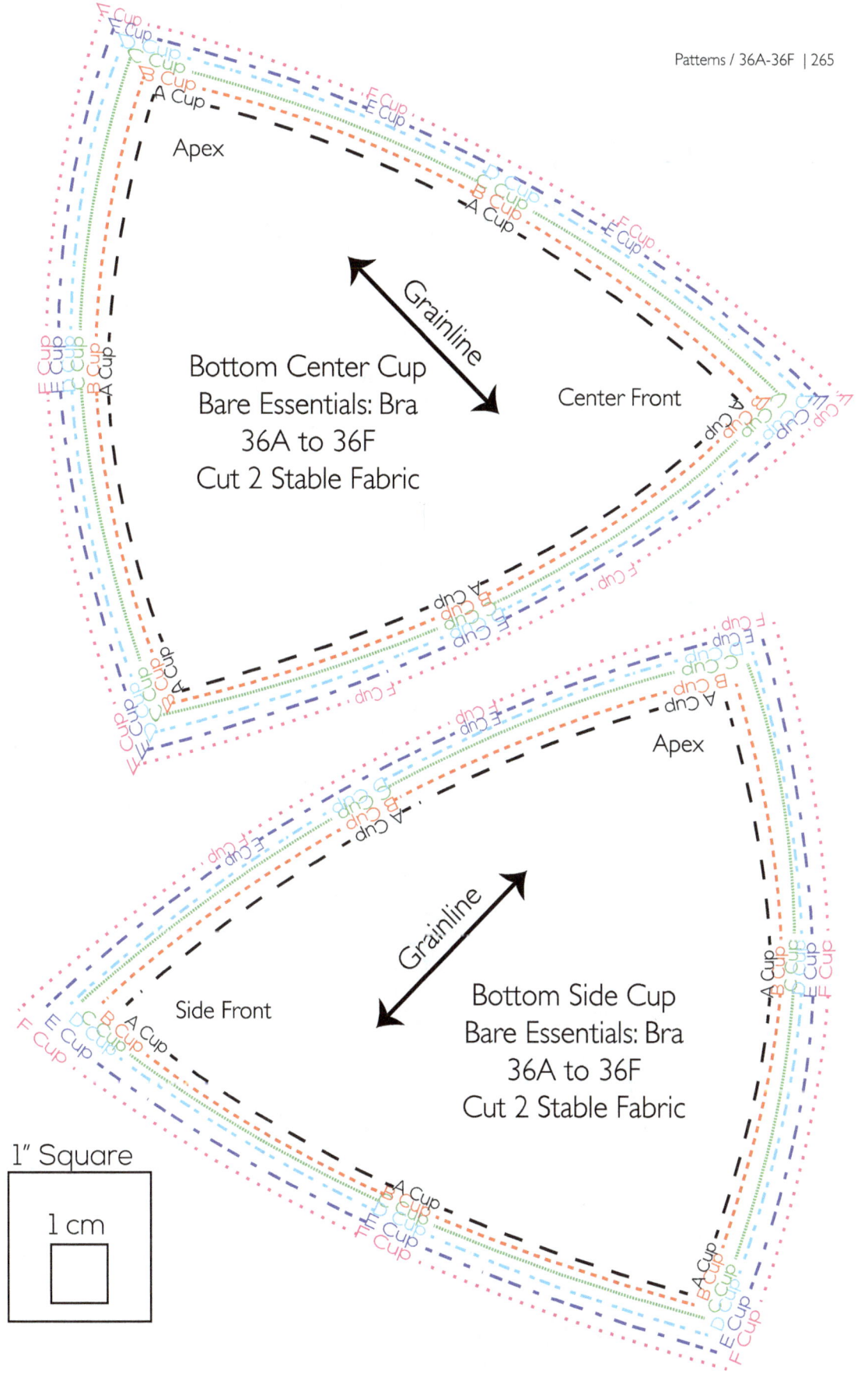

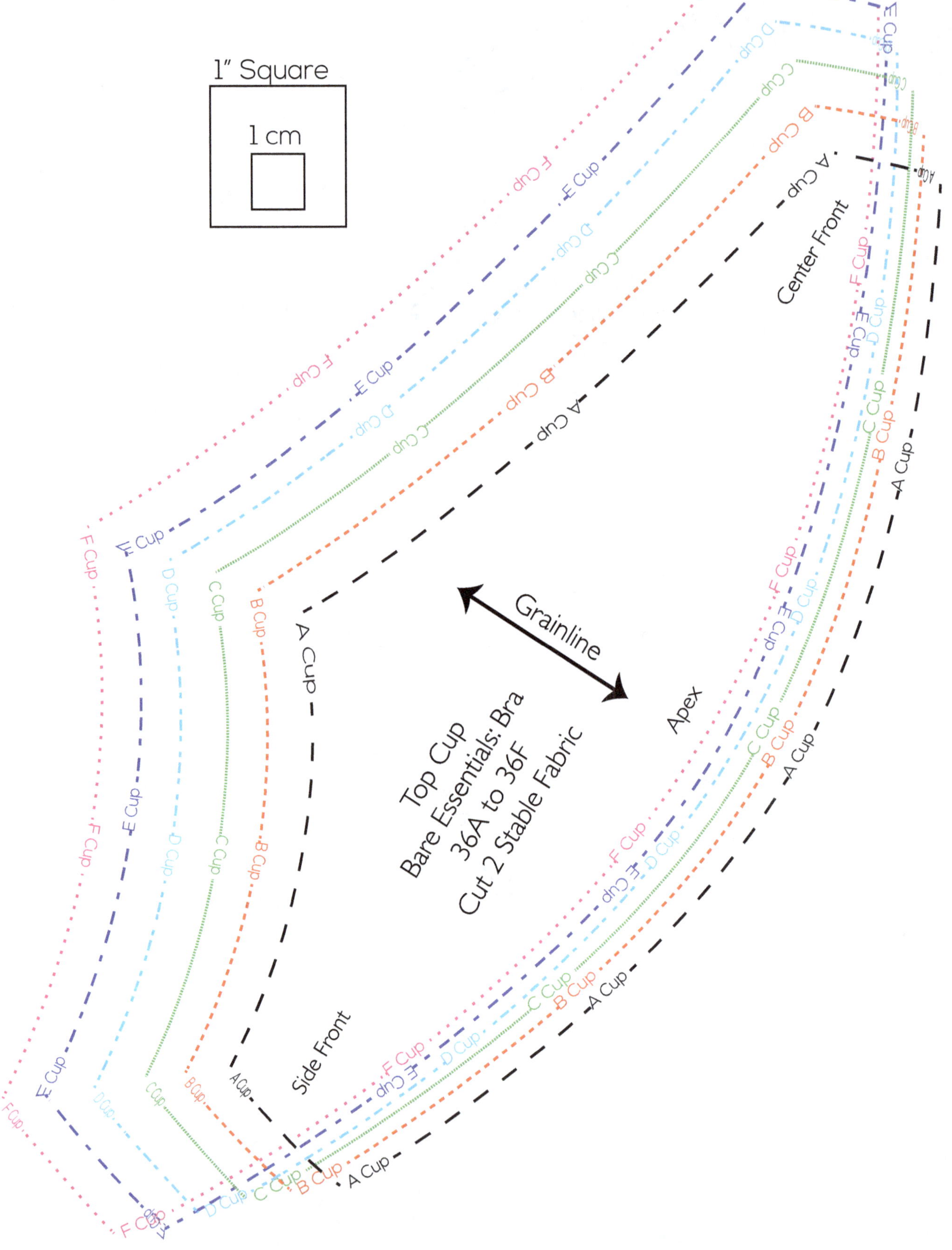
1" Square
1 cm
Top Cup
Bare Essentials: Bra
36A to 36F
Cut 2 Stable Fabric
Grainline
Apex
Center Front
Side Front
A Cup
B Cup
C Cup
D Cup
E Cup
F Cup

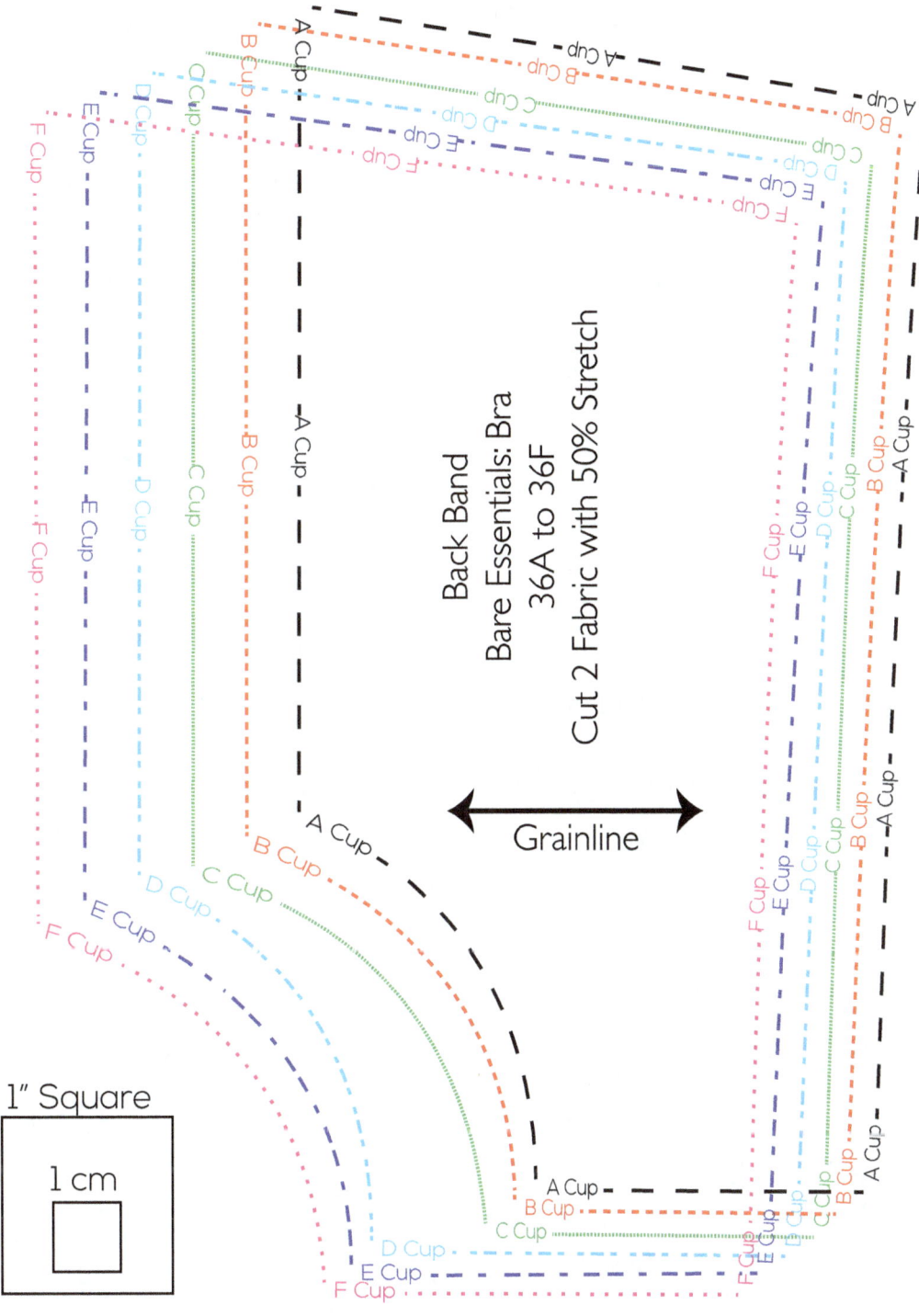

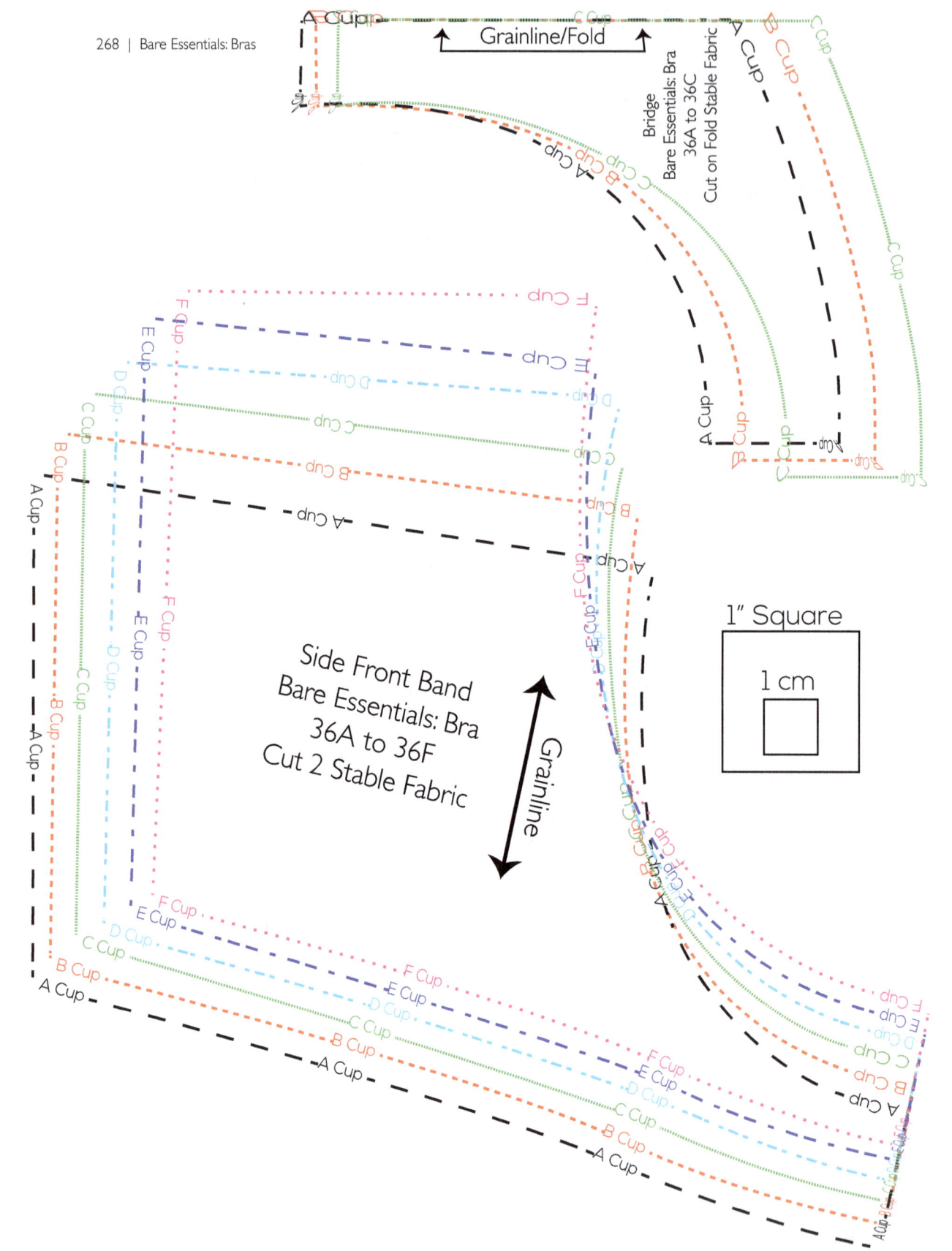

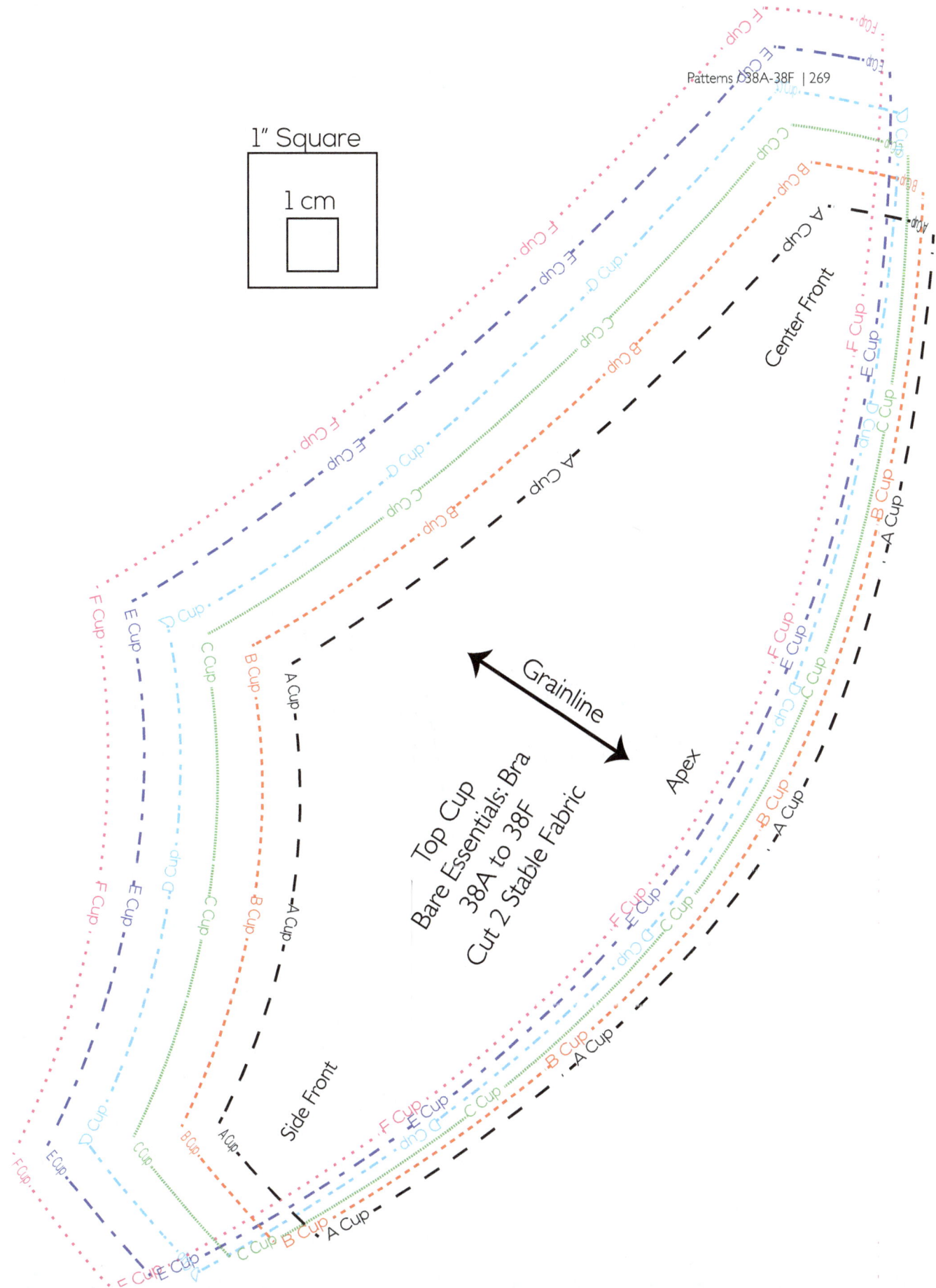

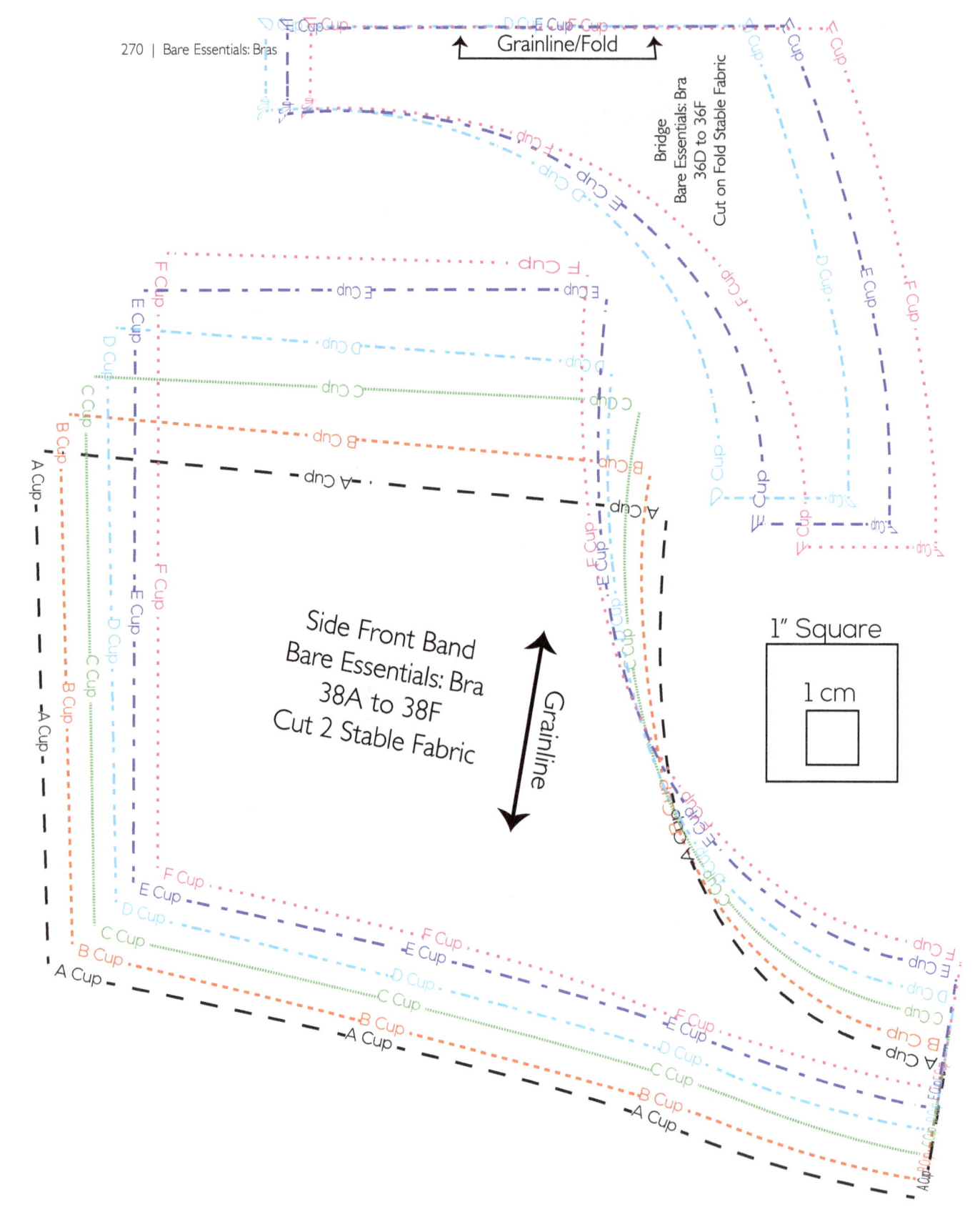

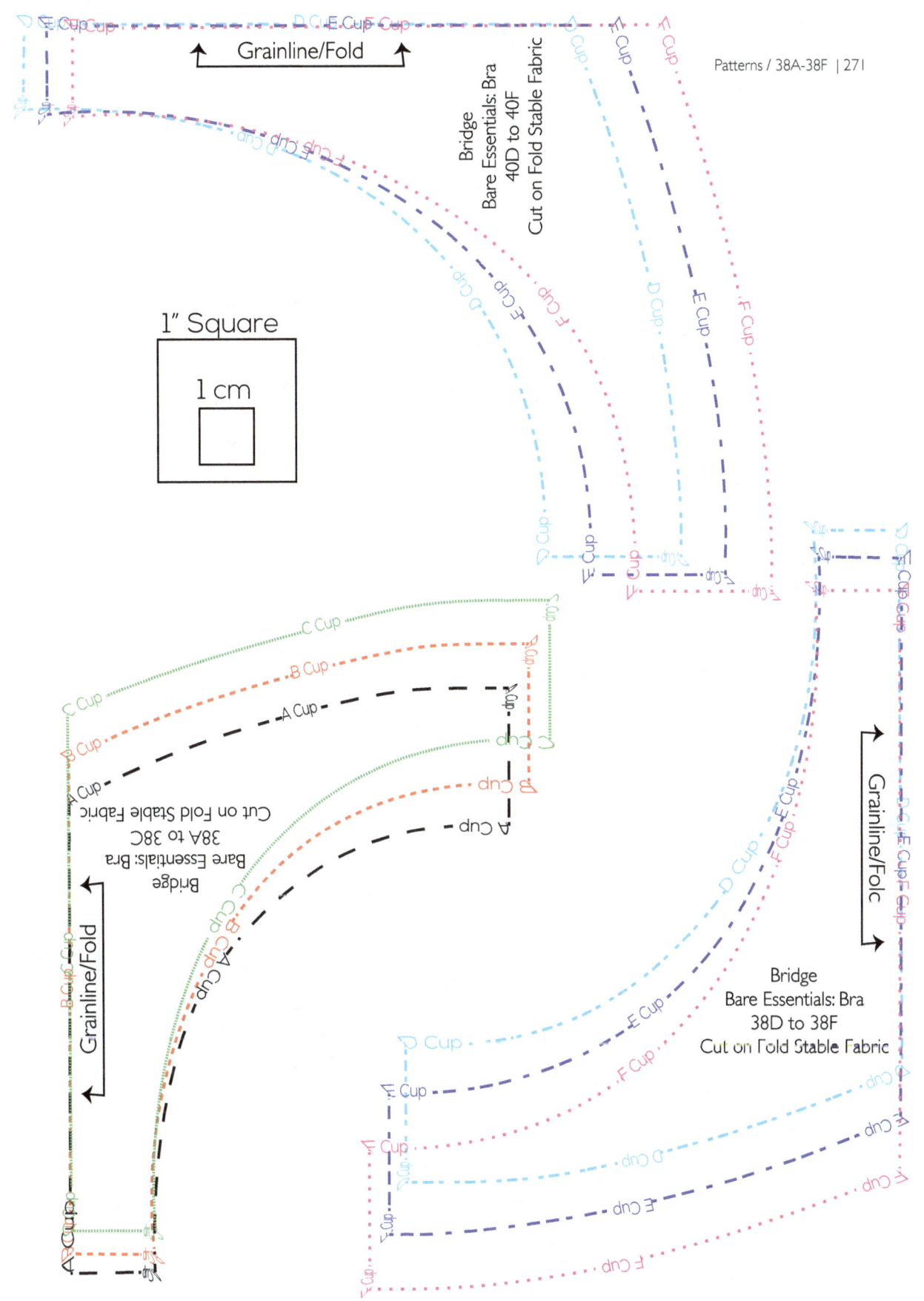

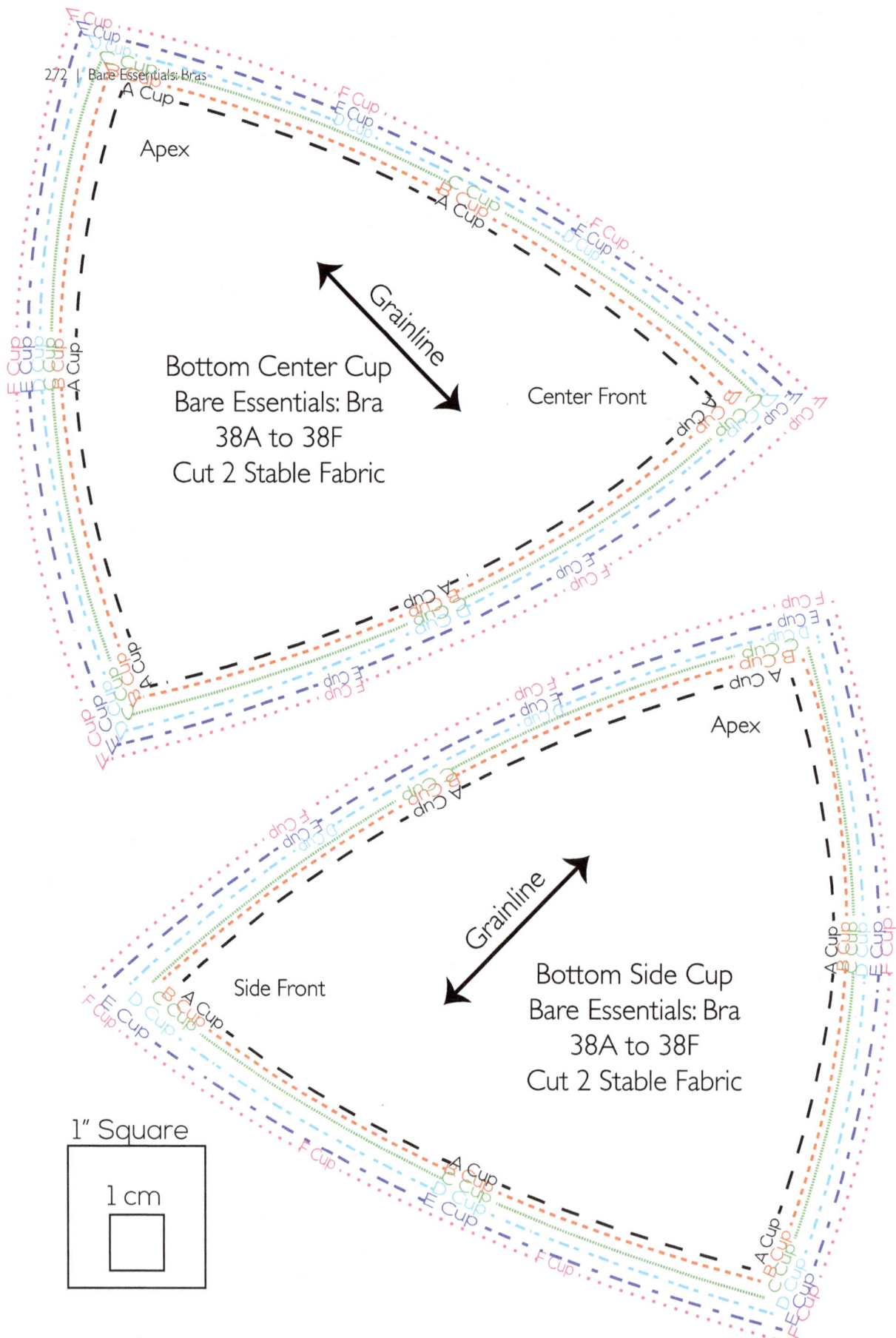

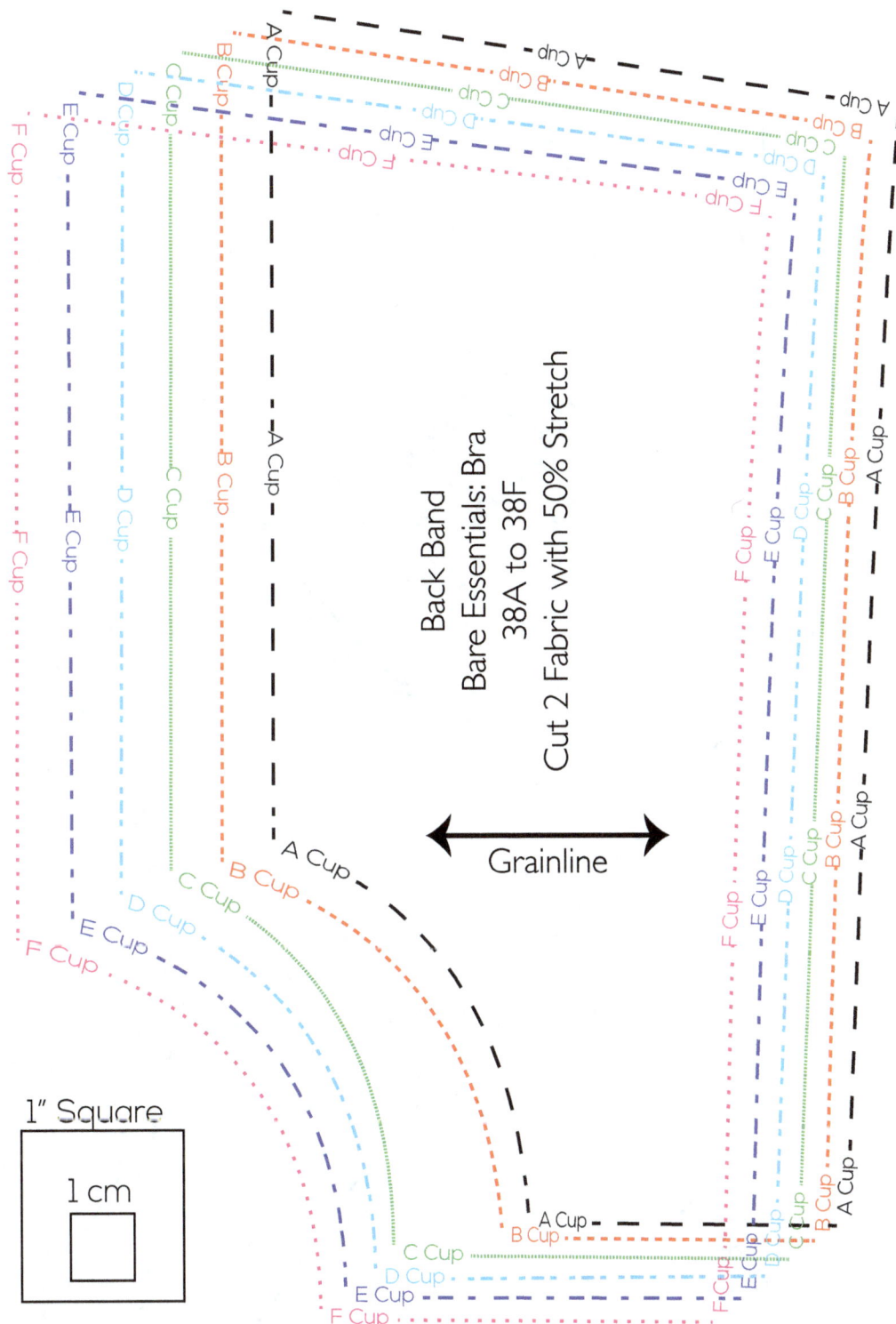

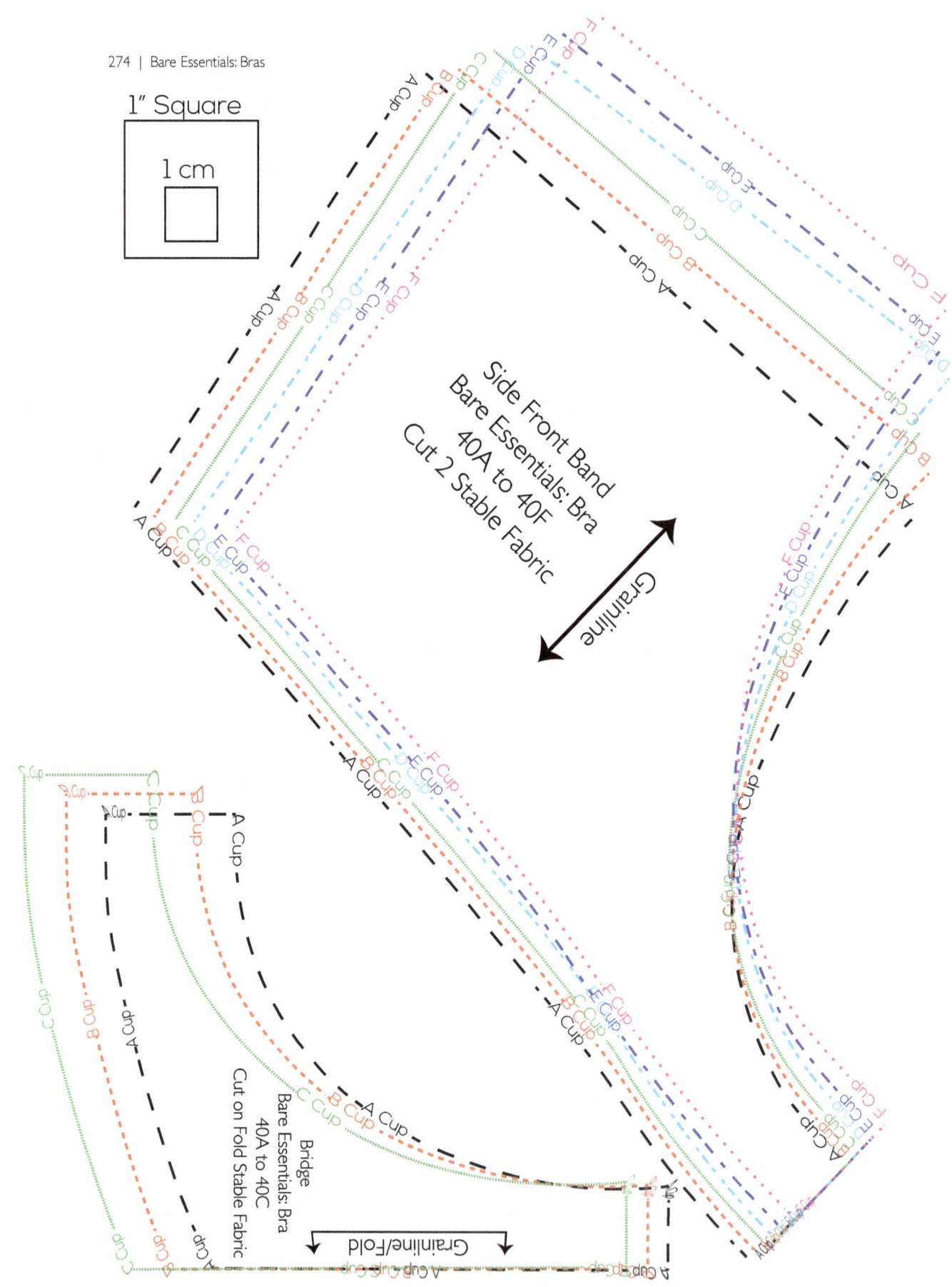

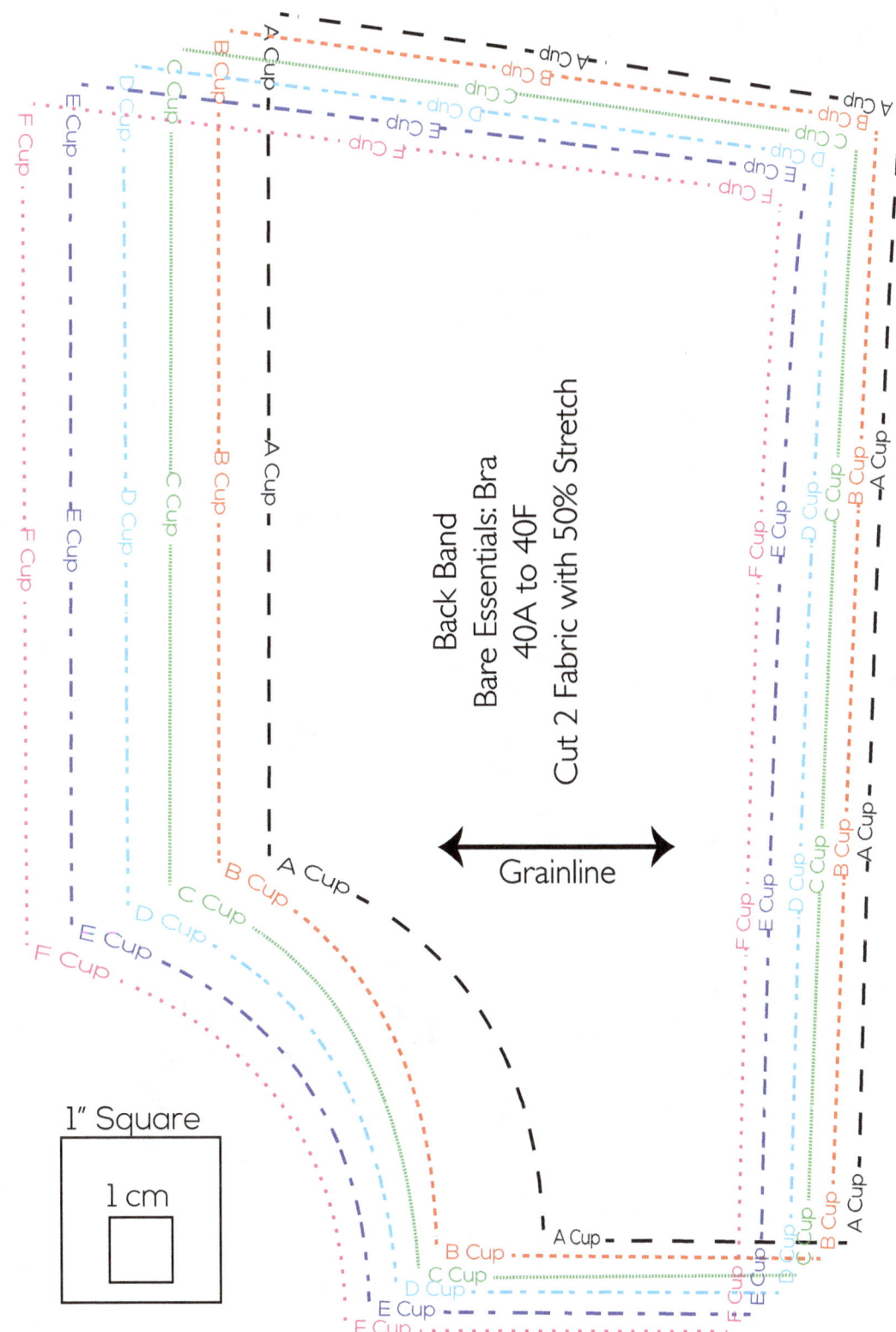

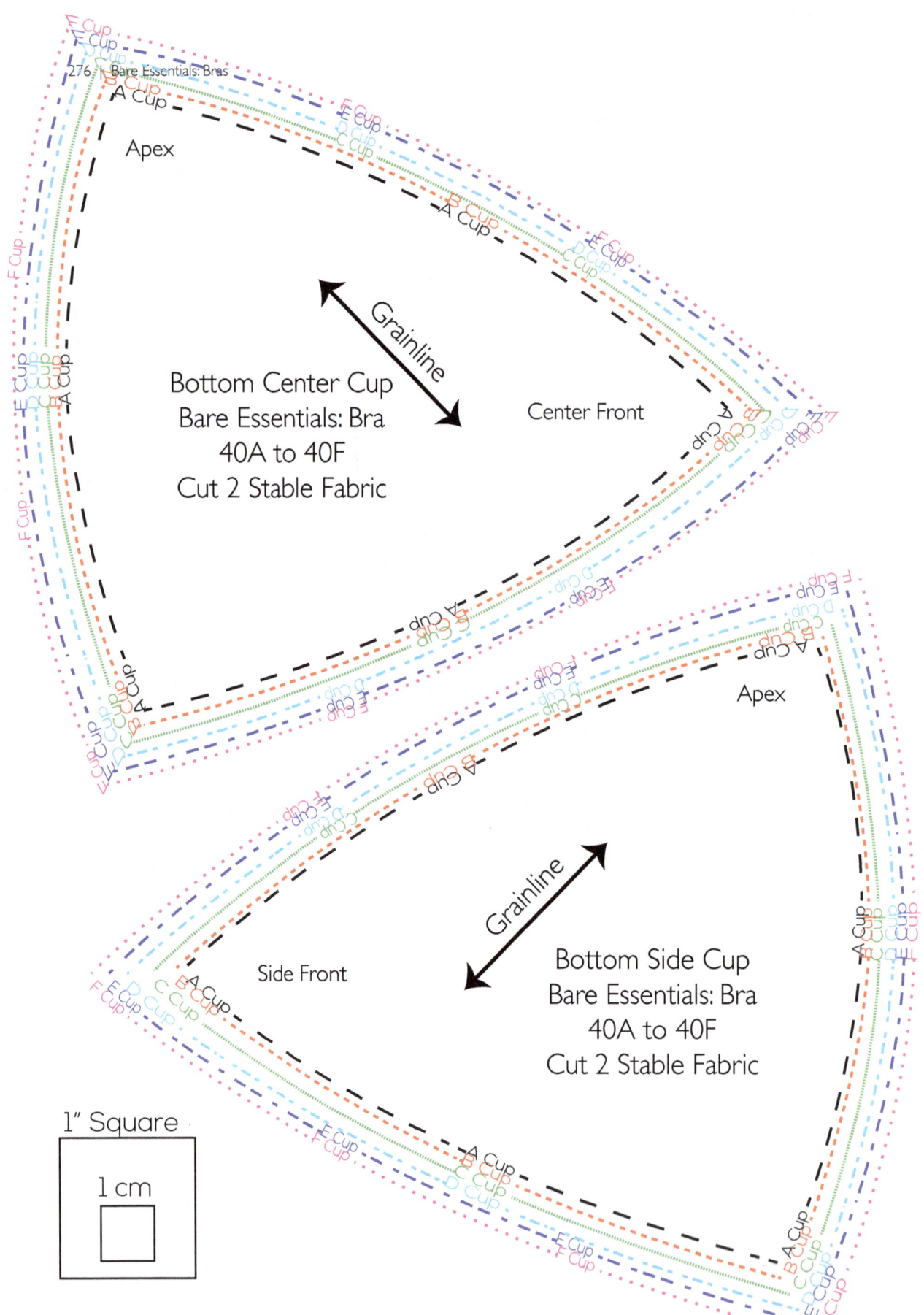

Patterns / 40A-40F | 277

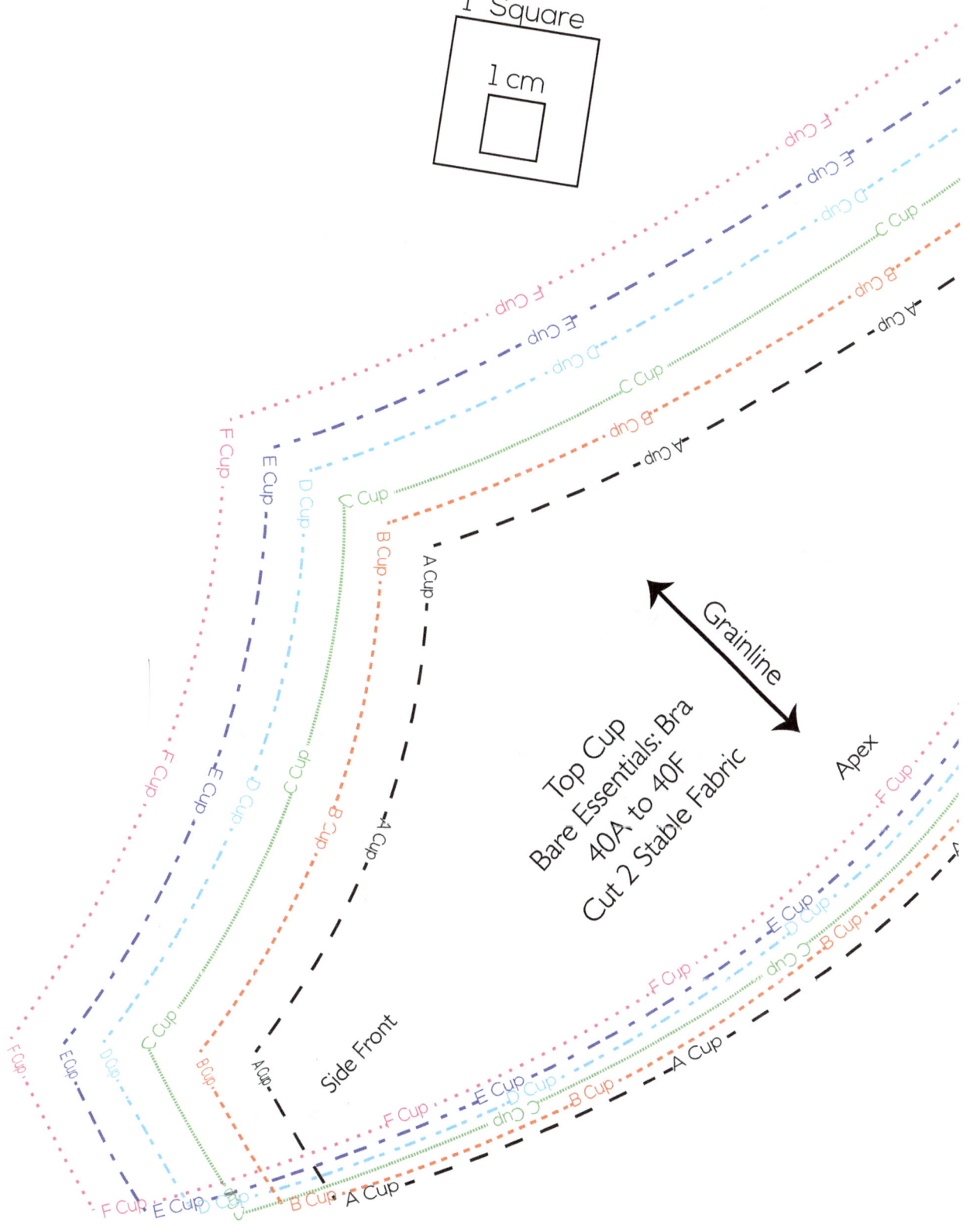

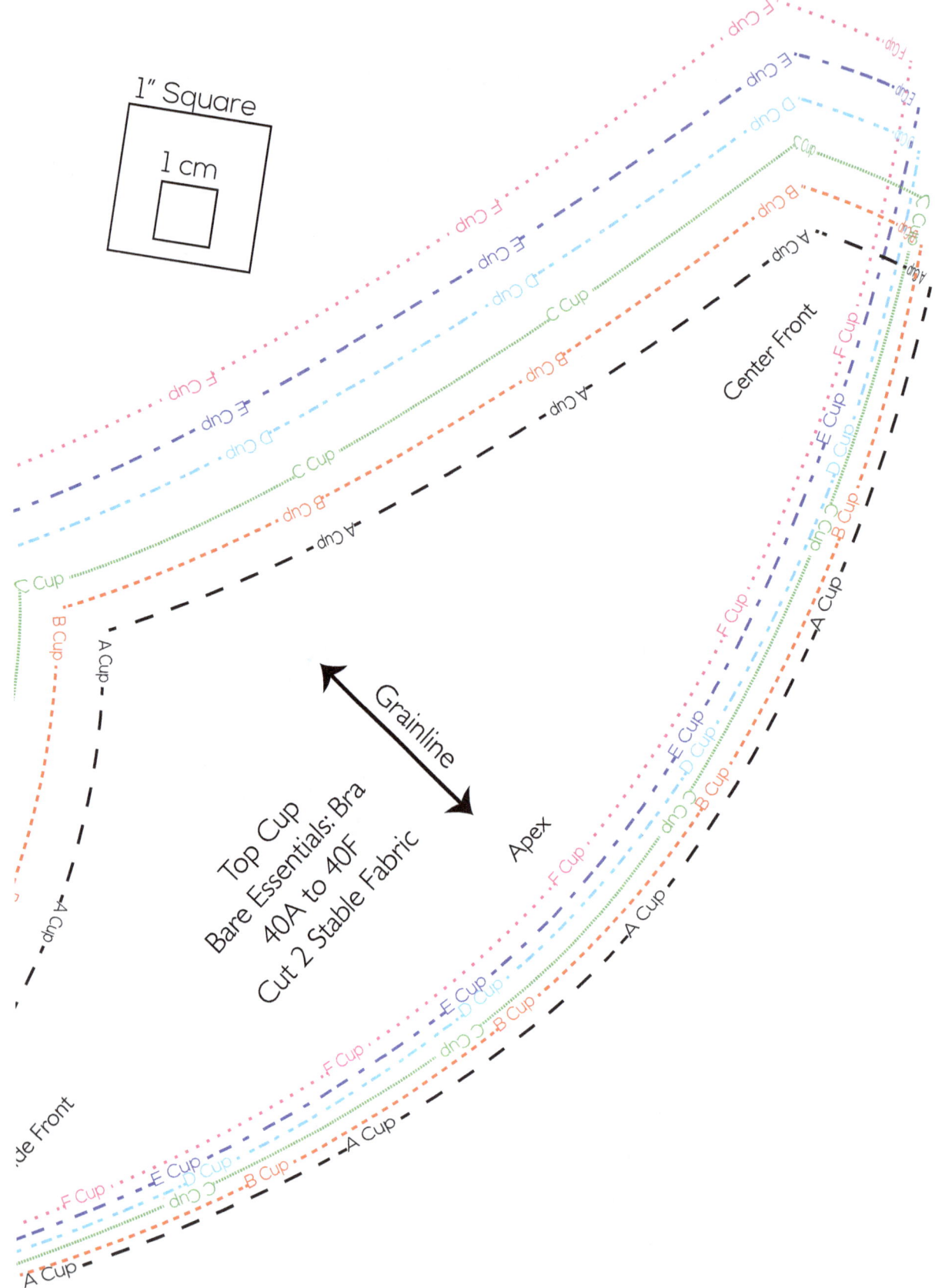

APPENDIX A
POLYPATTERN® BY POLYTROPON

All my drafted patterns are created in the CAD software PolyPattern®. My design business, Porcelynne, is the United States and Canadian partner of PolyPattern. For more information on this software, go to Courses.Porcelynne.com.

PolyPattern® is an easy to use CAD software for any designer, pattern maker, production team or home enthusiast. Digitize and grade existing patterns or draft from measure all within the program.

PolyPattern® is a software by Polytropon. The software is available by subscription or for purchase. A trial version is available on Courses.Porcelynne.com.

When I began using this software, I was looking for a solution that I could optimize and expedite grading. I am very pleased with the software and am glad I found an alternative to drafting in Adobe® Illustrator®. This software is an ideal solution for small to medium sized businesses.

You can import patterns into Illustrator® for creating downloadable patterns. Print patterns from PolyPattern® as PDFs and manipulate the patterns in any illustration software.

ABOUT THE PROGRAM

PolyPattern® is compatible with many other CAD systems including Lectra, Investronica and Gerber and can communicate with most plotters, digitizers, cutters, databases, spreadsheets and software applications.

The interface is easy to understand without the clutter of too many tools or extras. PolyPattern®'s thoughtfully-designed construction tools, combined with its unique "snaps" and keyboard input, allow you to make patterns with greater speed, accuracy, control, and unbelievable ease, no matter what pattern construction method you use.

PATTERN FEATURES:

- Geometric tools for quickly creating rectangles, circles, polygons, curves, and construction lines
- The use of absolute or relative measurements anywhere
- Pattern tools to cut and join any shaped edge
- Tools to rotate, mirror, and unfold patterns
- Notching tools for creating and editing notches and drill holes
- Facing tools for automatically creating perfect facings and hems
- A text tool for notes and reminders
- The ability to annotate patterns with text and shapes
- Automatic seam allowances and seam corner types

SPECIAL FEATURES

- Automatic opening of any type of pleat, dart, or pleated dart
- Automatic dart definition, reversal, shifting, and cut out
- Edge walking to determine the "fit" of two pieces
- The ability to fold a pattern across a line or to bring two points together
- The ability to extract a pattern from existing patterns and drafted lines
- Spiral tools to create accurate single or double spiral shaped patterns for flounces
- Pleating tools to quickly open multiple pleats with an option to smooth ruffle pieces
- Tools to define complex matching criteria for plaid and stripe matching in the marker

Since 1990, PolyPattern customers have enjoyed higher productivity.

Use Match Rules to Handle Fabric Motifs

Different Patterns In Different Sizes

Instantaneous Multiple Pleats

Easily manage drop sizes → *Size Set 1* *Size Set 2* *Composite Sizes*

Shift All or Part of a Dart

GRADING FEATURES:

- The ability to use any size names you choose
- The ability to save size group templates
- Classical X-Y grading and a graphical grading tool
- Tools to copy, add, subtract, mirror, and combine grade rules
- The ability to change the nest reference point for comparing nests
- The ability to add new sizes at any point which get automatically graded
- The ability to separate a pattern nest into individual patterns
- Tools to quickly measure all sizes in the nest
- Advanced measuring tools to add and subtract measurements across many patterns and see the result, in relative or absolute terms, in one table

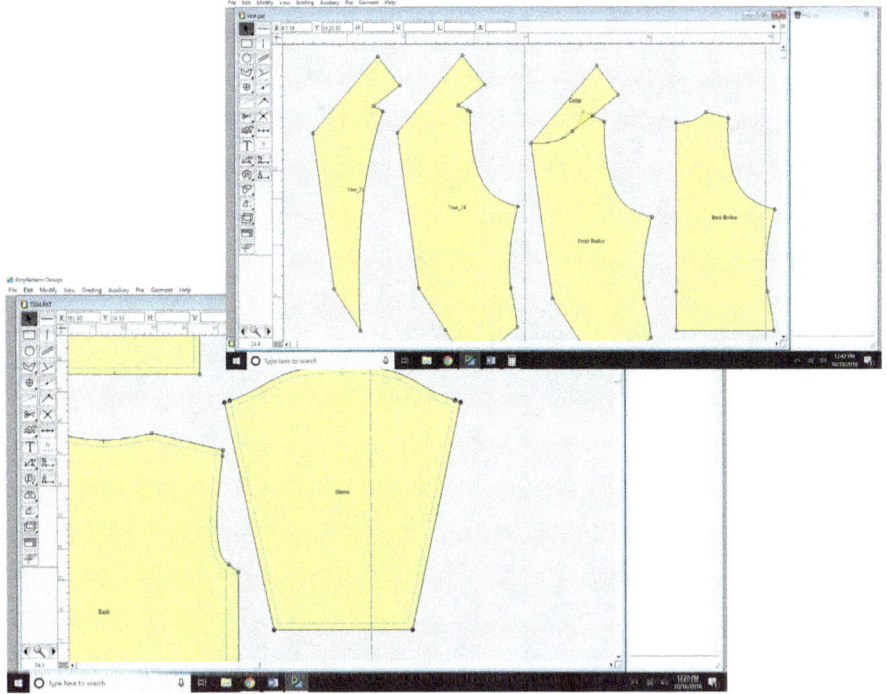

www.ingramcontent.com/pod-product-compliance
Lightning Source LLC
Chambersburg PA
CBHW080536300426
44111CB00017B/2746